OECD *Economic Surveys* Electronic Books

The OECD, recognising the strategic role of electronic publishing, issues the OECD ***Economic Surveys***, both for the Member countries and for countries of Central and Eastern Europe covered by the Organisation's Centre for Co-operation with Economies in Transition, as electronic books – incorporating the text, tables and figures of the printed version. The information will appear on screen in an identical format, including the use of colour in graphs.

The electronic book, which retains the quality and readability of the printed version throughout, will enable readers to take advantage of the new tools that the ACROBAT software (included with the diskette) provides by offering the following benefits:

- ❑ User-friendly and intuitive interface
- ❑ Comprehensive index for rapid text retrieval, including a table of contents, as well as a list of numbered tables and figures
- ❑ Rapid browse and search facilities
- ❑ Zoom facility for magnifying graphics or for increasing page size for easy readability
- ❑ Cut and paste capabilities
- ❑ Printing facility
- ❑ Reduced volume for easy filing/portability

Working environment: DOS, Windows or Macintosh

Subscription: FF 1 800 US$317 £200 DM 545

Complete 1994/1995 series on CD-ROM:

FF 2 000 US$365 £220 DM 600

Please send your order to OECD Electronic Publications or, preferably, to the Centre or bookshop with whom you placed your initial order for this Economic Survey.

OECD ECONOMIC SURVEYS

1995-1996

UNITED STATES

ORGANISATION FOR ECONOMIC CO-OPERATION AND DEVELOPMENT

ORGANISATION FOR ECONOMIC CO-OPERATION AND DEVELOPMENT

Pursuant to Article 1 of the Convention signed in Paris on 14th December 1960, and which came into force on 30th September 1961, the Organisation for Economic Co-operation and Development (OECD) shall promote policies designed:

- to achieve the highest sustainable economic growth and employment and a rising standard of living in Member countries, while maintaining financial stability, and thus to contribute to the development of the world economy;
- to contribute to sound economic expansion in Member as well as non-member countries in the process of economic development; and
- to contribute to the expansion of world trade on a multilateral, non-discriminatory basis in accordance with international obligations.

The original Member countries of the OECD are Austria, Belgium, Canada, Denmark, France, Germany, Greece, Iceland, Ireland, Italy, Luxembourg, the Netherlands, Norway, Portugal, Spain, Sweden, Switzerland, Turkey, the United Kingdom and the United States. The following countries became Members subsequently through accession at the dates indicated hereafter: Japan (28th April 1964), Finland (28th January 1969), Australia (7th June 1971), New Zealand (29th May 1973), Mexico (18th May 1994), the Czech Republic (21st December 1995), Hungary (7th May 1996) and Poland (1996). The Commission of the European Communities takes part in the work of the OECD (Article 13 of the OECD Convention).

Publié également en français.

Table of contents

Boxes

Tables

Figures

Text

BASIC STATISTICS OF THE UNITED STATES

THE LAND

Area (1000 sq. km)	9 373	Population of major cities, including their metropolitan areas, 1992:	
		New York	19 670 000
		Los Angeles-Anaheim-Riverside	15 048 000
		Chicago-Gary-Lake County	8 410 000

THE PEOPLE

Population, 1995	263 057 000	Civilian labour force, 1995	132 385 417
Number of inhabitants per sq. km	28.1	*of which:*	
Population, annual net natural increase (average 1988-93)	1 871 170	Employed in agriculture	3 456 000
		Unemployed	7 401 333
Annual net natural increase, per cent (1988-93)	1.06	Net immigration (annual average 1988-93)	806 000

PRODUCTION

Gross domestic product in 1995 (billions of US$)	7 253.8	Origin of national income in 1995 (per cent of national income[1]):	
GDP per head in 1995 (US$)	27 575	Agriculture, forestry and fishing	1.6
Gross fixed capital formation:		Manufacturing	17.6
Per cent of GDP in 1995	17.2	Construction and mining	5.3
Per head in 1995 (US$)	4 752.6	Government and government enterprises	14.1
		Other	61.4

THE GOVERNMENT

Government consumption 1995 (per cent of GDP)	17.7
Revenue of federal, state and local governments, 1995 (per cent of GDP)	31.3
Federal government debt held by the public (per cent of GDP), FY 1995	51.4

Composition of the 104th Congress 1996:

	House of Representatives	Senate
Democrats	198	47
Republicans	235	53
Independents	1	–
Vacancies	1	–
Total	435	100

FOREIGN TRADE

Exports:		Imports:	
Exports of goods and services as per cent of GDP in 1995	11.1	Imports of goods and services as per cent of GDP in 1995	12.4
Main exports, 1995 (per cent of merchandise exports):		Main imports, 1994 (per cent of merchandise imports):	
Food, feed, beverages	8.7	Food, feed, beverages	4.4
Industrial supplies	24.3	Industrial supplies	15.8
Capital goods (ex. automotive)	40.2	Capital goods (ex. automotive)	29.3
Automotive vehicles, parts	10.6	Automotive vehicles, parts	16.5
Consumer goods (ex. automotive)	11.1	Consumer goods (ex. automotive)	21.1

1. Without capital consumption adjustment.

Note: An international comparison of certain basic statistics is given in an annex table.

This Survey is based on the Secretariat's study prepared for the annual review of the United States by the Economic and Development Review Committee on 12th September 1996.

•

After revisions in the light of discussions during the review, final approval of the Survey for publication was given by the Committee on 7th October 1996.

•

The previous Survey of the United States was issued in November 1995.

Assessment and recommendations

Output has remained near its potential growth path

The United States has enjoyed another year of good economic performance. The economy's momentum was deliberately slowed from an unsustainably rapid pace in 1994 to one which stabilised the unemployment rate near a 20-year low, thereby achieving the elusive objective of a ''soft landing'' in 1995 and allowing the expansion to enter its sixth year. Since then there were initially some signs of weakness in demand and more recently of a robust rebound which might begin to press against capacity limits, but output does not seem to have strayed far from its potential growth path. Nearly 2¼ million non-farm jobs were created during 1995, an increase of nearly 2 per cent, once again the highest rate of any of the major seven OECD Member countries. And during the first two-thirds of this year employment has risen a further 1.9 million, bringing the cumulative rise to nearly 12 million since the beginning of this cycle in 1991, an impressive record by any standards. This recent acceleration has been buffered by some pickup in the rate of labour force growth, with the result that the unemployment rate has been confined to a range around 5 to 5½ per cent since the beginning of 1995.

There have been few signs of inflation pressure

Based on past experience, such a low rate might be expected to have put slight upward pressure on wages and prices, but thus far there has been only limited and tentative evidence of such tensions. The consumer price index rose only 2.5 per cent over the course of 1995, continuing the downtrend in inflation begun in 1991. Although the increase thus far in 1996 moved up to an annualised rate of 3.2 per cent, that has been entirely due to the effects of the jump in energy and food prices. And while the increase in the core index (excluding the food and energy components) edged up from 2.6 per cent in 1994 to 3.0 per cent in 1995, it has since fallen back again. What signs of incipient inflation acceleration there have been in 1996 have, therefore, been largely limited to private-sector wages and salaries: by the second quarter these had picked up to a 3½ per cent year-on-year rate of increase, the fastest gain since the first quarter of 1992. Based on average hourly earnings, wage pressures continued to mount in the third quarter. So far, however, the pickup in wage gains this year has been buffered by persistent moderation in the non-wage component of compensation, some very recent improvement in productivity performance and declining unit capital costs, leaving little in the way of overall cost pressures on prices for the moment.

Recent outcomes have some especially favourable aspects

Other features of recent outcomes have also continued to be favourable for short- and medium-term prospects. First, despite the abrupt slowdown in activity last year, business investment has remained buoyant, with robust increases in spending, especially for high-technology productivity-enhancing equipment. No doubt this is attributable in part to the healthy state of business finances. The persistent strength of the stock market in the face of higher long-term interest rates is testimony to the sharp recovery in profits: in the second quarter of 1996 unit profits of non-financial corporations were over 50 per cent higher than four years before. Second, in the spring of 1995 export growth also began to exceed import growth, with a substantial degree of slack in foreign economies still to be taken up. This, together with higher private and public saving, allowed the current account deficit to edge down for the first time in four years. However, this nascent export boom seems to have petered out in 1996, possibly due to the substantial effective appreciation of the dollar. Third, the share of general government consumption and investment spending in GDP has continued to decline: it has now fallen by nearly 3 percentage points over the past decade. Finally, the moderate overhang in business inventories that developed during the first half of 1995 as a result of the sudden and partially unexpected slowdown has now been corrected, and sectoral inventory-sales ratios have moved back down to their longer-term trends.

But macroeconomic risks remain

There are, to be sure, a number of areas of possible macroeconomic vulnerability. First, the substantial rise in long-term rates thus far this year could cause interest-sensitive components of demand to weaken. However, such a weakening would be most likely to merely restore the economy to its non-inflationary growth path from which it might otherwise have diverged on the upside, especially given the strength of recent labour-market outcomes. Nevertheless, both housing starts and motor vehicle purchases are at very high levels, well beyond replacement needs, and therefore carry a risk of a larger correction. Also of possible concern is the state of household finances. This is important for the sustainability of the current expansion, for if consumers are forced to retrench significantly, continued growth would be jeopardised. Signs of household financial stress are several: debt has risen sharply in relation to income over the past three years; the payment burden has climbed; personal bankruptcies are rising; and for more than a year delinquency rates have been rising for credit cards and other consumer loans as well. But delinquency rates for mortgages remain low, the saving rate is not unusually low, and while overall indebtedness is at a record level, in the aggregate it is more than offset by the rapid rise in the value of household assets, especially financial assets: indeed, net financial wealth has now reached more than three years of average income, up from 2½ only five years ago. The problem, if any, is therefore largely distributional: those faced with burdensome indebtedness may not be those with rising wealth. It is unclear whether households with healthy balance sheets will boost their consumption sufficiently to offset the drag from those who are reaching the limits of their spending capacity. In addition, some observers question whether the level of household wealth is sustainable, given the enormous gains in equity prices recorded since the end of 1994.

Real GDP is projected to stay near potential

The context then is one of both upside and downside influences on activity, but with the balance clearly weighted towards the former: with strong job creation, consumers are likely to continue to have the confidence and the wherewithal to maintain their expenditure growth, despite much-publicised anxieties; businesses cannot escape the need to invest in order to remain competitive in increasingly contestable markets; and exporters have the products and the cost structures which should allow them to again make modest gains in market share. The projection, therefore, calls for real GDP growth to ease to an annual rate of around 2 per cent over the next 18 months, with the moderation concentrated on interest-sensitive and government demand components. The implication of such an outcome for the labour market would be that the unemployment rate would edge up very slightly, for 2 per cent per year is probably not far below the economy's potential growth rate. There are those who believe it is or could easily be made much higher; but to avoid an acceleration in inflation, annual growth of 2 to 2½ per cent is all that the economy can manage unless there is a pickup in available labour supply, largely constrained by demographic trends, or an improvement in labour productivity growth from its trend over the past 20 years (slightly over 1 per cent per year). Boosting productivity growth trends is a difficult challenge, one which is feasible only in the medium term.

But inflation could pick up

Inflation outcomes should remain gratifyingly low by historical standards: the GDP deflator, for example, is expected to rise less in both 1996 and 1997 than in any year since 1965. However, the risks with regard to prices and wages are asymmetric. There remains little chance that the economy has much, if any, spare capacity: if it did, then signs of excess supply in terms of declining market tensions would become visible over time. On the contrary, there are some tentative signs of emerging labour market tightness and resulting modest wage pressures. This is projected to continue, with a slight further acceleration in compensation and some resulting pickup in underlying inflation.

The costs of inflation are many

The choice confronting monetary policymakers is, thus, a difficult one. There is widespread agreement that policy should be set with a view to achieving the long-run objective of price stability and that this goal has not yet been reached, despite the much-discussed biases in the consumer price index. Where there is room for debate is whether it is sufficient to contain inflation in the current expansion and wait for the next downturn in order to reduce inflation further or whether that goal is worthy of a more deliberate disinflationary push. This depends in part upon the costs of inflation, which are obvious at higher rates but less so at current rates. The Chairman of the Federal Reserve has often defined price stability as a state in which economic agents can neglect inflation in their economic plans; this is appropriate, as the efforts made to avoid or protect against inflation are one of its costs. It is likely that these costs are not trivial, especially to the degree that they may bring about quite distorted investment behaviour in the context of an imperfectly indexed system of capital income taxation.

More tangibly, the Treasury has implicitly recognised the lengths some investors will go to in order to avoid the ravages of inflation by proposing to issue indexed government debt. Workers too fear the power of inflation to eat away arbitrarily at their negotiated wage gains, and some unions, albeit a declining number, continue to bargain for cost-of-living adjustment clauses in their labour contracts.

Monetary policy makers should be vigilant

Given the outcomes over the past two years, it appears that current rates of resource utilisation are too high to achieve further progress towards price stability. In such an environment, the balance of inflation risks appears asymmetric. Thus to heed the call for higher growth and lower unemployment rates would be ill advised, whereas a slight easing in resource use should sustain the medium-term disinflation process. Ideally, even tighter fiscal policy would contribute to this effort. But in view of the protracted budget decision-making process, it falls to monetary policy alone to play this role. While the level of interest rates needed to reduce pressures on capacity is uncertain, it is the Committee's view that some insurance against any re-emergence of upward trends in inflation should prudently be bought in the form of a monetary stance conducive to slowing the growth of aggregate demand relative to that of potential output for some time. This is embodied in the Secretariat's projections. It is unlikely that such a move would seriously jeopardise the expansion.

National saving rose in 1995 but remains low

Over the medium term the major macroeconomic problem facing the United States remains the inadequacy of national saving and the impacts that this is probably having on global interest rates, domestic investment and the nation's net foreign indebtedness (which has now reached 11 per cent of GDP). Some improvement has occurred over the past year, with a rebound in the private sector saving rate.

But the government sector has also contributed, with its dissaving reduced from a peak of over 3 per cent of GDP in 1992 to less than 1 per cent in 1995. A further decline is likely in 1996. This is the payoff from the fiscal tightening that has been steadily pursued since 1990 as well as the elimination of the output gap.

An end to declining budget deficits may be imminent

But the outlook for further progress on the fiscal front is poor unless policies are strengthened. Official projections envisage a moderate-sized rise in the deficit already in 1997, even with a complete freeze in discretionary spending at the 1996 level and the favourable interest rates assumed to result from a successful agreement to balance the budget by 2002. With less optimistic assumptions, the budgetary situation would deteriorate to an even greater degree, and the deficit could reach some $400 billion (3.3 per cent of GDP) within a decade, wiping out virtually all of the progress made since 1992. It is the pressures on entitlement spending which are expected to play the biggest role in the re-emerging imbalance. And these are expected to worsen even faster once the baby boom generation begins to retire later in the next decade. It is, therefore, crucial that an early start be made to confronting these problems – health care spending in particular. As well, attention should be devoted to the long-term actuarial imbalance in Social Security before its financial situation becomes critical. Eliminating the federal deficit by 2002, as targeted by both the Congress and the Administration last winter, would be a good first step. But the two sides could not agree on the details; in particular, the Congress wished to make larger tax cuts and, therefore, required larger spending cuts in order to reach a zero deficit. Making the tax cuts conditional on actually achieving the spending cuts would seem the best solution to the impasse.

Structural reforms have been attempted on a wide front

Past progress in extending the role of market competition throughout the economy has meant that the agenda for further structural reform is limited relative to that in most OECD countries. Nevertheless, there has again been a number of initiatives to further structural reform, but only some of them have been successfully carried through. The biggest achievement was the passage of the new Telecommunications Act which will allow inter-sectoral competition in the telephone, cable television and broadcast industries and will speed the dismantling of price regulation for cable service providers. Also commendable was the new farm legislation which decouples crop payments from production, ends mandatory set-asides and lowers or phases out support prices for other farm products; but the overall budgetary implications of the new regime are disappointing, as spending is set to be higher in the near term than it would have been under the previous system. The recently passed health insurance reform eases portability of coverage and authorises small-scale testing of ''medical savings accounts'' in order to try to create incentives for patients to limit their demands for care, but it will bring about a worsening in adverse selection problems by allowing the healthiest to reduce risk-sharing by opting out of existing group plans. Efforts are ongoing to bring needed reforms to environmental laws and regulations, but with limited success to this point. Finally, yet another attempt to repeal the Glass-Steagall Act and desegment the financial services sector has unfortunately been abandoned, and the savings institutions' deposit insurance fund has yet to be properly recapitalised.

But there are continuing concerns over trade policy

Throughout the post-war era the United States has helped guide the world towards freer trade. This policy has been in its own self-interest, but it has provided possibly even greater benefits to its trading partners. Most recently, the United States was a leader in bringing the Uruguay Round of multilateral trade negotiations to a successful conclusion which included the establishment of the World Trade Organisation, and it has been a key instigator of the talks at the OECD over a Multilateral Agreement on Investment. But concern has been expressed in the Committee about certain other aspects of recent US trade policy, in particular the recent enactment of the Helms-Burton Act and other similar legislation which would extend US law beyond US borders, with potentially important multilateral trade implications. In various international services negotiations – financial services, telecommunications and maritime services – the United States found that a critical mass of offers for obtaining meaningful liberalisation was absent; multilateral agreements have not been reached to this point. Also, the recent OECD shipbuilding agreement has not yet been approved by the Congress. The hope has been expressed in the Committee that the United States will provide the leadership necessary to bring these ongoing negotiations to a successful conclusion.

The labour market functions well overall

Private and public institutions in the United States have created an environment where input and product markets function well, resulting in high and effective use of labour resources. The unemployment rate is at the low end of the range exhibited over the past twenty five years, and long-term unemployment remains scarce. Labour force participation rates are higher, unemployment rates are lower and labour productivity is greater than in most other OECD countries. In recent years, the performance gap has been dramatic, with a majority of OECD job creation occurring in the United States. Popular misconceptions notwithstanding, these jobs have, for the most part, been in the higher paying occupations.

But average real take-home pay has hardly risen and outcomes for the low-skilled have worsened

But the stagnation in average real wages and the widening of the income distribution over the past twenty years or so have troubled many commentators and the public at large. A large portion of the widening reflects demographic factors and the distribution of non-labour income, but important components result from increased dispersion in the distribution of wages and reduced labour force attachment of the low-skilled (which may be related to some degree). The United States appears to have a less equal distribution of wage rates, but a more equal distribution of employment than is found in Europe, for example. Efforts to reduce inequality in the United States should focus on measures that, to the extent possible, do not hamper the distribution of employment possibilities. That is why, in principle, the Committee does not support the recently enacted increase in the minimum wage. Even though its level relative to average wages will still be low and the increase may reduce overall income inequality, it is a blunt instrument which may put the least skilled at risk by reducing their job opportunities. On the other hand, the Earned Income Tax Credit has proven to be an effective means of boosting incomes of low-income adults without discouraging work effort or reducing employment, and could well be expanded to the extent overall budget pressures allow. Over the longer term, however, the greatest potential for alleviating the labour-market problems of the least skilled and for enhancing real wages overall is by boosting human capital formation, in particular by strengthening the skills and competences of those who currently fail to achieve even minimum standards.

In the long run these problems should be dealt with by better education and training

As stated in previous *Surveys*, the US education and training system presents a mixed picture in terms of performance. The diverse structure of higher education is a major competitive strength. By contrast, the effectiveness of many primary and secondary schools has been mediocre at best, and as noted in the two previous surveys, the high variability of service quality – particularly the very poor results achieved in large parts of the urban school system – is a factor perpetuating not only earnings inequality but also weak social cohesion and high crime rates. While the benefits from improved schooling come through only in the fairly long run, this is an argument for moving ahead as rapidly as feasible. The federal government has taken some limited steps to improve the average level and decrease the inequities in the system. While funding is not the only reason for uneven quality, the federal government should reinforce its efforts to reduce funding disparities, and the states should do the same. The heated debate over curriculum content indicates that the strategy of developing rigorous albeit voluntary national standards may not be feasible for all subjects. Continued experimentation with non-traditional kinds of schools may be more promising. Further, more attention needs to be devoted to bettering the quality of vocational studies at the secondary level. Finally, the adult part of the system would benefit from strengthening the quality of public training programmes by consolidating them around those that work best, increasing information on the performance of institutions that receive direct and indirect public funding and devolving responsibility toward the individual, as the Administration has recently proposed through its advocacy of tax deductions for retraining.

But some social assistance programmes could still usefully be adjusted

While other settings are favourable to well functioning labour markets in general, adjustments should be made to some social assistance programmes. A major overhaul of the Aid to Families with Dependent Children and Food Stamp programmes was signed into law this year which will impose time limits and work requirements on beneficiaries and encourage states to provide job training for welfare recipients. The time limits should greatly reduce the work disincentives and the resulting unemployment trap from which these programmes suffered. But the reform may not provide enough support in terms of training, child care and access to medical insurance. Moreover, several features will further shrink an already limited safety net for the non-aged, non-disabled poor and virtually eliminate it for legal immigrants. Poverty among children might also become more widespread, especially if states choose to reduce their welfare spending as permitted by the legislation. Reform at the federal level is also needed to deal with access to health insurance by the working poor. The disability assistance programmes have grown quite rapidly, even after passage of the Americans with Disabilities Act which, among other goals, was designed to promote the employability and self-reliance of disabled persons. Therefore further efforts should be made to identify strategies to increase employment of current and potential disability beneficiaries.

The case for abandoning the shareholder value-based system of corporate governance is unproven

The rapid pace of business restructuring as manifest in the recent trend to corporate downsizing has led many experts and the public at large to question the advantages of the US system of corporate governance and especially its market-enforced focus on shareholder value. But downsizing is just the embodiment of the dynamism of the US business sector and the acuity of competition in US product markets both of which are great sources of competitive strength. Moreover, the social and human costs associated with quick corporate downsizing are mitigated by the particular strengths of the US labour market with respect to its high degree of flexibility and mobility. This suggests more generally that a proper evaluation of any system of corporate governance cannot be made independently of a consideration of other characteristics of the economy. Overall then the case for abandoning the central premise of the US capital allocation system – profit maximisation – in favour of an alternative ''stakeholder'' approach to business governance (where an important role is allocated to employees, creditors and local communities) remains unproven.

But some "stakeholder" features could be adopted

But that does not mean that the stakeholder view has nothing to offer. First, it might be argued that all debtholders, and banks in particular, should be allowed to hold equity as well (without the benefit of deposit insurance coverage on such holdings of course). At the margin such a change might increase their voice in governance fora, especially given the unusual tendency of the bankruptcy system to reprioritise claims. And, in a nation where union representation is marginal, all employees, and not just those in managerial positions, should have a decision-making role which is commensurate with the firm-specific capital they contribute to the enterprise. This may justify widespread use of equity-based compensation and the policies which are in place to encourage it. Any more interventionist proposals to encourage "good corporate citizenship", however, seem unlikely to yield positive results.

The costs of separating ownership from control are potentially large

Beyond that broad debate lie many others. Most important is the question of whether the current set of institutions, laws and regulations does a good job in minimising agency costs, given the separation of ownership from control that results from the delegation by shareholders of decision-making power to management. These agency costs can be substantial, as can be seen in the huge premiums usually offered to shareholders in takeover situations. It is only natural that managers, when not given appropriate incentives, use their discretion to further their own aims: they may seek to maximise the firm's size, to hoard cash flow, to choose low-risk/low-return strategies, or to pay themselves excessively, and they may try to entrench themselves.

But they can be controlled in several ways

In theory, this behaviour can be controlled: by aligning management's interests with those of shareholders through an ownership stake and/or equity-based compensation; by choosing a level of debt which responds not only to direct cost and risk considerations but also to its advantage in terms of forcing the disbursement of free cash flow; and by various forms of monitoring. The board of directors has traditionally proved to be a weak monitor, due primarily to a lack of independence from senior management. But boards have become more assertive of late, probably because directors are more likely to be outsiders and their compensation is to a greater extent equity-based. Bank-based monitoring is prevalent in a number of other OECD Member countries, but this seems to be diminishing somewhat; in the US case it has been effectively ruled out by Depression-era laws which split commercial from investment banking. Monitoring can also be carried out by different kinds of shareholder voice. The major disadvantage of this mechanism is the free-rider problem; this can be overcome by concentrated shareholdings. US anti-trust law prevents industrial groups from serving this purpose, so it is left to institutional investors to play this role. Some – especially public pension funds – have become quite activist over the past decade, encouraged by significant payoffs to governance changes they have sought and by limited regulatory changes that have, since 1992, somewhat expanded the scope for institutional investors to exercise an active monitoring role. But such regulatory changes could easily go further in order to strengthen the potential for effective shareholder monitoring.

In the US case the most important is market-based monitoring

Yet it is left to the markets to do much of the monitoring in the US context. Highly competitive factor and product markets are an important disciplinary device, but one which operates rather slowly to correct managerial failure, as bankruptcy is an extreme outcome. Costly though it is, the "market for corporate control" acts more quickly to correct substandard performance or to exploit *ex ante* potential. But there is no doubt that some of the 83 000 mergers and acquisitions which have taken place since 1968 were driven by objectives other than increasing efficiency, factors such as managerial empire-building, tax minimisation and rent-seeking at the expense of both employees and bondholders. Nonetheless, the attempts by both firms and state governments to crimp or even shut down this mechanism have fortunately proved largely unsuccessful.

US corporate competitiveness is strong, and the governance system seems to work as well as any

The evidence that there is a time-horizon problem in US financial markets and that the business sector suffers from "short-termism" is unconvincing. While to many it appeared that US firms were losing competitive ground to their foreign rivals during the 1980s, this was largely the result of the substantial real appreciation of the dollar during the first half of the decade. Since the subsequent reversal of that uptrend, US firms have been regaining competitive ground: they dominate many export markets; their foreign subsidiaries are formidable players on the domestic scene in many other economies; they are leaders in the research and development field, helping to generate substantial royalties and licence fees; and while they may not invest as much as some others in fixed capital, they seem to be exceedingly good at managing it productively in order to create profits and, ultimately, wealth. Thus, whatever faults the corporate governance system has cannot be impeding performance to any significant extent. And the readiness with which new governance forms are emerging stands the system in good stead for the future.

A wrap-up

US macroeconomic outcomes continue to be favourable in absolute terms as well as relative to trading partners'. The economy is for all intents and purposes at full employment with fairly low inflation, and, while some risks certainly exist, it looks likely to continue that way over the next two years. Also, the current account deficit appears to have peaked, the dollar has rallied, and the budget deficit has been reduced. However, future fiscal prospects are mediocre in the near term and poor looking further out unless an agreement is reached to balance the federal budget by reining in entitlement spending. And full price stability has not yet been achieved. Some valuable structural reforms have been legislated, but several other efforts – in financial services deregulation and, especially, in health care, and other areas affecting social objectives – remain to be completed, while other domains, such as taxation and Social Security financing, have been reformed in the past but are in need of further attention in the future. It is to be hoped that these reforms will be successfully brought to fruition in the years to come.

I. Recent economic trends and prospects

The economy has expanded at about a 2 per cent pace since the end of 1994 with some quarters showing real GDP growth well above that rate while others have been close to zero (Figure 1). Other indicators such as unemployment rates, wages and prices have also exhibited a somewhat sawtooth pattern, but also have shown little systematic movement. These are the signs of an economy operating near trend capacity in both levels and growth rates. If the economy was not yet near capacity in level terms, then there would be a significant amount of underutilised resources, and wage rates and prices would be decelerating noticeably, which they are not. Likewise, if potential growth rates were not being realised on average, then unemployment rates would be rising, which also has not occurred. Thus, to a first approximation, the economy has achieved trend growth at (reasonably) high levels of resource utilisation. In such a situation, analysts have strained to try to tease emerging trend shifts out of incoming data.

Demand-side developments

After registering growth rates of a meagre $^1/_2$ per cent (annual rates, using the chain-type indexes now being emphasised by the Bureau of Economic Analysis; see Box 1) in each of the first two quarters of 1995, the pace of activity re-accelerated to a 2 per cent rate, on average, in the second half of the year. But, around the turn of the year, the economy was again showing signs of weakness, partly due to temporary factors such as the two government shutdowns, several work stoppages and severe winter weather. Indeed, in the fourth quarter, total domestic demand fell. But as 1996 has progressed, the economy has strengthened again. Real GDP rose 2 per cent in the first quarter, and growth accelerated to $4^3/_4$ per cent in the second quarter. Income-side measures of real GDP growth indicated substantially stronger growth in activity than product-side accounts

Figure 1. **AN ECONOMY NEAR EQUILIBRIUM**

Per cent change, annual rate

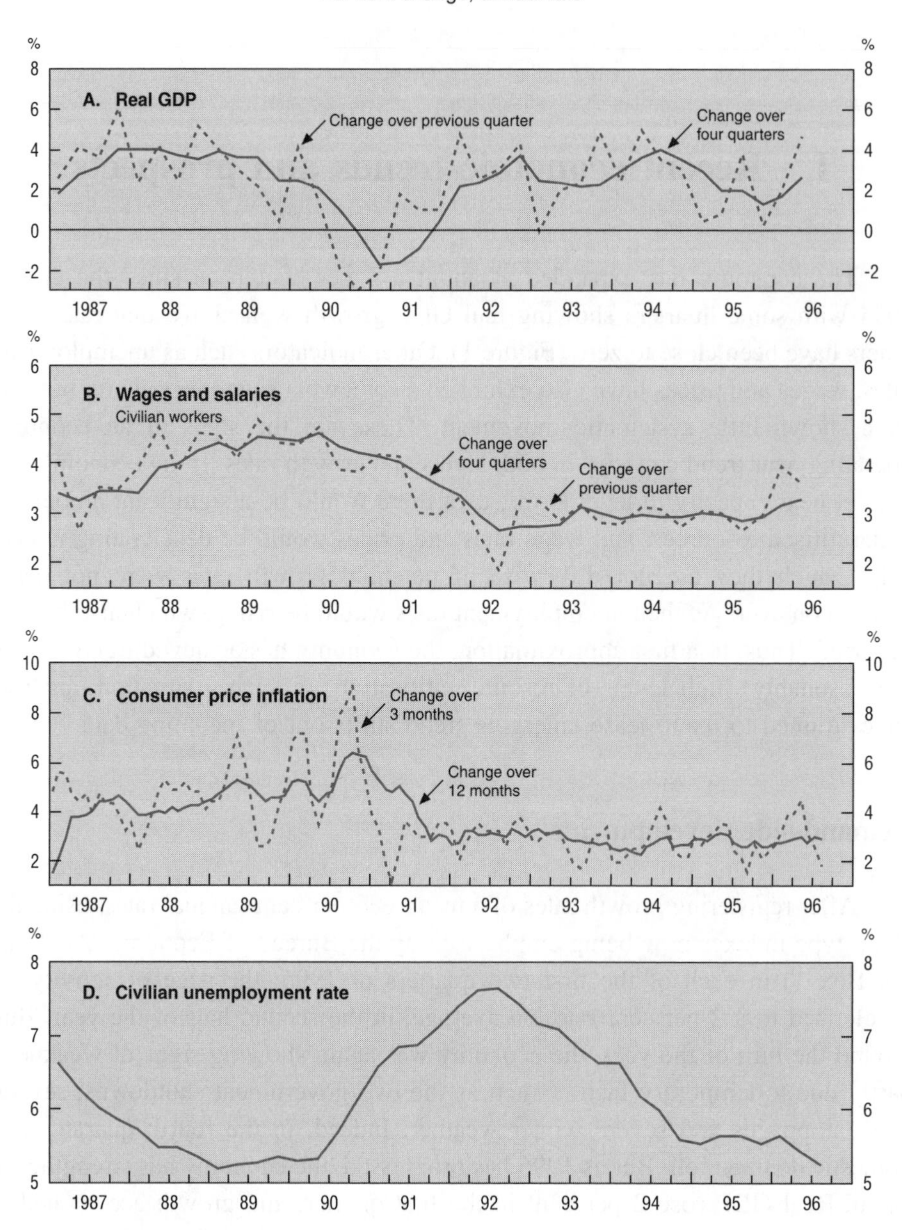

Source: Bureau of Economic Analysis; Bureau of Labor Statistics.

Box 1. **The revised national accounts**

In December 1995, the Bureau of Economic Analysis (BEA) published comprehensive revisions to the national accounts. The most noteworthy change was a shift to feature a chain-type weighted measure of GDP. As foreshadowed by the BEA, GDP growth calculated with the chain-type index was lower in recent years than that using the former featured measure, 1987 fixed-weight GDP. (Much of the reduction would have occurred with a rolling forward of the fixed weight index to a more recent year.) Price deflators were revised up to the same degree that growth was revised downward owing to the methodological change.

The major conceptual change was to account separately for government consumption and investment, bringing the national accounts closer to the System of National Accounts recommendations. The service flows from government investment are set equal to depreciation; thus, the rate of return is assumed to be zero. These newly recorded service flows boost GDP by about 2 percentage points.

Newly available data also had an important impact on the revisions. For example, the personal saving rate was revised upward for most years and the slowdown in economic growth in 1995 is now much more pronounced than in initial estimates.

during 1995, but the two measures registered similar rates of growth during the first half of 1996.

Much of the slowdown in 1995 can be traced to a shift in accumulation of stocks. In 1994, real stockbuilding averaged 0.9 per cent of GDP, but by the beginning of 1996 inventory levels were being reduced, particularly for farm products and retail trade (Figure 2). The inventory correction shaved nearly a percentage point off aggregate demand growth over the four quarters ending in the first quarter of 1996. The reduction in farm stock accumulation (from $12 billion in 1994 to –$3 billion in 1995) primarily reflects the bumper crop in 1994 and the poor harvest in 1995, but increased net exports were also a factor. The downshift in non-farm stockbuilding has allowed stock-to-sales ratios to retrace their earlier rise. The stock correction appeared to be completed by the end of the second quarter.

In addition to the slowdown in stockbuilding, demand growth eased in 1995 owing to a rise in the personal saving rate, foreign economic developments and their impact on export demand and a retrenchment in housing demand. The government sector continued to be a drag on the economy, but business

Figure 2. **STOCKBUILDING EASES**

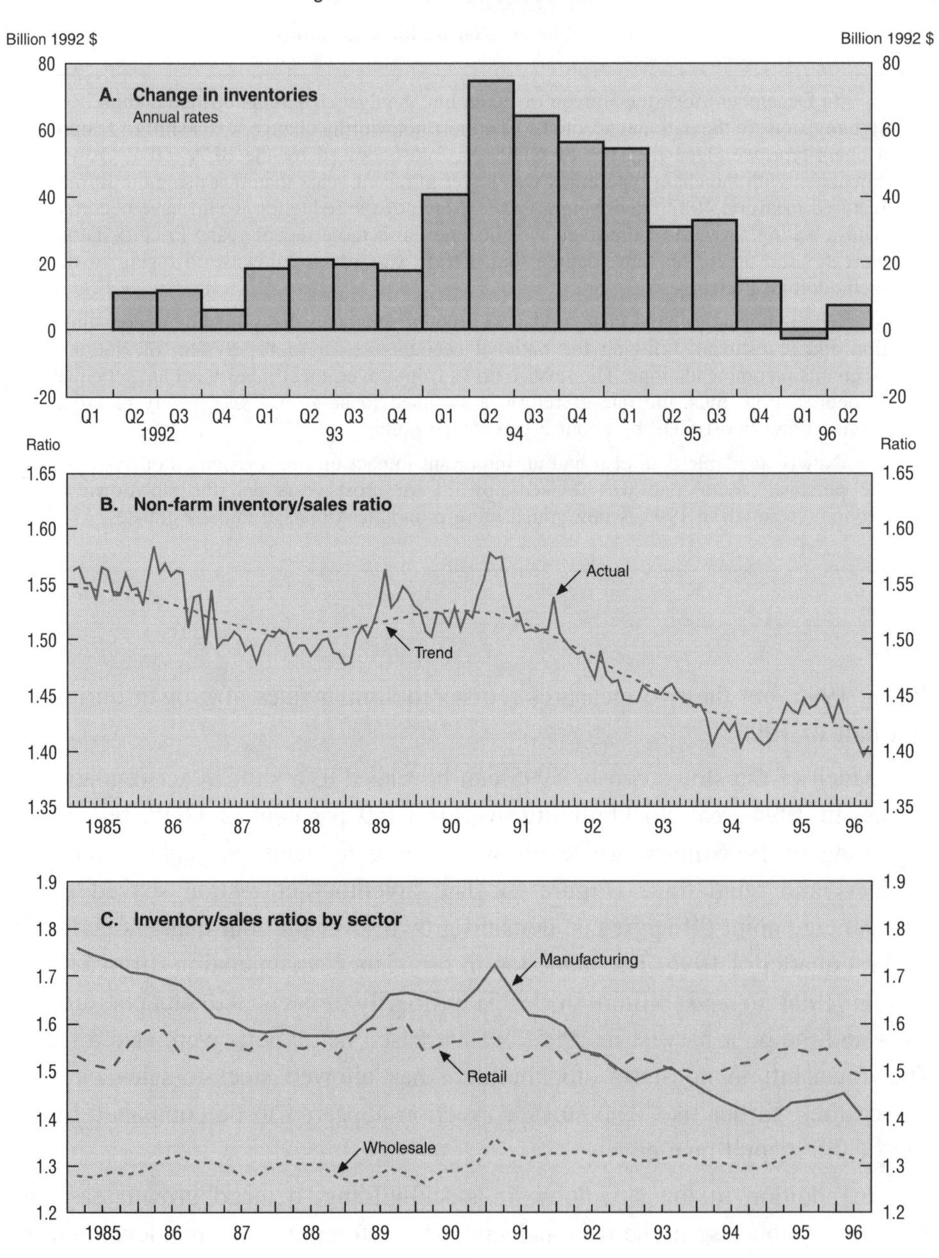

Source: Bureau of Economic Analysis.

investment remained robust. Recent data indicate that many of these factors have reversed themselves in the first half of 1996.

Real private consumption rose 2½ per cent in 1995, somewhat stronger than overall real GDP growth, but weaker than real disposable personal income gains, so that the saving rate rose ¾ percentage point. Consumption accelerated in the first half of 1996, and the saving rate has declined somewhat.

Many analysts have pointed to the state of household balance sheets as the key to consumption prospects. Some point to net financial assets, which rose spectacularly in 1995 and the first half of 1996, as a reason for consumption to race ahead of income in 1996 (Table 1). Others have stressed that data on liabilities point to a risk that consumers will have to slow consumption to reach sustainable levels. Historically, assets and liabilities have tended to be built up by the same households, and thus net worth is the determinant of household finances and consumption. But to the extent that this has not been the case in recent years, and that holders of assets and debt have different propensities to consume out of wealth, the two sides of the balance sheet should be examined separately.

Concerns about household liabilities are driven by rising debt payment burdens, and especially the sharp rise in credit card delinquency rates (Figure 3). The latter is consistent with the hypothesis that the increases in assets and liabilities are accruing to different segments of the population. Indeed, while the proportion of credit holders with high debt repayment to income ratios remained relatively constant from 1989, the proportion of low income households with high debt burdens has risen. The Federal Reserve's Senior Loan Officer Survey indicates that banks have begun to tighten standards on consumer credit, and the growth rate of bank credit to consumers has slowed since the beginning of the year. However, mortgage delinquencies have remained near historically low levels, and the marked increase in financial assets and the more widespread holding of equities may point to relatively healthy balance sheets for many consumers.

Residential investment fell sharply in the first half of 1995 and then rose rapidly over the second half of the year and into the first half of 1996. Housing starts and construction data indicate that residential investment was expanding briskly in the second quarter. Much of the plunge and subsequent rebound reflect lagged effects of mortgage interest rates on demand (Figure 4). With interest rates rising sharply in the first half of 1996, housing starts appeared to have reached a

Table 1. **Household balance sheets**

$ billion, year end

	1990	1991	1992	1993	1994	1995[1]	Average annual per cent change 1990-95	Average annual per cent change 1994-95
Tangible assets	8 775	9 286	9 557	9 970	10 544	11 030	4.7	4.6
Financial assets	14 202	15 697	16 572	17 763	18 418	20 842	8.0	13.2
Deposits	3 351	3 363	3 359	3 330	3 347	3 565	1.2	6.5
Credit market instruments	1 466	1 545	1 619	1 677	2 003	2 011	6.5	0.4
Mutual funds	472	593	741	998	1 059	1 265	21.8	19.5
Corporate equities	1 760	2 653	2 919	3 285	3 168	4 166	18.8	31.5
Life and pension reserves	3 686	4 061	4 488	4 940	5 194	5 974	10.1	15.0
Equity in non-corporate business	2 629	2 521	2 458	2 476	2 565	2 643	0.1	3.0
Other	838	961	988	1 057	1 082	1 218	7.8	12.6
Liabilities	3 764	3 972	4 173	4 461	4 837	5 231	6.8	8.1
Mortgages	2 491	2 654	2 816	2 970	3 165	3 360	6.2	6.2
Consumer credit	811	797	802	864	990	1 132	6.9	14.3
Other	462	521	555	627	682	739	9.9	8.4
Net financial assets	10 438	11 725	12 399	13 302	13 581	15 611	8.4	14.9
Net worth	19 213	21 011	21 956	23 291	24 125	26 641	6.8	10.4
Memorandum:								
Ratios to disposable income:								
Assets	5.42	5.66	5.51	5.66	5.62	5.87		
Liabilities	0.89	0.90	0.88	0.91	0.94	0.96		
Net worth	4.53	4.76	4.63	4.75	4.68	4.91		

1. For 1995 tangible assets is an OECD estimate.
Source: Board of Governors of the Federal Reserve System, *Flow of Funds Accounts.*

plateau in the February-June period; the effects on construction should be felt in the months ahead.

Business fixed investment was a major contributor to overall demand growth in 1995 and led the surge in activity in the first half of 1996. Business investment in producer durable equipment (PDE) typically rises with changes in the growth rate of demand as firms need to expand capacity to meet the additional demand. A simple accelerator model which links growth in PDE to the change in growth of output (Figure 4) indicates that growth in PDE may be greater than

Figure 3. **HOUSEHOLD FINANCES**

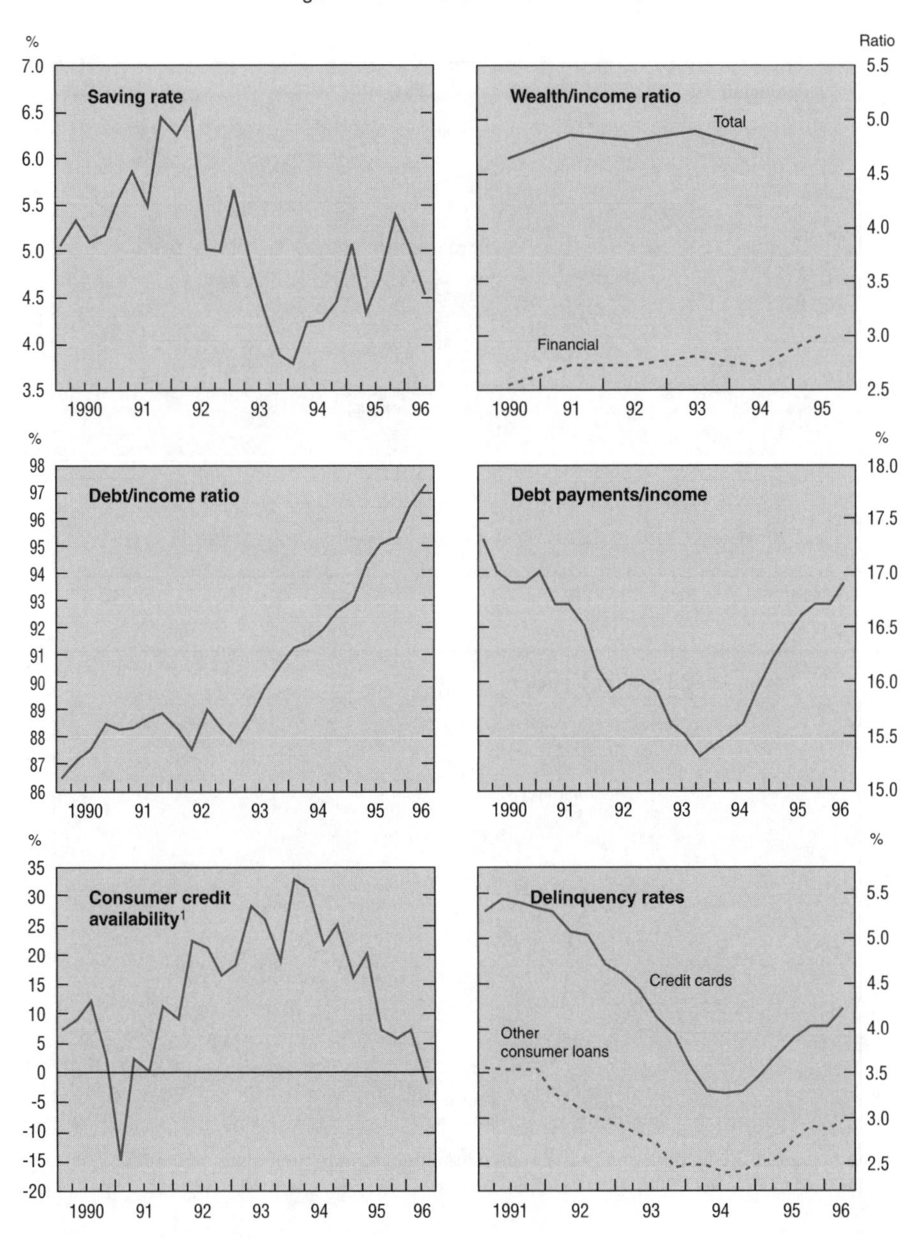

1. Senior Loan Officers Survey.
Source: Federal Reserve Board and OECD.

Figure 4. **INVESTMENT DEVELOPMENTS**

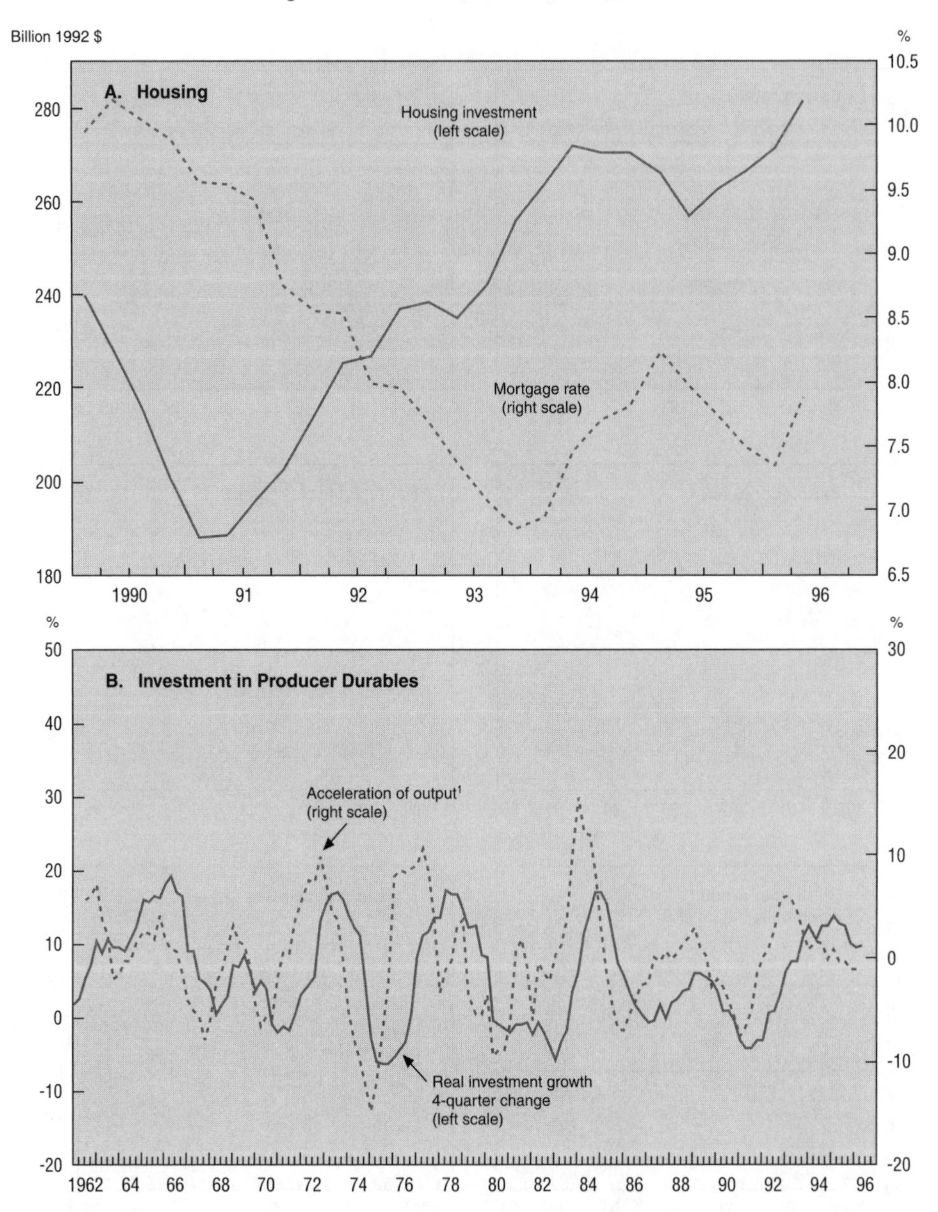

1. The eight-quarter per cent change in non-farm business output less the year-earlier eight-quarter change at annual rates.

Source: Bureau of Economic Analysis; OECD.

expected for current rates of demand growth. This may reflect reductions in the user cost of capital – particularly falling computer prices – and rising profitability. While computers and peripherals have drawn much attention, industrial equipment has remained an important component of PDE growth. Construction of non-residential structures, the other component of fixed investment, picked up in 1995, led by growth in hotel, industrial and other commercial (including retail) construction. Although vacancy rates of office buildings have tumbled over the past two years, this component has not been an important source of the recent buoyancy.

The government sector continues to be a drag on demand, both from reductions in its own purchases as well as the effects of higher effective tax rates. The federal government reduced military spending and shed labour in non-defence functions in 1995. Deficit-cutting efforts have also constrained federal government investment, which is now classified separately in the national accounts. Investment is largely a state and local affair (72 per cent of total public investment in 1995); there, real investment rose 20 per cent from 1991 to 1995, reflecting its somewhat procyclical nature.[1] State and local consumption has grown slowly, however, reflecting budget restrictions (see Chapter II).

In 1995 real exports of goods and services rose more rapidly than imports for the first time since 1991, as growth of imports slowed more rapidly than that of exports. Merchandise export growth slowed substantially in the first half of 1995 owing to the weakening in activity in many OECD countries, especially Mexico (Figure 5). However, the effect on export volumes was mitigated by gains in market share, perhaps reflecting the good relative cost performance of US exporters in recent years. Although there were wide swings in some bilateral exchange rates, which may have affected goods flows, the real effective exchange rate remained in the range it has been in since the late 1980s. The easing of domestic demand, especially for automotive products, led to a slowing in the growth of merchandise imports in 1995. All told, the merchandise trade deficit peaked in the first half of 1995 and shrank considerably in the second half. The surplus on non-factor services continued to expand, although imports grew faster than exports. US trade in non-factor services has grown more slowly than that in goods since 1990, but the balance on non-factor services has doubled over the past five years. During the first half of 1996, the merchandise trade deficit

Figure 5. **MERCHANDISE EXPORTS AND IMPORTS**

Per cent change from previous period, annual rates

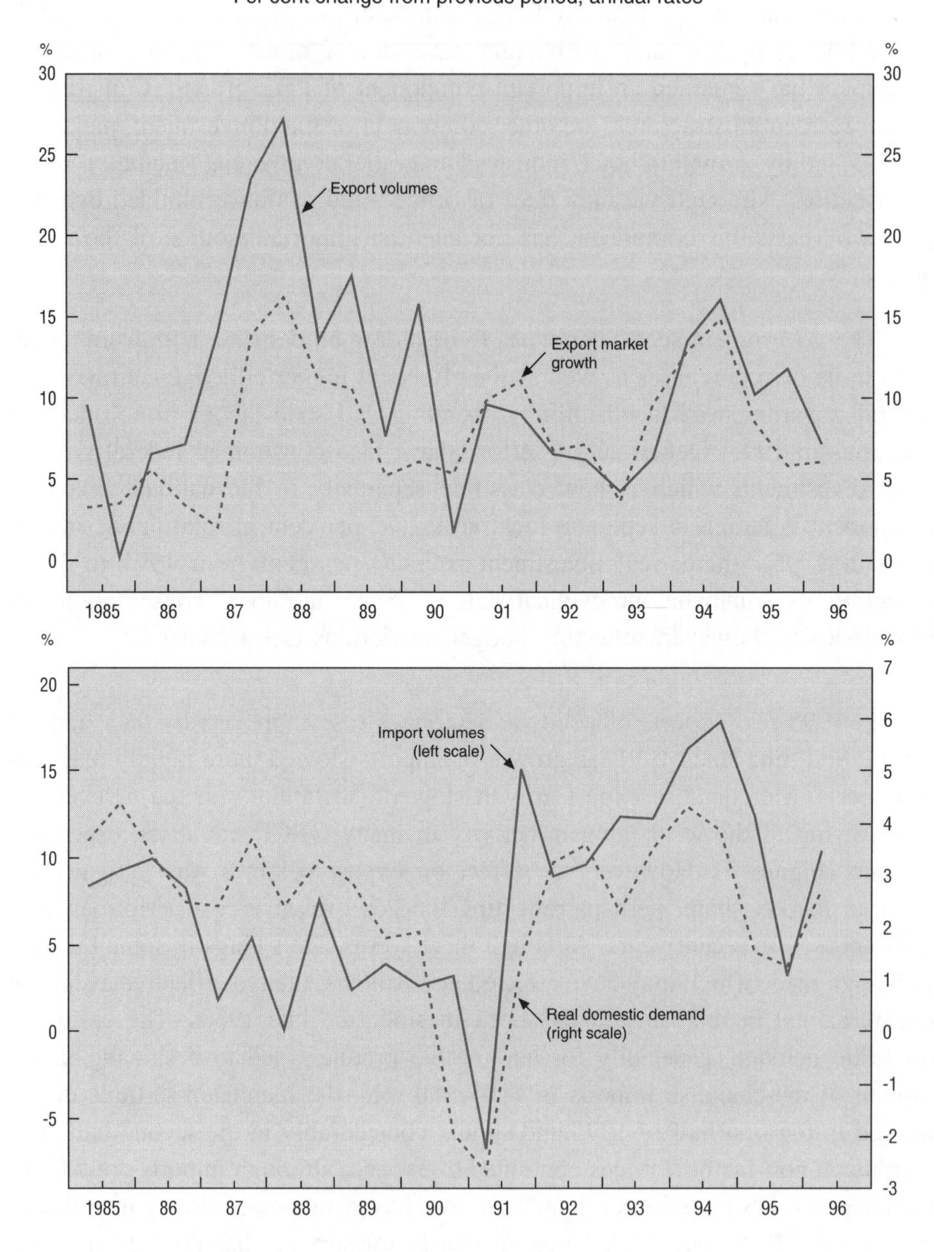

Source: Bureau of Economic Analysis; OECD.

expanded a bit, as import volume growth rebounded, reflecting the pickup in domestic demand, and export growth slowed sharply.

There has been a shift in both markets for exports and origins of imports in recent years, in part reflecting divergent growth rates in various economies, but also the market-opening policy changes made by many developing countries (Table 2). Compared with 1990, export markets and import suppliers have shifted towards NAFTA members, the rest of Latin America and the dynamic Asian economies, while non-NAFTA OECD countries have lost somewhat in relative importance.

After expanding since the end of the last recession, the current account deficit peaked in the second half of 1994, shrank throughout 1995 and began to expand in 1996, largely reflecting developments in the trade account (Table 3). In addition, the deterioration of investment income was not as great as would be expected from the worsening of the US net investment position, in part because the rates of return on direct investment rose more for US investors than for foreign investors (Table 4). A minor factor in the improvement of the current account in 1995 was the delay of US payments to foreign countries that resulted from the budget problems (which will boost the deficit in 1996). But more

Table 2. **US merchandise exports and imports by trading partner**

Per cent of total except as noted

	Exports				Imports			
	1985	1990	1994	1995	1985	1990	1994	1995
World ($ billion)	213.1	393.0	509.4	581.4	345.3	495.3	677.0	757.0
OECD	68.5	71.8	67.9	65.8	69.5	65.7	65.3	64.7
Canada	22.2	21.1	22.3	21.6	20.0	18.4	19.4	19.5
Mexico	6.4	7.2	9.9	7.9	5.5	6.1	7.5	8.3
Japan	10.6	12.4	10.4	11.0	19.9	18.1	17.9	16.6
Other	29.3	31.1	25.3	25.3	24.1	23.0	20.4	20.2
Non-OECD	31.4	28.1	32.0	34.1	30.5	34.3	34.7	35.3
Latin America	6.7	5.4	7.2	7.6	7.0	6.2	5.3	5.3
Dynamic Asian [1]	11.1	13.1	15.6	17.2	13.7	17.0	19.6	20.5
Other	13.6	9.7	9.3	9.3	9.7	11.0	9.9	9.6

1. China, Hong Kong, Chinese Taipei, Korea, Malaysia, Philippines and Singapore.
Source: OECD.

Table 3. **Current account**

$ billion, seasonally adjusted annual rates

	1994	1995	1995				1996	
			Q1	Q2	Q3	Q4	Q1	Q2
Current account balance	–148	–148	–156	–164	–151	–122	–139	–155
of which:								
Exports of goods, services and income	840	969	932	966	978	1 001	1 011	1 030
Imports of goods, services and income	949	1 082	1 054	1 097	1 093	1 086	1 106	1 148
Net unilateral transfers	–40	–35	–35	–33	–36	–37	–44	–37
Balances:								
Goods	–166	–173	–180	–192	–170	–152	–171	–187
Non-factor services	62	68	62	64	73	75	74	76
Investment income	–4	–8	–4	–3	–17	–8	1	–6
Private transfers	–20	–21	–20	–20	–20	–22	–23	–24
Official transfers	–20	–14	–14	–13	–16	–14	–21	–13

Source: Bureau of Economic Analysis.

Table 4. **Rates of return on foreign direct investment**

Per cent

	1981-85	1986-90	1991	1992	1993	1994	1995
Direct investment[1]							
US investment abroad	7.5	9.3	8.3	8.0	9.0	9.2	10.7
Foreign investment in United States	3.2	2.2	–0.7	0.1	1.1	3.8	5.2
Portfolio investment[2]							
US investment abroad	10.0	7.1	6.2	4.8	3.9	4.4	5.2
Foreign investment in United States	9.1	7.2	6.5	5.2	4.6	5.0	5.6

1. Rate of return in US dollars. Numerator is direct investment receipts or payments (balance of payments accounts) and denominator is the average of year-end figures for the value of direct investment for the current and previous year, evaluated at current cost.
2. Rate of return in US dollars.

Source: Bureau of Economic Analysis.

fundamentally, the decline of the current account deficit as a share of GDP reflects the narrowing in the net saving and investment balance as both public and private saving rose and domestic investment remained constant as a share of GDP.[2]

The supply side and prices

Employment, as measured by the household survey, grew at the same rate as the working-age population from the fourth quarter of 1994 until the end of 1995.[3] And because the labour force participation rate remained around 66.6 per cent, the unemployment rate stayed in a narrow range centred around 5½ per cent. Over the first eight months of 1996 employment growth has accelerated, and the unemployment rate fell to 5.1 per cent in August. Thus the unemployment rate has been below the OECD's view of the natural rate of unemployment for nearly 2 years, though not outside the inevitable normal range of error surrounding these estimates (Figure 6, top panel). The last time that the unemployment rate dropped below the estimated natural rate, at the end of the 1980s, wage rates and employee compensation began to accelerate (middle and lower panels). No acceleration in either compensation or wages was evident through 1995. Over the twelve months ending in December 1995, the growth in the employment cost indexes (ECI) for compensation and wages were essentially unchanged from the previous twelve month period. But in the first half of 1996, some evidence of acceleration of wages has been evident in the ECI wage index and average hourly earnings,[4] while growth of total labour compensation has picked up only slightly. The extent to which this reflects tight labour markets, higher inflation expectations of workers, and/or a lagged pass-through to wages from smaller increases in non-wage costs, is still an open question.

With a quiescent labour market, it is not surprising that consumer price inflation has been subdued. Overall consumer prices rose 2½ per cent over the twelve months ending December 1995, the fifth year in a row in the 2½ to 3 per cent range (Figure 7). Over that time period, core inflation, defined by consumer prices excluding the volatile energy and food components, has generally been higher, as energy prices, in particular, have tended to fall. More importantly, core inflation showed some signs of acceleration in 1995, advancing 3.0 per cent compared with 2.6 per cent in 1994. But during the first eight months of 1996 evidence of this acceleration has withered; by August the twelve-month change had receded to 2.6 per cent. Meanwhile, overall consumer inflation surged during the first five months rising at a 4.1 per cent annual rate, reflecting soaring energy costs. But since May overall CPI inflation has slowed markedly,

Figure 6. **LABOUR MARKET PRESSURES**

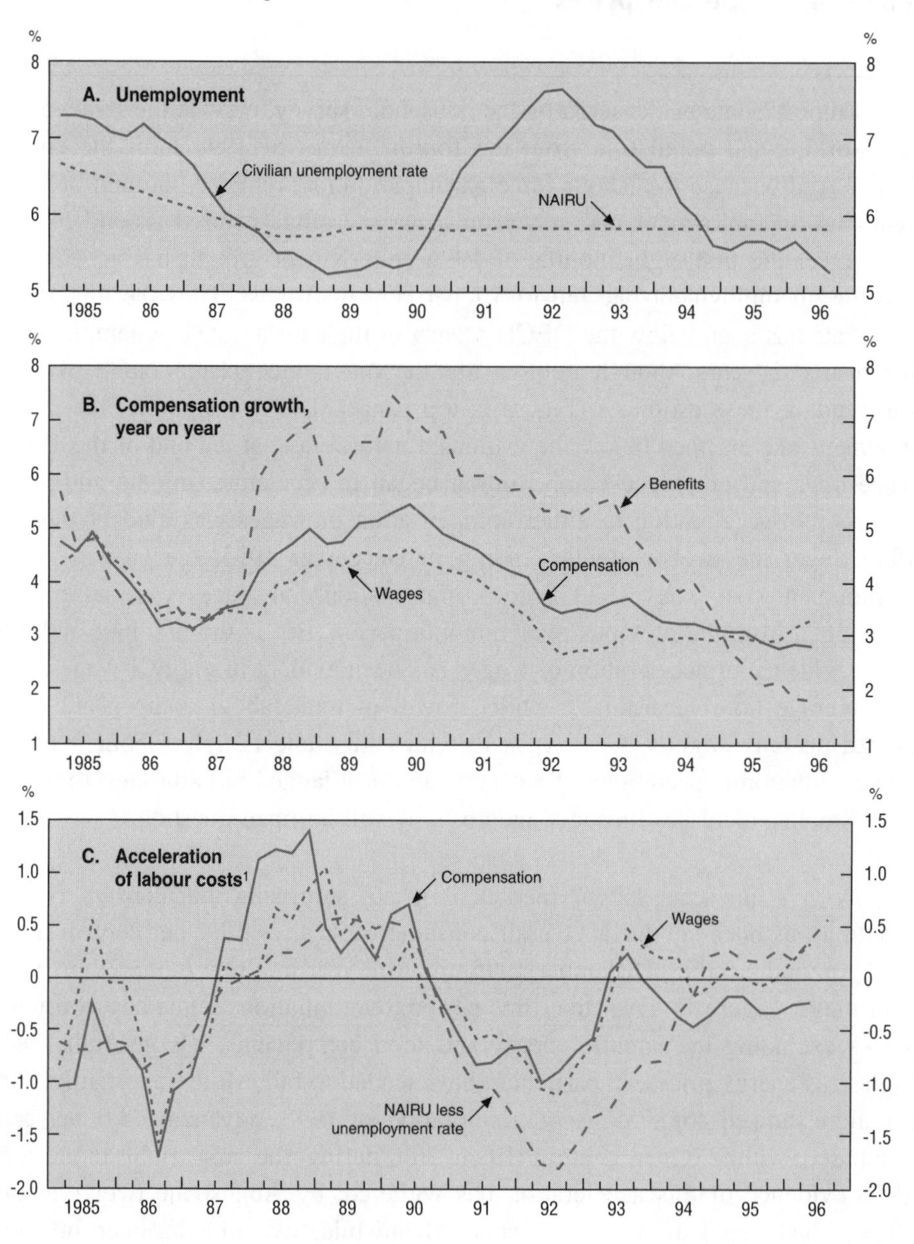

1. Twelve-month growth rate minus year-earlier rate.
Source: Bureau of Labor Statistics; OECD.

Figure 7. **INFLATION REMAINS TAME**

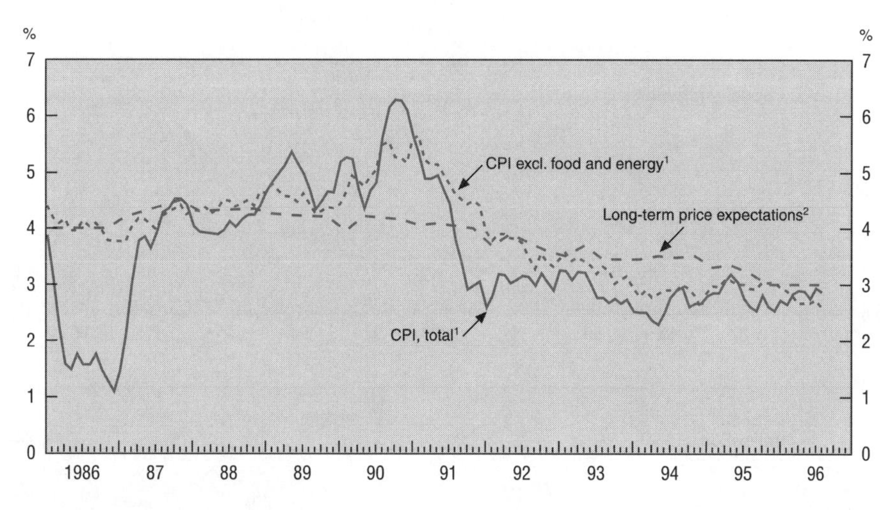

1. Per cent change over 12 months earlier.
2. Survey of Professional Forecasters.

Source: Federal Reserve Bank of Philadelphia; OECD.

held down by both falling energy prices and subdued core inflation, and was only 3.2 per cent (at an annual rate) over the first eight months.

The success in keeping inflation at historically low levels has changed expectations about inflation prospects. Surveys of professional forecasters indicate that this group's long-term inflation expectations have fallen a full percentage point since the late 1980s. Consumers' inflation expectations, however, have fallen less.

One factor holding down consumer price inflation may have been the easing of capacity constraints in the manufacturing sector (Figure 8). Manufacturing capacity has been growing quite rapidly of late, reflecting rising labour productivity (in part due to capital investment) as manufacturing employment has been steady, at roughly 18¼ million, since the end of the last recession.[5] Capacity utilisation has some bearing on price developments in the goods market, particularly for intermediate goods, although this is certainly attenuated by import and export possibilities and, thus, global capacity considerations. While manufacturing capacity constraints have eased since the end of 1994, this may have been

Figure 8. **MANUFACTURING SECTOR INDICATORS**

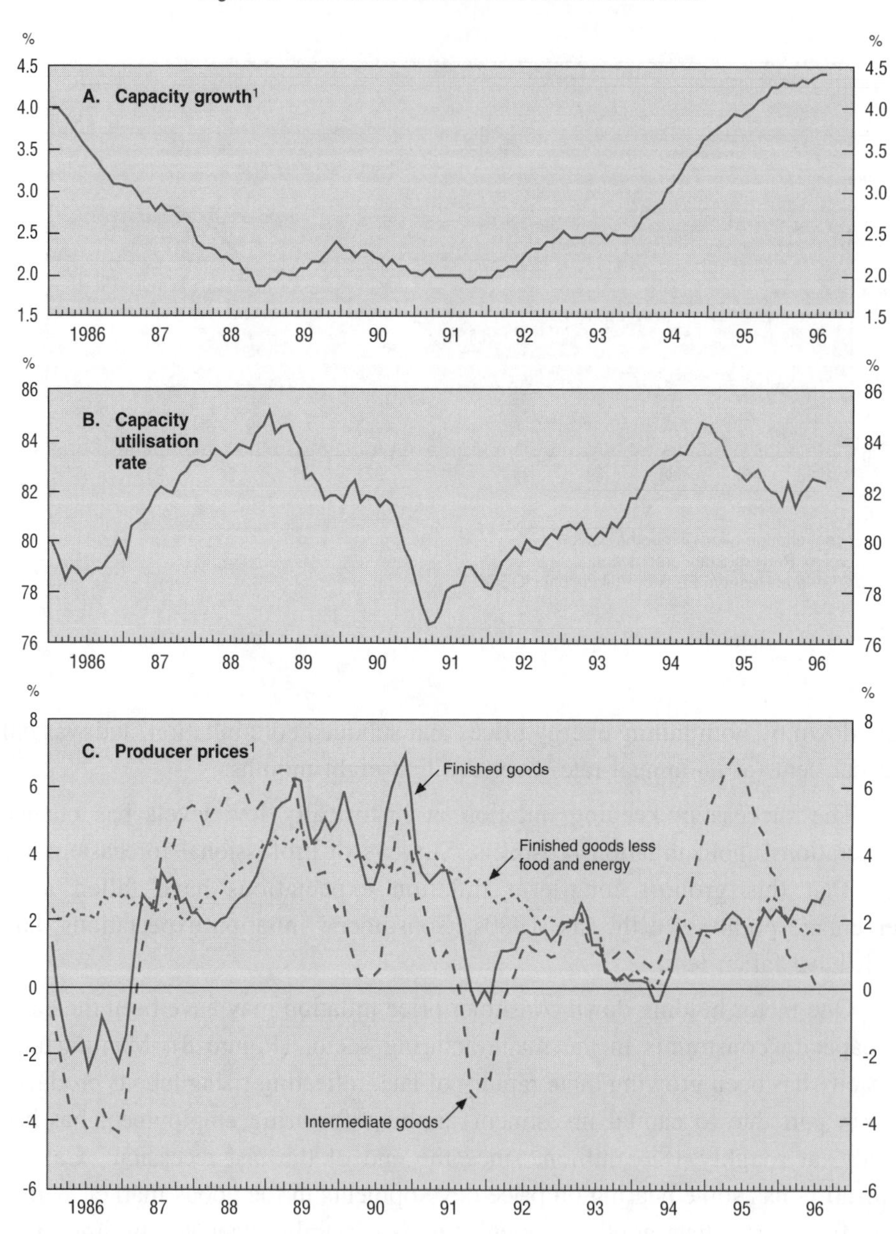

1. Per cent change over 12 months earlier.
Source: OECD.

offset by tightening constraints in other sectors, as the overall labour market has tightened, and thus lower price pressures in the manufacturing sector may not have translated into lower price pressures overall.[6]

Considerable interest has emerged about the sustainable rate of economic growth. The growth of capacity is determined by the supply of labour and physical capital as well as improvements of the quality of labour (human capital) through education and training, technological innovation and improvements in management practices. Statistically, the effects of all the factors except the quantity of labour are captured in measures of labour productivity. Abstracting from cyclical variations, the growth rate of labour productivity in the non-farm business sector (essentially covering gross domestic product less farms, government and owner-occupied housing) has averaged 1.1 per cent since 1973 with little variation (Figure 9).[7] As trend labour productivity has been fairly constant, the evolution of non-farm business output has been determined by aggregate hours worked in the business sector. Aggregate hours can be disaggregated into several components: growth of the working-age population, the employment-population ratio (labour force participation and the unemployment rate), and average weekly hours per worker (Table 5). In recent years, aggregate hours have been growing at around 1 per cent per year, chiefly due to growth in the working-age population component. In sum, sustainable growth of 2 to 2¼ per cent can be expected with current demographic trends.

There has been much speculation regarding the factors behind the continued slow productivity growth in recent years despite the widespread incorporation of computer and information technologies. The responses fall into four categories, some of which conflict with one another. Some argue that there is no mystery, because computers make up only a small share of physical capital (Sichel and Oliner, 1994). Others argue that a delay between incorporation of new technologies and productivity increases is often measured in decades, and, thus, the gains will be realised in future years.[8] Many now argue that tight monetary policy has kept growth below potential. This line of argument, while common, seems to lack a basis in macroeconomic models for two reasons. Lower average inflation rates are often associated with higher output growth due to a reduction in relative price distortions. In addition, overly tight monetary policy would result in slow job creation, rising unemployment and falling inflation rates, reflecting the underutilised capacity, which does not appear to be the case in the United States.

Figure 9. **LABOUR PRODUCTIVITY GROWTH**[1]

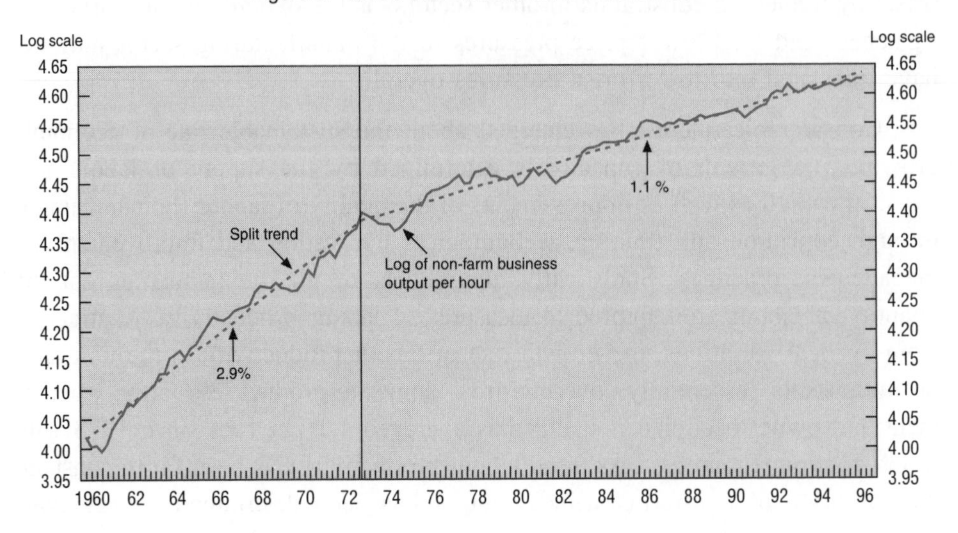

1. Non-farm business (excluding owner occupied housing).
Source: Bureau of Labor Statistics.

Table 5. **Growth of real GDP**

Average annual per cent change

	Period			
	1960-73	1973-79	1979-90	1990-95
Real GDP	4.3	2.9	2.6	1.9
Non-farm business output[1]	4.7	3.1	2.7	2.1
Labour productivity, non-farm	3.0	1.1	1.0	1.0
Labour input, non-farm business	1.6	1.9	1.6	1.1
Population growth	1.8	1.9	1.2	1.1
Employment rate	0.2	0.6	0.4	0.1
Average weekly hours	–0.4	–0.6	–0.1	0.0
Other[2]	0.1	0.1	0.1	0.0

1. GDP excluding government, owner-occupied housing, farm output and non-profit institutions.
2. Shifts in the share of labour between business and non-business sectors, etc.
Source: Bureau of Economic Analysis and Bureau of Labor Statistics.

A different line of argument assumes that larger productivity gains have in fact been made, especially in sectors such as services where the increases in real output are particularly difficult to measure. This view has some empirical support from the work that has been done on biases in the consumer price index (see Box 2). Many observers suggest that problems with this index in measuring the cost of living lead to a bias of around 1 percentage point in the growth rate of consumer prices. The Bureau of Labor Statistics (BLS) has embarked on a series

Box 2. **CPI bias**[1]

In recent years much work has been carried out to examine the bias in the consumer price index (CPI) as a measure of the cost of living. Analysts have identified five possible sources of bias: 1) substitution bias; 2) new goods bias; 3) formula or elementary index bias; 4) outlet substitution bias and 5) quality adjustment bias or linking bias. *Substitution bias* is the difference between the CPI index and a cost of living index. The CPI, as developed by the BLS is not designed to measure the change in the cost of living, rather it measures the change in prices of a fixed basket of goods.[2] Some analysts estimate that there may be a 0.2 percentage point wedge between the growth rates of the two measures. *New goods bias* also exists because the CPI, as a price index and not a cost of living index, is not designed to measure the welfare gain from new products. There are no good aggregate measures of this, but some individual products which have been studied carefully suggest that while it is difficult to estimate precisely, it may be substantial. *Formula bias* is due to the choice of sub-optimal index formulas instead of Fisher ideal index formulas for price quotations at the lowest level of aggregation (0.5 percentage point bias). *Outlet substitution bias* arises because the BLS assumes that all of the shift to low cost outlets reflects different quality of service, whereas, unless there are changing tastes, some of the shift represents a shift to lower cost providers (0.2 to 0.4 percentage point bias). *Linking bias* occurs because the current method of linking one good to its successor product may not adequately take into account the improved quality of the new product. There are no good aggregate estimates for this problem.

1. This box draws heavily on Diewert (1996). The sources of bias estimates, as cited by Diewert, are Aizcorbe and Jackman (1993) for substitution biases, Reinsdorf and Moulton (1996) and Armknecht, Moulton and Stewart (1995) for elementary index bias, Reinsdorf (1993) for outlet substitution bias and Diewert (1996) for quality adjustment and new goods bias.
2. The difference being that as relative prices change consumers shift their baskets of goods towards those whose prices have risen the least. A cost of living index captures this substitution, while the CPI is not designed to do so. The CPI is a price index rather than a cost of living index, though some of its most common uses are to measure the cost of living.

of improvements to be incorporated in the index over a period of several years beginning in 1995 that would shave about ½ percentage point from the growth rate of the index.[9] A national commission is scheduled to report on its findings and recommendations at the end of 1996; its preliminary findings stated that the bias was in the range of 0.7 to 2.0 percentage points.

Short-term economic prospects

The US economy is projected to grow moderately over the remainder of 1996 and in 1997 (Table 6). After the pickup in growth over the first two quarters of 1996, the economy should begin to slow again towards sustainable rates. The slowing is expected because the rise in long-term interest rates over the first half of the year should begin to work its way through the economy, and the temporary boost to production from renewed stockbuilding should wane. Over the entire projection period private investment is expected to remain above trend, and government consumption and investment are projected to continue to be subdued by ongoing fiscal reform. In this context, monetary policy is assumed to allow short-term interest rates to rise modestly in order to guard against a further build-up in demand pressures. As 1996 comes to an end long-term rates should recede as the surge in demand evident in the spring and summer is seen to be temporary. All told, real GDP growth for 1996 is projected to be 2¼ to 2½ per cent, slowing to 2 per cent in 1997.

Consumer price inflation is projected to remain well contained. Over the first half of 1997 overall price increases should be held back by the unwinding of the oil price rise that occurred in the first half of 1996. With continued tight product and labour markets, underlying inflation may show some slight upward drift, however. Wage pressures have been coming into focus and may mount over the projection horizon. But with the economy operating only slightly above potential, the current degree of wage and price tensions should not translate into any significant pickup in inflation.

The current account as a share of GDP is expected to remain near 2 per cent of GDP. The deficit in goods and non-factor services may narrow as the other OECD economies pick up steam. Without wider differentials on factor returns, the expanding net negative international investment position of the United States should lead to further deterioration on factor services.

Table 6. **Near-term outlook**

Percentage change from previous period, seasonally adjusted at annual rates, volume (1992 prices)

	1995	1996	1997	1995		1996		1997	
				I	II	I	II	I	II
Private consumption	2.3	2.6	2.1	2.0	2.3	2.9	2.4	2.0	2.0
Government consumption	–0.3	0.3	0.0	–1.2	–1.0	0.9	0.7	–0.3	0.0
Gross fixed investment	5.3	5.6	2.9	5.2	2.6	7.5	4.8	2.4	1.9
of which:									
Private residential	–2.3	5.6	–2.2	–6.6	2.4	9.2	1.9	–4.8	–1.0
Private non-residential	9.5	6.5	5.4	11.5	3.9	7.4	7.5	5.5	3.2
Government	1.9	2.3	0.5	1.3	–1.5	5.9	–0.9	0.9	1.0
Final domestic demand	2.4	2.8	2.0	2.1	1.8	3.4	2.6	1.8	1.7
Stockbuilding [1]	–0.4	–0.3	0.1	–0.5	–0.6	–0.6	0.7	–0.3	0.1
Total domestic demand	2.0	2.5	2.0	1.5	1.2	2.7	3.2	1.5	1.8
Exports of goods and services	8.9	5.8	7.2	6.7	9.5	4.7	4.6	8.3	7.4
Imports of goods and services	8.0	6.1	5.7	9.3	1.5	8.0	7.1	4.9	5.7
Foreign balance [1]	0.0	–0.1	0.1	–0.4	0.9	–0.5	–0.4	0.3	0.1
GDP at constant prices	2.0	2.4	2.1	1.1	2.1	2.2	2.9	1.8	1.9
Memorandum items									
GDP price deflator	2.5	2.1	2.1	2.8	2.1	2.0	2.1	2.0	2.3
Private consumption deflator	2.3	2.1	2.3	2.5	1.8	2.2	2.2	2.2	2.4
Unemployment rate	5.6	5.4	5.5	5.6	5.6	5.5	5.3	5.4	5.5
Three-month Treasury bill rate	5.5	5.2	5.5	5.7	5.3	5.0	5.3	5.5	5.5
Ten-year Treasury note rate	6.6	6.6	6.8	7.1	6.1	6.3	6.8	6.8	6.8
Net lending of general government									
$ billion	–143	–129	–138						
Per cent of GDP	–2.0	–1.7	–1.7						
Current account balance									
$ billion	–148	–159	–163						
Per cent of GDP	–2.0	–2.1	–2.1						

1. The yearly and half-yearly rates of change refer to changes expressed as a percentage of GDP in the previous period.
Source: OECD estimates.

At this stage of the cycle there appear to be two, potentially related, types of risks attached to the projection: those relating to growth and those to inflation. On the growth side, the upside risks seem to dominate in the thinking of the financial markets, driven by concerns that the expected surge in output during the first half of the year may be more persistent than projected. In this view, consumption is powered by the rise in wealth and investment forges ahead in order to incorporate new technologies and boost capacity. This scenario is balanced by downside possibilities suggested by strains emerging in household balance sheets and falling capacity utilisation rates in the manufacturing sector. Even with moderate growth, there is considerable uncertainty about the tightness of labour and product markets. While the wage and price developments over the past year and half have been consistent with full employment, they are also consistent with output above capacity and its attendant price pressures being masked by favourable transitory productivity or cost shocks, for example the unexpectedly small increases in non-wage labour costs. However, the slow rise in labour compensation and solid productivity gains as well as the recent moderation in underlying inflation may be signalling that there is some slack in the economy and that price pressures may ease.

II. Policy developments

Monetary and exchange rate policy and developments

Strategy and objectives

The Federal Reserve continues to aim for the longer-term stability of prices. It has come to see the achievement of that goal as not inconsistent with but rather a necessary precondition for the lowest possible array of interest rates and hence the maximisation of output and employment, given the lack of any long-term trade-off between output and inflation. The Federal Reserve has not taken an official position on attempts to make price stability the sole objective of monetary policy as set out in proposed reforms to the Federal Reserve's enabling legislation such as the Economic Growth and Price Stability Act of 1995.[10] In terms of strategy, there is no clear consensus among its members on whether it is sufficient to prevent an increase in inflation during the current economic upturn and await an inevitable eventual recession to make the final disinflationary push (the recently named ''opportunistic approach''), or whether it would be less costly over time to move more immediately and deliberately to move to price stability (Orphanides and Wilcox, 1996).

Observers are obviously of one opinion or the other largely because of the view they hold as to the efficiency costs of the current modest rates of inflation – which themselves seem likely to be estimated with some upward bias (see Chapter I). While it is now fairly widely accepted that inflation has negative effects on output growth (Barro, 1995), it is less clear if they apply equally to all ranges of inflation. If inflation is still pernicious, even at these historically low levels, then it would be advisable to absorb some limited short-term costs in order to reap the permanent benefits of its elimination. The evidence from the literature on this question is by no means clear-cut: while experience does suggest that there are net benefits to lowering inflation from somewhat higher levels, there are too few episodes of countries moving from low to zero inflation to allow strong conclusions (Edey, 1994). Much depends on what discount rate one uses for the permanent benefits[11] and whether the negative effects of inflation are merely on the level of output or also on its growth rate. And here, too, research is hampered by the dearth of experience: effects which are statistically insignificant because of the paucity of observations may still be economically relevant (Thornton, 1996). Yet the interaction of inflation with the inefficient system of capital income taxation in the United States may provoke such distortions that, even without growth rate effects, the benefits may far exceed the costs of disinflation in the current range (Feldstein, 1996). Additionally, tensions in the international monetary system could mount, if the United States, the principal reserve currency country, were to have a higher inflation objective than most of its major trading partners. On the other hand, moving to zero from low inflation rates eliminates the opportunity of generating negative real interest rates which might be desirable to stimulate recovery from recession, and it may prevent equilibrating real wage cuts if nominal wages are downwardly rigid, thereby preventing adjustment (Card and Hyslop, 1996). Indeed, it has recently been argued that such mechanisms might even lead to a permanent increase in the sustainable rate of unemployment (Akerlof *et al.*, 1996).

Recent changes in short- and long-term interest rates

In 1994-95, with the economy showing signs of a further pickup in momentum, the intent of the Federal Reserve was to be pre-emptive: ''to head off an incipient increase in inflationary pressures and to forestall the emergence of imbalances that so often in the past have undermined economic expansions'', as the then-Vice Chairman of the Board of Governors put it. In the event, policy makers were extremely successful, and by raising rates more quickly and substantially than had been the case in previous episodes, they were able to hold down the peak in the federal funds rate to 6 per cent in early 1995, well below market expectations as proxied by futures contracts (Figure 10).[12]

Once 1995 began, the economy slowed surprisingly quickly, reducing the risk of any pickup in wage and price inflation. As it became clear that demand pressures had moderated and that tensions in labour and product markets were not intensifying further, the Federal Open Market Committee (FOMC) felt able to withdraw some of the monetary tightness that it had previously imposed by easing

Figure 10. **FEDERAL FUNDS FUTURES**

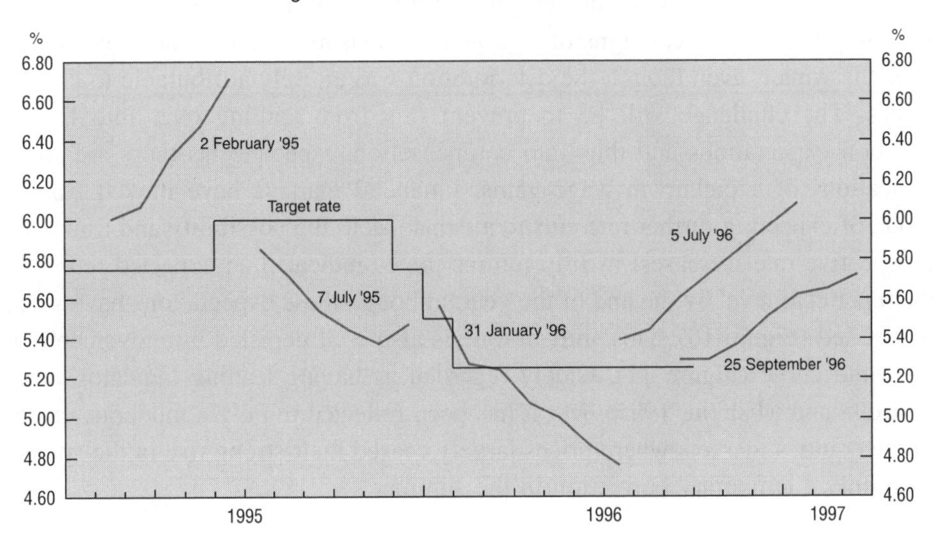

Source: Wall Street Journal Europe.

reserve market conditions in July 1995. At that point investors expected a series of further easing moves in the following months (Figure 10); but with some signs of a rebound over the summer, these hopes were not immediately realised.[13] Nevertheless, with renewed demand weakness in the autumn, a risk of prolonged sluggishness and further signs of lower inflation expectations, by year-end the FOMC cut the target rate on federal funds another quarter point to 5½ per cent. Similarly, early in 1996, the economy appeared to be still sputtering, even though many of the shocks it was being buffeted by were widely acknowledged to be temporary. And again inflation was proving more benign than expected, rising at only a 2 per cent annual rate in the final quarter of 1995 and 2½ per cent rate for the year as a whole, over ½ percentage point less than the mid-year central-tendency forecast by the Governors and Reserve Bank Presidents. Thus, at the end of January a third slight easing in reserve conditions was agreed to, bringing the target federal funds rate to 5¼ per cent. At the same time the discount rate was shaved to 5 per cent, the first decline of less than ½ percentage point since 1978, and banks cut their prime rates for the third time – to 8¼ per cent.

Since February, with the termination of the aforementioned shocks, the economy has given clear signs of resurgence. Measured price inflation worsened over the winter, even though the deterioration was entirely attributable to energy prices. The challenge will be to prevent this from spilling over into higher inflation expectations and thus into compensation, especially as there are some indications of a pickup in wage gains. Financial markets have moved from a mode of expecting further rate cuts to a debate as to the possibility and timing of prospective rate increases: in July futures prices indicated an expected return to the 6 per cent level by the end of the year, although these expectations have since moderated (Figure 10). This shift in tone is also well depicted by movements in the yield curve (Figure 11), widely regarded as having leading indicator value (Estrella and Mishkin, 1995). But it has been reflected to only a moderate extent in the equities markets where prices largely ceased their strong rise in the spring, with only a temporary correction in the summer.

The pattern of long-term interest rates over the past year has very much followed that of the real economy. This has not always been the case in the past, but it is by no means unusual (Figure 12, Panel A). Last year long-term rates fell steadily in the first half, as the economy cooled and the risks of a pickup in inflation ebbed, edged up briefly during the summer, as activity rebounded, and then resumed their downtrend before the third quarter was over, assisted by spreading hope for an imminent agreement between the Administration and the Congress to move to a balanced federal budget by early in the next decade. While long-term interest rates also fell abroad, in line with widespread demand weakness, the US decline was greater than for many other countries. For example, from the spring of 1995 for about a year an unusual interest-rate spread spread in favour of Germany opened up, with the ten-year differential reaching nearly ¾ percentage point at the end of June 1995. The gap of US over Japanese long-term rates remained over 3 percentage points for most of the year.

However, almost simultaneously with the 31 January cut in the federal funds rate, the year-long bond market rally came to an end. Besides the recognition that the economy was strengthening anew, there may have been some additional upward impetus to long-term rates from the crumbling of any residual hope for a budget balancing agreement. From the trough, 10-year Treasury note rates rose as much as 140 basis points, bringing them back to the 7 per cent level, last seen in the spring of 1995 before some moderation in August and September. The spread

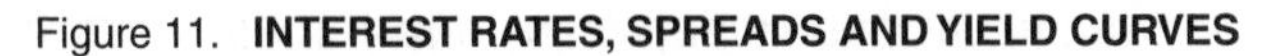

Figure 11. **INTEREST RATES, SPREADS AND YIELD CURVES**

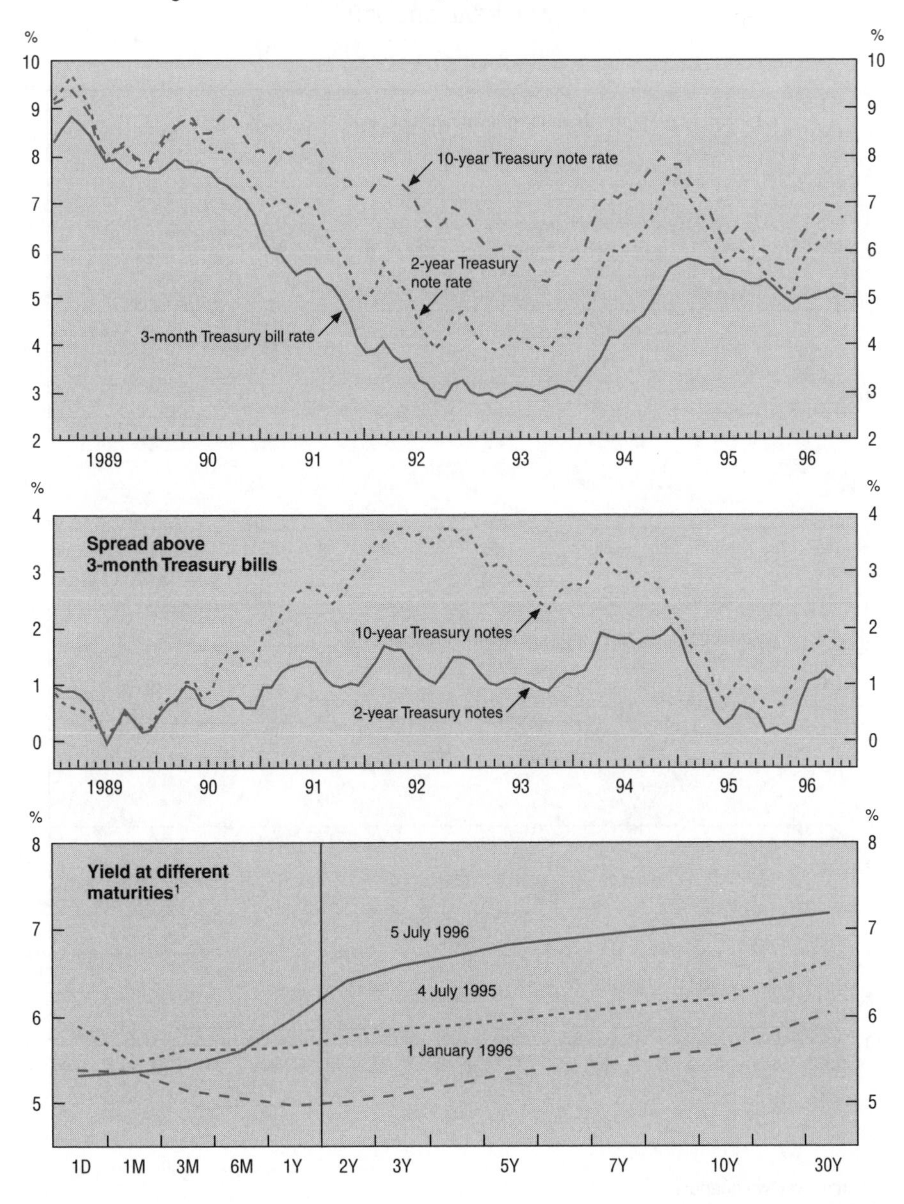

1. One-day rates are for Federal funds; one month to 1 year are treasury bills; two-year to 30-year rates are redemption yields for benchmark bonds.

Source: Datastream; Federal Reserve Board.

Figure 12. **THE RELATIONSHIP BETWEEN LONG-TERM INTEREST RATES AND REAL GROWTH**

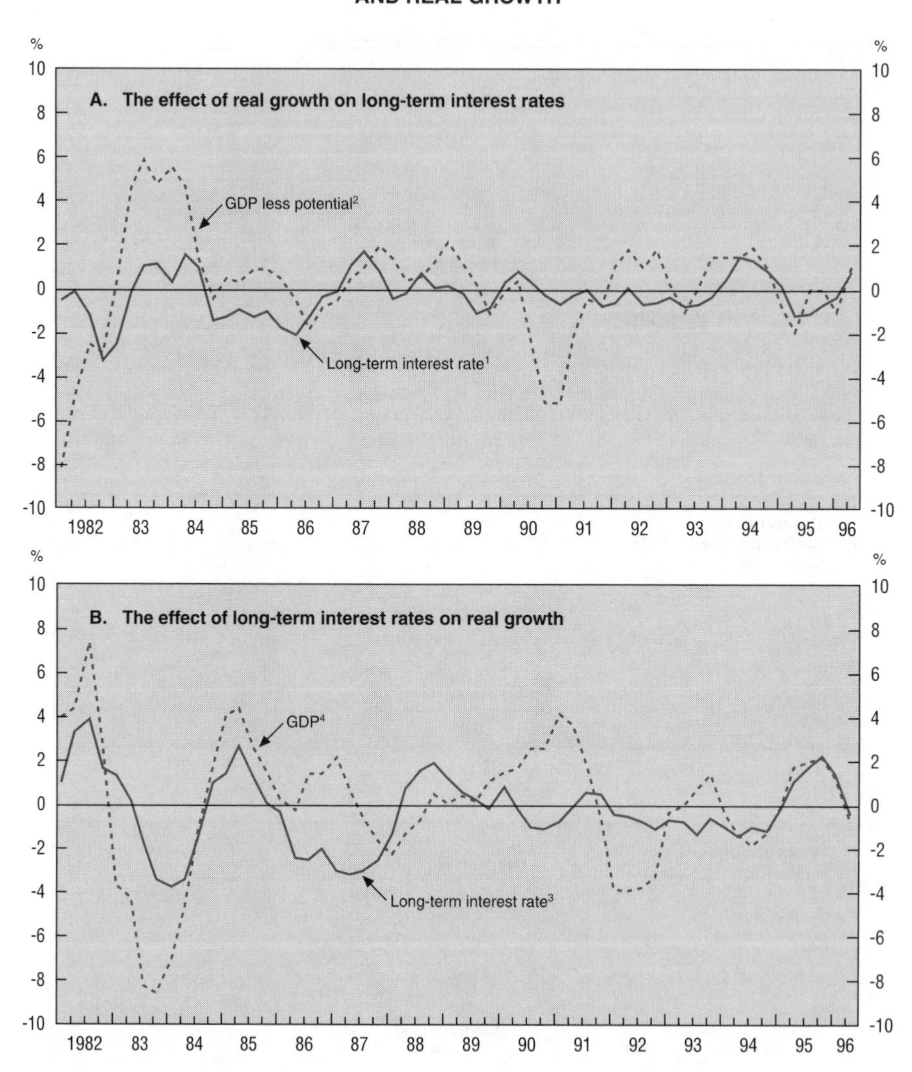

1. Change over two quarters.
2. The two-quarter per cent change in real GDP at annual rates less the two-quarter per cent change in potential GDP at annual rates.
3. Change over four quarters.
4. The four-quarter per cent change in real GDP less the year earlier four-quarter change at annual rates.

Source: OECD.

vis-à-vis Germany reversed and widened to nearly 1/2 percentage point, and that against Japan also widened by more than a percentage point. Likewise, interest rates on 30-year fixed rate mortgages rose from below 7 1/4 per cent to a peak of about 8.4 per cent in early summer and 8 per cent more recently. There was some regularity to the pattern of these rate increases. A majority occurred in immediate reaction to just five data releases: the February, March, May and June employment reports and the first estimate of the first-quarter growth in GDP. In each case there was some subsequent reversal when the monthly producer and consumer price inflation figures were published. This is consistent with an alternative view that while demand is growing strongly, supply may be greater than widely assumed, leaving some capacity still spare. This learning process might also be bringing about the steady reduction in inflation expectations (see Chapter I).

As was pointed out in last year's *Survey*, long-term rates seem to be much more correlated with short-term rates than in the past. A slight variation on this theme is that fluctuations in long-term rates may be doing more of the work in equilibrating the economy. It has already been argued above that for the last few years long-term rates have been more responsive to the real economy; here the hypothesis is advanced that such fluctuations have indeed been serving to stabilise activity. A four-quarter change in long-term rates is associated with a subsequent change in four-quarter real GDP growth of the opposite sign and this association has been especially tight in the last couple of years (Figure 12, Panel B). Thus, some commentators are arguing that there is little or no need for the Federal Reserve to change policy-controlled rates in response to demand shocks, as the financial markets do the work for them. While there is some validity to this argument, it must be remembered that many market participants are merely trying to guess what the monetary authorities will do, and that if they are wrong, and their expectations are not ratified, then at least the shape of the yield curve will change. For example, at the time of writing the markets are expecting the federal funds rate to rise some 30 basis points over the next six months or so, compared with an even larger decline expected near the beginning of the year (Figure 10). This has been reflected in a much larger increase in one-year forward rates at a medium-term horizon than at a longer-term horizon. Presumably, if the markets come to expect less of an increase in short-term rates for a given trajectory of demand, that difference would reverse, and the yield curve would steepen further due to heightened expectations of increased future inflation. Only if long-term rates rose more than proportionately would they provide restraint on activity, and the risk is that this increase could bring about an eventual recession.

The Treasury to issue indexed bonds

In May 1996 the Treasury announced its intention to make quarterly issues of indexed bonds (''Inflation-Protection Securities''). In September it provided some details (they will be issued quarterly beginning in January and the inflation compensation will be based on the unadjusted Consumer Price Index). The initial intent is to provide a niche product primarily for small investors (they will be available in units of as little as $1 000) to provide for education and/or retirement, but also for financial institutions with long-term real liabilities, such as pension funds. Several benefits are expected. First, public borrowing costs should be shaved by broadening the overall market for Treasury securities and by eliminating what remains of the inflation risk premium:[14] that risk would be transferred to taxpayers who are in a good position to bear it, as tax revenues are correlated with inflation. Second, personal and national savings might be boosted. Third, they may impart some information on real interest rates and inflation expectations that might be useful to policy makers and others; however, movements in the gap between the two yields could reflect other factors as well. Fourth, their introduction might open the way for other new financial products. Finally, they will provide policy makers with added impetus to oppose inflation, as in the presence of indexed bonds a rise in inflation would raise borrowing costs more quickly than otherwise. On the other hand, holders of these securities will constitute a group whose resistance to inflation is reduced.

Developments in money and credit

While the monetary aggregates no longer carry much influence in Federal Reserve policy discussions, given their lack of leading indicator properties, it is worth noting that M2 growth has continued to follow a pattern more consistent with predictions based on its historical determinants than was the case in the early 1990s when there was a downshift of some $500 billion or 15 per cent (Carlson and Keen, 1995). After a period of slow growth in early 1995, M2 increased fairly steadily in the 5 to 7 per cent (annual rate) range for a time, although renewed weakness has been in evidence since the middle of April with annualised growth rates of below 2 per cent. Around the middle of 1995, the outward shift in demand for currency seems to have come to an end, perhaps due to the impending introduction of new $100 notes and/or to a stabilisation of the average economic situation in a number of foreign countries where dollars have displaced local currencies as units of transaction and stores of value. There were some signs of a renewed acceleration over the summer months, however. Chequable deposits have been shrinking continuously at about a 5 per cent annualised rate, largely attributable to the spread of sweep accounts (at a rate of $8 to $10 billion per month or about 9 per cent of M1 per year); however, this does not depress M2.

Overall bank loan growth has slowed from the vigorous double-digit pace of late 1994 and early 1995; in May loan growth actually turned negative. The Federal Reserve's Senior Loan Officer Survey indicates that most of this reflects demand-side influences, as credit supply conditions are still good. The first component to decelerate (late in 1994) was consumer loans. Banks' willingness to make such loans has fallen steadily over the past year and a half, as delinquencies on credit cards and other instalment credit began to rise, possibly more quickly than bankers had expected (see Chapter I). Business loan growth has most recently fallen to less than a 6 per cent annualised rate; the aforementioned Survey shows that the nearly three years of steady easing in terms and conditions was interrupted in the first quarter of 1996, but terms remain attractive, and banks are still actively seeking loan customers, especially among small and medium-sized firms. The availability of household mortgages has followed a similar pattern, with low albeit rising delinquencies and some tightening of supply.

The balance of payments and the dollar's appreciation

After reaching a relatively low average value in the spring of 1995 the dollar has staged a strong recovery over the past 18 months. Not only has it gained some 10 per cent on a nominal effective (trade-weighted) basis,[15] but it has thereby succeeded in breaking out of the range in which it has traded since the beginning of the decade (Figure 13). It has also made an even more substantial recovery against the yen, some 37 per cent, in part reflecting substantial monetary easing by the Bank of Japan. US policy-makers have generally welcomed the orderly reversal in the movements of the major currencies since 11 April 1995, indicated their support for a strong dollar and otherwise largely refrained from

Figure 13. **EXCHANGE VALUE OF THE DOLLAR**

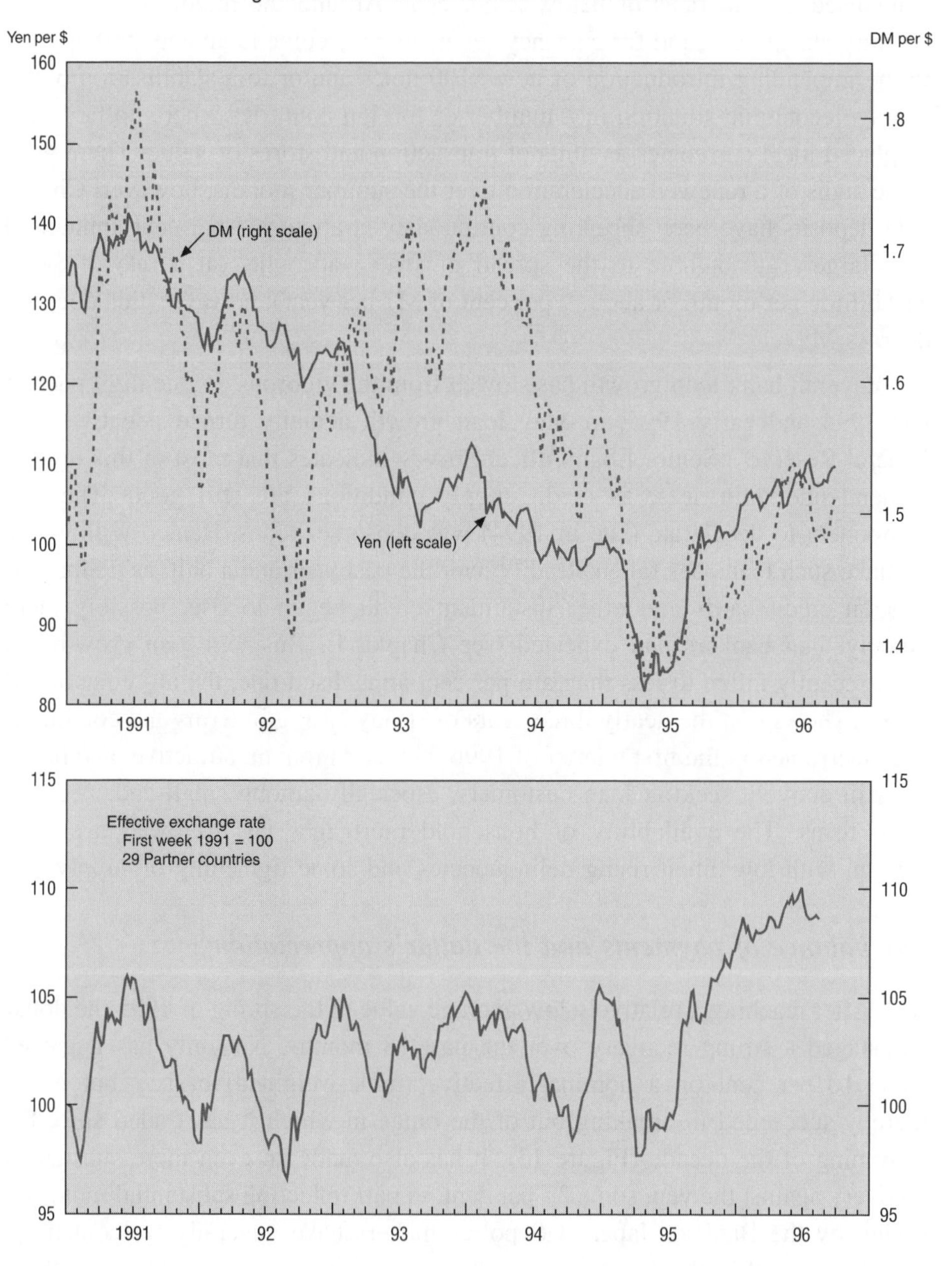

Source: OECD.

comment. The US authorities have not undertaken any exchange market intervention since 15 August 1995. Accordingly, other than valuation changes, official foreign currency holdings have reflected only changing arrangements with the Mexican authorities; in that regard, the Bank of Mexico repaid all its outstanding short-term swap borrowings ($2 billion) in October 1995 and January 1996. A total of $3.5 billion in medium-term swap borrowings from the US Treasury remains outstanding after a $7 billion repayment in August 1996.

The dollar's strong performance reflects fundamental factors in a number of countries, including developments in the US balance of payments (Table 7). The current account deficit stabilised in 1995 and the first half of 1996, albeit at a high level. At the same time recorded capital inflows were picking up substantial steam, with net foreign assets in the United States increasing $425 billion in 1995, nearly half again as much as in 1994. What is perhaps the most notable development, however, is the even further acceleration in foreign official asset holdings in the United States: the stock of such holdings rose $110 billion (20 per cent) in 1995. Preliminary estimates for the first half of 1996 indicate a further acceleration to $130 billion (annual rate). This reflects both exchange-market intervention to support the dollar on the part of several industrial countries and rapid reserve growth by some developing countries, combined with an increase in the dollar share of global reserves from 61 to 65 per cent in 1995 (according to the Bank for International Settlements).

The majority of these official flows have been toward US Treasury securities; indeed, in 1995 foreign central banks bought around half of all new Treasury issues, nearly $70 billion worth, and that pace has quickened further thus far in 1996. And last year their decisions were echoed by those of private foreign investors – in large part hedge funds domiciled in a small number of offshore tax havens[16] – who bought a further $100 billion of such securities, thereby boosting holdings by 46 per cent. Thus, overall net foreign purchases slightly exceeded the US federal budget deficit and more than entirely financed total US Treasury borrowing for the first time since uninterrupted deficits began in 1970 (Figure 14). By year-end foreigners held 26 per cent of total US public debt securities, equalling the 1978 peak.[17] Private foreign investors also made substantial net purchases of other US securities, especially in the form of corporate and other bonds, in part a result of heavy Eurobond issuance by US corporations. But foreign purchases of corporate equities were not unusually large, despite the

Table 7. **Capital flows and international investment position**

$ billion

	1994 flows	End-year position	1995 flows	End-year position	1996 S1 flows (annual rates)
Current balance	–148.4	–492.5 [1]	–148.2	–773.7 [1]	–147.3
Per cent of GDP	2.1	6.9	2.0	10.5	2.0
US assets abroad	150.7	2 825.8	307.9	3 352.9	235.8
US official reserve assets, net	–5.3	163.4	9.7	176.1	1.0
Other US government assets, net	0.3	81.3	0.3	81.5	1.2
US private assets, net	155.7	2 581.2	297.8	3 095.3	233.7
of which:					
Direct investment	54.5	1 058.9	95.5	1 301.1	46.2
Foreign securities	60.3	556.2	99.0	721.7	109.0
Bonds	12.2	232.3	48.3	310.7	n.a.
Equities	48.1	324.0	50.7	411.1	n.a.
Other claims reported by:					
US non-banking concerns	32.8	273.7	34.2	311.1	n.a.
US banks	8.2	692.3	69.1	761.3	6.9
Foreign assets in the United States	285.4	3 318.3	424.5	4 126.6	359.6
Foreign official assets	40.3	546.0	109.8	677.9	130.4
of which:					
US government securities	36.8	415.0	72.5	498.9	107.1
Other US government liabilities	2.3	24.9	1.1	25.9	0.0
US liabilities reported by US banks	3.6	73.3	32.9	106.1	21.2
Other foreign official assets	–2.5	32.9	3.3	46.9	2.1
Other foreign assets	245.1	2 772.3	314.7	3 448.7	229.1
of which:					
Direct investment	49.8	771.9	60.2	1 019.2	78.8
US Treasury securities	34.2	266.6	99.3	388.9	87.0
Other US securities	57.0	752.8	95.3	998.6	129.1
Bonds	53.6	413.9	81.9	533.2	n.a.
Equities	3.4	338.9	13.4	465.4	n.a.
Other liabilities reported by:					
US non-banking concerns	–7.7	197.3	34.6	232.9	n.a.
US banks	111.8	783.7	25.3	809.0	–78.9
Errors and omissions	13.7	–	31.5	–	23.6

1. Net international investment position of the United States with direct investment positions at market value. Using the alternative current cost evaluations the end-year positions would be –$580.1 billion (8.2 per cent of GDP) and –$814.0 billion (11.0 per cent of GDP). For this purpose GDP is measured by the mean of the data for the final quarter of the year and the first quarter of the following year, rather than for the calendar year as a whole. End-year positions are determined by beginning-of-year positions, capital flows, price changes, exchange rate changes and other changes including changes in coverage and statistical discrepancies.

Source: Bureau of Economic Analysis.

Figure 14. **FOREIGN SHARE OF US FEDERAL BORROWING AND DEBT**

Per cent of total private ownership

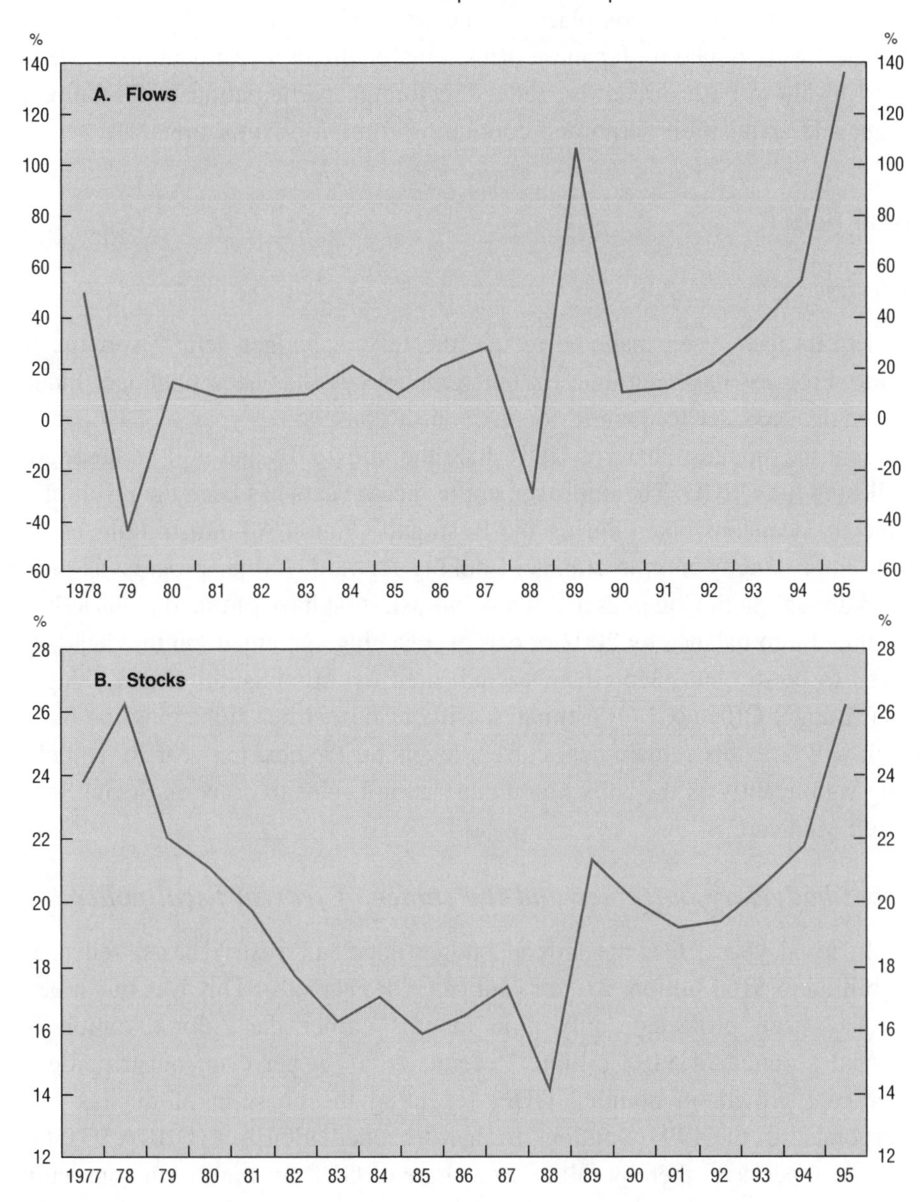

Source: Department of the Treasury.

surge in US stock market prices recorded last year. For their part, US net purchases of foreign securities rebounded after their 1994 decline, as further portfolio diversification took place; on the equity side a large share the securities purchased were issued by Japanese firms. Finally, direct investment flows were at record levels in both directions, reflecting foreign participation in the domestic merger and acquisition boom and continuing foreign privatisations.

Fiscal policy

Overview

Efforts have been made to reduce the federal budget deficit over the last decade. Progress has been uneven, but some success has been obtained. Indeed, the deficit looks set to decline for the fourth consecutive year in 1996; it will represent the smallest share of GDP since the mid-1970s and will be among the smallest in the OECD. The improvement in recent years has been the result of the budgetary decisions taken during the Bush and Clinton Administrations as well as the improving economic climate. Looking forward, further progress is uncertain. Although both Congress and the Administration have outlined plans to bring the budget into balance by 2002 or earlier, reaching agreement on the details has proved to be difficult. Moreover, as indicated by Administration and Congressional Budget Office (CBO) estimates, without further belt tightening the budget deficit will probably remain near current levels for the next ten years or so before rising significantly as the baby boom generation begins to draw on Social Security and Medicare.

Recent budgetary outcomes and the stance of federal fiscal policy

In fiscal year 1995, the federal budget deficit (Treasury basis) fell nearly $40 billion to $164 billion, 2¼ per cent of GDP (Table 8). This was much better than had been projected: only nine months earlier the Administration had expected a deficit of $193 billion. Receipts rose 7¾ per cent, outstripping the 5 per cent growth in nominal GDP, reflecting the phase-in of the tax hikes incorporated in the 1993 Omnibus Budget Reconciliation Act (OBRA 93). Outlays rose 4 per cent, thereby falling as a share of GDP for the fourth consecutive year. In recent years, outlay growth has been restrained by the caps imposed on discretionary spending (see Box 3 for a description) which have allowed total

Table 8. **Recent budget outcomes**

$ billion

	FY 1994	FY 1995			FY 1996			
	Actual	Feb. 94 [1]	Feb. 95	Actual	Feb. 95	Feb. 96	*Memo.:*	
							Change	Per cent
Receipts	1 257.7	1 342.2	1 346.4	1 355.2	1 415.5	1 426.8	11.3	0.8
Individual income taxes	543.1	597.2	588.5	590.2	623.4	630.9	7.5	1.2
Corporate income taxes	140.4	141.0	150.9	157.0	157.4	167.1	9.7	6.2
Social insurance taxes	461.5	492.1	484.4	484.5	509.3	507.5	–1.8	–0.3
Excise taxes	55.2	55.8	57.6	57.5	57.2	53.9	–3.3	–5.8
Other	57.6	56.1	65.1	66.0	68.1	67.4	–0.7	–1.1
Outlays	1 460.8	1 518.9	1 538.9	1 519.1	1 612.1	1 572.4	–39.7	–2.5
Discretionary	543.9	542.4	553.8	545.7	549.0	541.2	–7.8	–1.4
National defense	282.3	271.1	272.1	273.5	262.2	266.3	4.1	1.6
Other	261.6	271.3	281.7	272.2	286.8	274.8	–12.0	–4.2
Non-interest mandatory	714.0	763.7	750.9	741.3	806.2	790.2	–16.0	–2.0
Social Security	316.9	334.5	333.7	333.3	351.4	348.1	–3.3	–0.9
Medicare	141.8	153.3	154.4	156.9	174.7	174.9	0.2	0.1
Means-tested programmes	170.4	192.0	184.5	181.6	197.0	191.7	–5.3	–2.7
Medicaid	82.0	96.4	88.4	89.1	95.9	94.9	–1.0	–1.0
Food stamps and nutrition	33.0	34.5	34.8	33.5	35.8	34.7	–1.1	–3.1
EITC	10.9	15.8	16.8	15.2	20.2	18.1	–2.1	–10.4
SSI	24.5	26.2	25.1	24.5	25.4	24.5	–0.9	–3.5
Family support	16.5	16.9	17.3	17.1	17.9	17.4	–0.5	–2.8
Other	3.5	2.2	2.1	2.2	1.8	2.1	0.3	16.7
Deposit insurance	–7.6	–11.1	–12.3	–17.9	–6.3	–13.5	–7.2	114.3
Other mandatory [2]	92.5	95.0	90.6	87.4	89.4	89.0	–0.4	–0.4
Interest	203.0	212.8	234.2	232.2	257.0	241.1	–15.9	–6.2
Deficit, total	203.1	176.7	192.5	163.9	196.6	145.6	–51.0	–25.9
Excluding deposit insurance	210.7	187.8	205.8	181.8	202.9	159.1	–43.8	–21.6

1. Excludes health care reform proposals.
2. Mostly federal employee retirement, unemployment compensation, veterans' benefits, student aid for higher education and agricultural subsidies.

Source: Budget of the United States Government.

Box 3. **The budget process in the United States**

Treasury Budget. Often called the unified budget, the Treasury budget includes taxes and other receipts and net outlays (outlays less certain fees and charges) of the US federal government, including the surpluses or deficits of some government enterprises, government employee pension and social security funds, and financial transactions such as asset sales of the savings and loan insurance agencies. A cash accounting system is used except in two major areas: interest payments on Treasury debt are accrued, and guaranteed and direct loans are entered based on their estimated subsidy value.

Fiscal year. Runs from 1 October to 30 September.

President's Budget. The President is required to submit a budget proposal for the coming five fiscal years by the first Monday in February.

Budget Resolution. The Budget Resolution must be approved by both chambers. It contains the broad outlines of Congressional policy and controls the ensuing appropriations and reconciliation bills. The Budget Resolution does not implement any policy changes and is not subject to presidential approval.

Appropriations bills. These thirteen bills fund discretionary spending for government agencies. They control about $550 billion, or one-third of federal government spending. Appropriations bills specify budget authority levels which grant authority to enter into obligations that will translate into immediate or future outlays. Thus, changes in budget authority result in changes in outlays that largely occur in the same year for personnel costs, but which occur over many years for many capital expenditures.

Reconciliation bill. This bill includes all of the changes to mandatory spending and taxes that are required to meet the net tax increases and spending cuts agreed to in the Budget Resolution.

Continuing Resolution (CR). CRs are used to temporarily authorise spending on programmes that have not been granted budget authority through an appropriations bill. A discretionary programme cannot be operated without budget authority granted through either an annual appropriations bill or a CR.

Discretionary spending. This category includes nearly all purchases of goods and services, in particular, compensation of active personnel. In addition it covers many of the grants-in-aid (such as education and highway) and some transfer programmes (such as Pell grants for education). The 1990 and 1993 Omnibus Budget Reconciliation Acts (OBRA 90 and OBRA 93) placed caps which limit aggregate spending on these programmes, except for designated emergencies.

Mandatory spending. Mandatory spending programmes include open-ended entitlements for individuals or businesses and net interest expenses. The major transfer programmes are Social Security, Medicare and low-income assistance, federal employee pensions, deposit insurance, student loan subsidies, agriculture subsidies and net interest. OBRA 90 and OBRA 93 restrained mandatory spending with the pay-as-you-go (PAYGO) caps which place parliamentary hurdles in front of any tax and mandatory spending legislation that is projected to increase the deficit.

discretionary outlays to grow minimally in nominal terms, as increases in non-defence spending have been roughly offset by reductions in defence spending. Mandatory spending increases slowed in 1995, reflecting a sharp slowdown in the growth of means-tested outlays and rising asset sales related to the deposit insurance cleanup. On the other hand, net interest payments surged as the rise in interest rates in 1994 was more fully reflected in the refinancing of maturing Treasury securities.

During the debate over the tax increases incorporated in OBRA 93 and since, some observers suggested that the increased marginal rates would discourage labour supply or shift income to less taxed forms, such as fringe benefits, to such an extent that much of the projected increase in revenue would not materialise (Feldstein and Feenberg, 1995).[18] Clearly substantial temporary tax avoidance was accomplished by shifting some personal income to earlier years. For example, year-end bonus payments amounting to some $15 billion were shifted from the beginning of 1993 and 1994 into the respective previous years in order to avoid higher personal income tax rates in 1993 and the boost to the Medicare portion of social insurance tax rates in 1994. But evidence of permanent changes in behaviour is scarce. Medicare tax receipts have risen more rapidly than other social insurance taxes, and personal income tax collections have been in line with Treasury projections, consistent with the substantial revenue gains expected by the Administration. However, these developments may reflect other factors, such as a surge in capital gains realisations. More informed assessment cannot be done until the temporary shifts are finished and disaggregated panel data becomes available.

Against the background of declining budget deficits, the Administration's FY 1996 budget proposal, presented in February 1995, was designed to keep the deficit near $200 billion over the following five years. In May, Congress passed a Budget Resolution (see Box 3) that outlined reductions in discretionary spending and major transfer programmes to balance the budget over seven years and fund a tax cut amounting to about 1/2 percentage point of GDP per year when phased in. The Administration responded with its own plan in June which balanced the budget in ten years. The Administration's plan was less aggressive on two counts: first, it spread the cuts over more years, and, second, it used somewhat more optimistic economic and technical assumptions, thereby requiring less action to reach balance. Both plans relied on cuts to many of the same programmes, and many of the tax changes were similar as well (OECD, 1995*c*).

Throughout the fall of 1995 the differences between Congress and the Administration narrowed substantially. By the time negotiations were suspended, the Administration had boosted the amount of deficit reduction to equal the Congressional proposal, but with smaller tax cuts which allowed smaller spending reductions. Yet final agreement could still not be reached.[19] During the process, portions of the government were closed because of failure to enact either appropriations bills or continuing resolutions (CRs) to fund many government agencies. This failure reflected divergent views about appropriate spending levels, first within Congress and then between Congress and the Administration.[20] Budgetary savings from these closures were minimal because employees were paid for the days lost when the government reopened, but the timing of spending by the government was affected as purchases and grants were delayed and output of government services was forgone.[21]

As a result of budget cuts imposed by Congress (as well as appropriations made in earlier years), discretionary spending is expected to fall about 2 per cent in nominal terms in FY 1996, reflecting decreased spending on both defence and non-defence programmes. Discretionary spending is projected to be somewhat higher than Congressional proposals, but lower than the Administration's revised FY 1996 budget. Owing to the collapse of budget negotiations, there were no major changes to tax or transfer programmes except the Farm bill, which is expected to boost outlays by a few billion dollars in the near term and reduce them in future years, and the expiration of several excise taxes that bring in about $6 billion per year. Thus, recent policy decisions are projected to have only a minor impact on the FY 1996 budget outcome. However, with buoyant personal and corporate income tax receipts and a surprising slowdown in outlay growth for some major means-tested transfer programmes, the FY 1996 deficit projection has now fallen to around $116 billion. This would be some $80 billion (more than 1 percentage point of GDP) less than in the FY 1996 budget proposal (Table 8).[22]

With the economy operating at roughly full employment over the past couple of years, the recent decline in the deficit has been largely structural. On a national accounts basis, which excludes financial transactions from the Treasury budget and adjusts the timing of certain taxes and spending, the deficit has declined from 2¾ per cent of GDP in calendar 1994 to a projected 1¾ per cent in

Figure 15. **FISCAL STANCE**[1]
Per cent of GDP

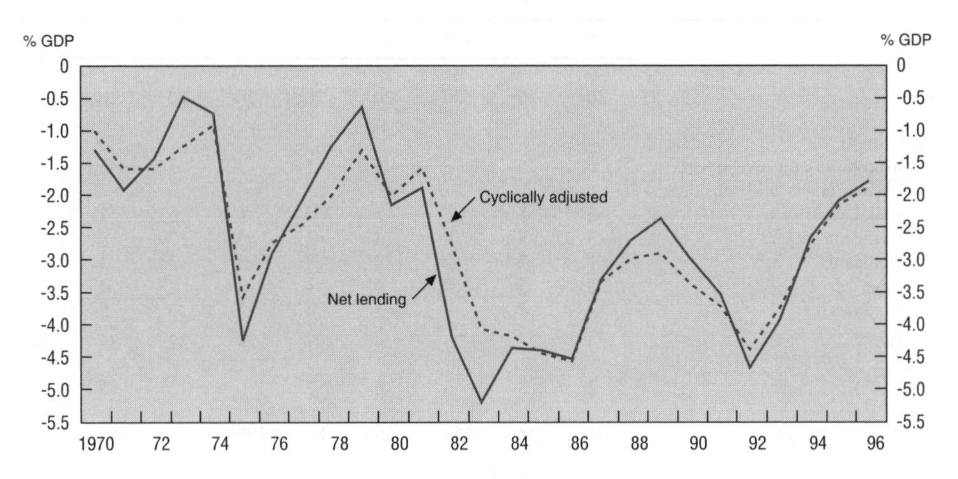

1. Federal government net lending on a national accounts basis by calendar years. 1996 is a projection based on 1996 data through Q2.

Source: OECD.

1996 (Figure 15), with all of the improvement due to structural factors. The exact timing and magnitude of the drag on demand is difficult to gauge precisely because of the uncertain effects of tax payments on consumption. For example, the increased payments by high-income earners beginning in 1994 may have begun to reduce consumption already in 1993 when the changes were put into law, and the adjustment may have extended over several years as these consumers are probably not liquidity constrained. Additionally, the portion of the rise in payments in 1996 owing to unexpectedly high capital gains realisations may be associated with increased, rather than depressed consumption.[23] Notwithstanding these uncertainties, it is clear that fiscal policy has been restraining demand throughout the recovery, perhaps by as much as ½ percentage point of GDP per year.

Projections and proposals

While the near-term deficit outlook is somewhat brighter than last year, the longer-term outlook is little changed. Indeed, the Congressional Budget Office

Table 9. **Long-term projection of the federal budget**[1]

As a per cent of GDP

	1995	2000	2005	2010	2015	2020	2025	2030	2050
Receipts	20	20	20	20	20	20	20	20	20
Expenditures									
Consumption and investment	6	6	5	5	5	5	5	5	5
Transfers, grants and subsidies									
Social security	5	5	5	5	5	6	6	7	7
Medicare	3	3	4	4	5	6	7	8	8
Medicaid	1	2	2	2	3	3	3	3	4
Other	5	5	4	4	4	4	4	4	4
Net interest	3	3	3	3	4	5	7	8	16
Total	23	22	23	24	27	29	32	35	44
Deficit	2	3	3	5	7	9	12	15	24
Debt held by the public	51	53	57	65	81	106	139	180	373
Memorandum:									
Gross domestic product ($ trillion)	7.2	9.2	11.6	14.6	18.1	22.1	26.9	32.8	72.1

1. Projections assume that deficits do not affect either interest rates or economic growth.
Source: Congressional Budget Office.

has produced long-term budget projections similar to the OECD's projections made for last year's *Survey* (Table 9). The current size of the deficit, as a share of GDP, is sufficiently small to stabilise the debt-to-GDP ratio at its current level of some 50 per cent of GDP. But demographic pressures from the retirement of the baby boom generation and the expected continuing rise in health care costs should put significant pressure on federal finances, particularly after 2005. Indeed, the Medicare hospital insurance trust fund is now projected to be bankrupt by the year 2001 and to reach a cumulative deficit of $408 billion by 2005. The Administrations's proposals should be sufficient to keep the trust fund solvent for the next five to ten years.

The Administration has proposed to balance the budget by 2002 through reductions in spending on the major health care programmes, further cuts to real discretionary spending, additional sales of the electromagnetic spectrum, and welfare reform (Table 10). Under Administration proposals, spending on national defence would continue to fall through 1998, after which it would begin to rise

Table 10. **The Administration's policy proposals**

Fiscal years, $ billion

	1996	1997	1998	1999	2000	2001	2002	Final year savings as per cent of that year's baseline level
Discretionary spending								
Baseline	548	549	549	564	580	596	613	
Proposal	541	542	539	536	537	548	573	
Change	–7	–6	–9	–28	–43	–48	–40	–6.5
Mandatory spending changes								
Medicare	0	–6	–10	–16	–25	–31	–37	–12.3
Medicaid	0	3	–1	–6	–11	–18	–27	–16.9
EITC	0	–1	–1	–1	–1	–1	–1	–4.0
Welfare reform	0	–5	–7	–6	–7	–7	–9	–8.3
Auction electromagnetic spectrum	0	–2	–3	–4	–3	–3	–18	n.a.
Veterans' programmes	0	0	0	–1	–2	–2	–2	–8.1
Other mandatory [1]	–9	2	4	0	–2	–7	–11	n.a.
Total mandatory	–9	–8	–17	–34	–51	–67	–104	–8.8
Tax changes								
Personal income tax cuts	–1	–17	–13	–16	–19	–20	–21	–2.5
Other tax cuts	0	–1	–1	–2	–2	–2	–2	n.a.
Business tax increases	0	4	6	8	8	9	10	4.2
Renew expired excise taxes	1	6	6	6	6	7	7	11.9
Other tax increases	0	2	2	2	2	2	2	n.a.
Total tax changes	–1	–6	–1	–2	–5	–5	–4	–0.2

1. Includes asset sales.

Source: Budget of the United States Government.

with inflation. Non-defence spending increases would offset the declines in defence spending over the next two years, keeping total nominal discretionary spending at the 1996 level. A small portion of these savings would be used to provide tax relief. The Administration has proposed personal income tax deductions or credits for families with children, education and training expenses or savings for retirement that amount to 1/4 percentage point of GDP.[24] Offsetting two-thirds of this are proposals to renew and raise the recently expired excise taxes and to boost corporate income taxes through base broadening.

While these proposals would balance the budget in 2001 under the Administration's assumptions, the Congressional Budget Office estimates that a $87 billion dollar deficit would remain in that year (0.9 per cent of GDP). The Administration's plan contains contingency proposals that would reduce or end the tax reductions and enforce tighter discipline on discretionary spending if the deficit is above a trigger point in 2000.[25] The CBO estimates that the contingency plan would be triggered and that the resulting savings would be enough to balance the budget in 2002.

Congress has passed a Budget Resolution that also calls for a balanced budget in the fiscal year 2002 based on larger cuts to spending as well as larger tax reductions. However, only the short-term discretionary spending proposals are likely to be enacted this year, as the stalemate between the President and Congress on reforms to taxes and entitlements has continued. The welfare reform legislation should reduce spending levels by 0.1 percentage point of GDP and the tax cuts incorporated in the minimum wage bill should reduce receipts by an equally small amount. Thus, it is unlikely that the major long-term spending problems will be addressed before next year. As highlighted in the CBO's analysis of long-term issues, bringing the budget into balance over the next few years will be a good beginning, but further action will be required if medical care spending trends persist.

The state and local sector

State and local governments have also been under budgetary pressures. Rising demands for state and local services, particularly education, prisons and the state portion of Medicaid, have led to expenditure growth much faster than overall GDP growth. Accordingly, their current and capital expenditures as a share of GDP rose 1 percentage point from 1990 to 1995 (Table 11). Rising

Table 11. **State and local finances**

Per cent of GDP

	1980-84	1985-89	1990	1991	1992	1993	1994	1995	1996[1]
Current expenditures	10.8	10.7	11.3	12.0	12.1	12.2	12.2	12.4	12.5
Taxes[2]	10.0	10.4	10.4	10.7	10.8	10.9	10.8	10.9	11.0
Grants-in-aid	2.7	2.3	2.3	2.6	2.8	2.8	2.8	2.8	2.8
Saving	1.9	1.9	1.4	1.3	1.4	1.4	1.4	1.3	1.3
Social insurance[3]	1.1	1.1	1.0	1.1	1.1	1.0	0.9	0.8	0.8
Other	0.8	0.8	0.4	0.2	0.3	0.4	0.5	0.5	0.5
plus:									
Consumption of fixed capital	1.1	1.0	1.0	1.0	1.0	1.0	1.0	1.0	1.0
less:									
Investment	2.0	2.0	2.1	2.1	2.1	2.1	2.1	2.2	2.2
equals:									
Net lending	0.9	0.9	0.2	0.2	0.3	0.3	0.3	0.1	0.1

1. Projection.
2. Receipts excluding grants-in-aid: taxes, fees and fines and social insurance contributions.
3. Contributions and investment income less benefit payments.

Source: Bureau of Economic Analysis.

grants-in-aid have financed some of this, but states and localities have also boosted taxes by ½ percentage point of GDP, mostly in the form of sales and property taxes.

Virtually all state and local governments have restrictions that require "balanced budgets", but these restrictions, particularly those written into state constitutions, frequently refer only to a portion of the budget, often excluding social insurance funds and capital spending for example. Usually, a balanced budget requires that revenues plus surpluses from prior years must be greater than outlays, and so current outlays may exceed current revenues. In addition, some of the restrictions are only to submit or pass a balanced budget, without provisions to cover unanticipated shortfalls that appear within the year. The closest concept to the general accounts budget is saving excluding social insurance funds, which rose from 0.4 per cent of GDP in 1990 to 0.5 per cent in 1995, reflecting the success state and local governments have had in improving their balance sheets. However, this saving rate, as well as net lending, is still below that recorded in the 1980s. The social insurance funds primarily fund public employee pensions. Contributions as a share of wages and salaries have fallen, and the funds'

Figure 16. **STATE AND LOCAL GOVERNMENT PENSION RESERVES**

Ratio to wages and salaries

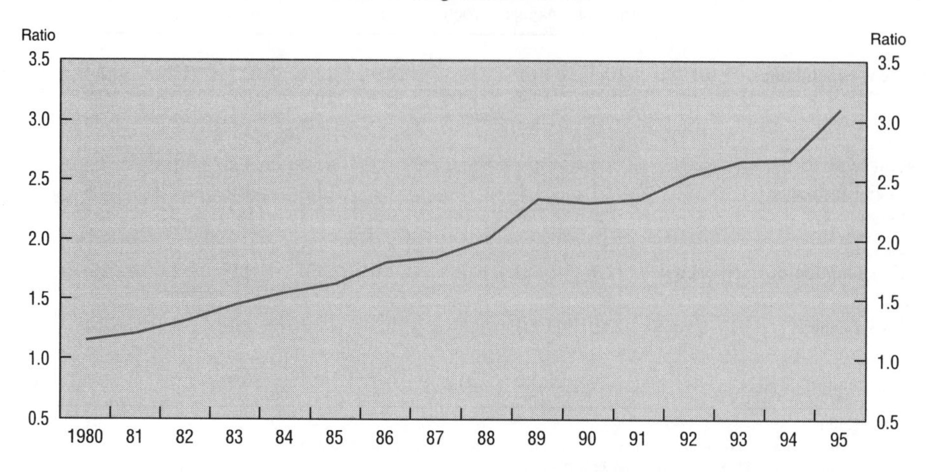

Source: Board of Governors of the Federal Reserve System, *Balance Sheets for the US Economy;* Bureau of Economic Analysis.

surpluses have declined in recent years. This may reflect the funds' substantial capital gains, as the ratio of assets to wages (used as a proxy for liabilities) has risen strongly (Figure 16).

A review of structural policy changes

The structural policy agenda in the United States covers a wide range of subjects. Since market mechanisms are already well implanted, initiatives to liberalise economic activity further are mainly the result of structural changes brought about by such factors as technological developments and international agreements. Social problems are also often the catalyst for reform efforts. But the coherence of these initiatives is limited by the political constraints imposed by the need for all legislation to be approved by both houses of Congress and the President and the inevitable false starts and compromises which ensue.

A number of important structural reforms have either been legislated over the past year or are under active consideration in Congress. The most important of these is the **Telecommunications Reform Act of 1996,** which the President signed into law 8 February 1996. Arguably the most important structural reform of his presidency, the new law will subject the telecommunications industry to the most extensive restructuring since 1984, when divestiture of the Bell System's local telephone exchange monopolies from its long distance and equipment manufacturing operations took place as a result of the 1982 AT&T antitrust consent decree. It is intended to open all sectors of the telecommunications industry to competition – including the now monopolised local telephone exchange and cable television sectors – by removing legal, regulatory and monopolistic barriers to entry. Incumbent local telephone companies, including the seven regional Bell companies, will be required to permit rivals to use their local networks and to make network elements available on an unbundled basis for resale. In return, the regional Bell companies will be allowed to enter the long distance and equipment manufacturing markets once they satisfy the Federal Communications Commission that their local networks have been satisfactorily opened to competition. The new law also removes regulatory barriers to competition among cable television firms, telephone companies and other service providers in providing videoprogramming. Cable television rates were deregulated immediately for small cable systems in areas where they serve no more than 50 000 subscribers. Rates for some other services are deregulated elsewhere after three years, or earlier where there is effective competition. Media concentration limits have also been eased: for example, in a market with 45 or more commercial radio stations, a single company is now permitted to own up to eight stations, with no more than five in the same service (AM or FM). In the wake of the new law, restructuring has already begun, with two pairs of regional Bell companies agreeing to merge, one regional Bell company offering to buy the nation's third-largest cable company, and a wave of consolidation in the radio sector.

New farm legislation covering the period through 2002 was signed by the President on 4 April 1996; it continues the process of injecting greater market influence into planting decisions. It replaces traditional subsidies for grains, oilseeds, cotton and rice with a system of fixed declining "transitional" payments over seven years, allowing farmers to plant what they want and ending mandatory set-asides; for these crops government intervention is largely eliminated. But given that the previous (1990) law allowed farmers 15 per cent crop flexibility and they were using only a small share of that, there will probably be very little impact on aggregate production outcomes. The Act also overhauls milk marketing orders (regional agreements) and phases out price supports for dairy products over four years; after 2000 there will only be a recourse (repayable) loan programme. But less change is effected for peanuts and sugar. For the former, loan rates (support prices) have been lowered, the edible use quota has been increased and quota trading will be allowed across county lines, while for the latter domestic marketing allotments (production quotas) have been eliminated. In order to clinch passage, extra spending had to be included (for example, on rural development, conservation and environmental programmes). This eliminated the budgetary savings included in earlier versions relative to the law which expired at end-1995; indeed, the new regime now looks set to be more expensive than its predecessor would have been over the near term (the CBO estimates the increase at $3.2 billion and $1.5 billion in FY 1996 and 1997, respectively), given the likelihood of market prices persisting at levels substantially above those that prevailed when the legislation was initially formulated.

Controversial legislation dealing with the **immigration** question has passed both chambers and is in conference.[26] The bill passed by the House would limit the number of refugees admitted, increase border controls, tighten measures to prevent illegal immigrants from getting jobs and make them ineligible for federal education and welfare benefits. An early version of the House-passed bill would also have cut levels of legal immigration, but this provision was dropped. The House version also contains a provision – which the Senate version does not – which allows states to deny illegal immigrants access to public schools; this has drawn the threat of a Presidential veto. In a related matter, the major welfare reform signed 22 August 1996 (described in detail in Chapter III) prohibits most new legal aliens from receiving means-tested benefits for five years after entry and bans current and future immigrants from Supplementary Security Income and Food Stamps. Refugees and asylees are limited to five years of benefits. Overall benefits to immigrants will be cut by nearly $4 billion per year, 40 per cent of the bill's total savings. It is unclear whether this will supersede some or all of the benefit provisions in the immigration reform legislation.

The United States **trade policy** position in multilateral negotiations has continued to move toward one of greater insistence on reciprocity. As occurred in

1995 with the Uruguay Round financial services negotiations, the United States decided in April 1996 that the set of existing offers in the telecommunications talks did not constitute a critical mass of sufficient weight for it to make a deal with the 52 other participants, and the initial deadline was missed. It cited specific disappointment in the areas of international and satellite services. In February it had revised its offer to improve access to US markets including local telephone service. Later, it indicated a desire to retain the right to refuse license applications by foreign firms able to abuse their dominant positions. The result is that the deadline for an agreement was put off until 15 February 1997, although liberalisation commitments are still to enter into force on 1 January 1998, as originally foreseen. Maritime services talks were also suspended. The US Trade Representative (USTR) announced on 14 June that the package of offers presented on 4 June by 23 participants in the negotiations "merely locks in place restrictive, anti-competitive measures", giving the United States no reason to submit an offer. The result was that the mandate of the negotiating group expired without an agreement being reached, and further negotiations will have to await the next round of overall services negotiations due to get underway by the beginning of the year 2000.

The United States has taken a leading role in the negotiations at the OECD over a Multilateral Agreement on Investment, due by mid-1997, which would make national treatment binding (which the 1976 OECD instrument does not) as well as provide for effective dispute settlement procedures, elimination of performance requirements and protection against expropriation. It remains to be seen whether the ultimate accord will cover direct investment alone or portfolio investment as well.

While no extension of so-called "fast-track authority" (which expired in 1994) has been granted to the President by the Congress, trade policy has been the focus of a number of other actual and expected bills. In September 1995 the "Super 301" provisions in US trade law were extended for a further two years. Legislation retroactively renewing the Generalised System of Preferences (which had expired 31 July 1995) until May 1997 was signed in August 1996. In June 1996 the House of Representatives passed legislation intended to implement the 1994 OECD Shipbuilding Agreement, already approved by all other signatories. However, it contains a number of provisions which appear to violate the terms of the Agreement; one provision would allow the government to continue to extend loan guarantees to US shipbuilders until 1 January 1999. No vote has as yet taken place in the Senate. Congressional hearings were held in April regarding the nation's antidumping procedures. In January 1996 the USTR established a permanent monitoring and enforcement unit.

In the first twelve months of its existence the WTO received 25 trade disputes to adjudicate, of which the United States was the complaining party in six and defending party in four. The United States lost a dispute settlement panel challenge by Venezuela and Brazil before the WTO as well as a subsequent appeal regarding standards applied to gasoline with a view to reducing exhaust emissions. But after USTR initiated WTO dispute settlement proceedings in February, Japan decided to submit a draft amendment of its Copyright Law to its Parliament in order to extend the term of retroactive protection for the rights of performers and producers of sound recordings to 50 years. Also, this year the United States has decided to challenge a number of foreign practices before the WTO, including: 1) the Canadian tax on advertising in US magazines with special Canadian editions imposed on 15 December 1995; 2) the EU decision to ban US beef containing hormones; 3) the EU banana import regime (for the second time); and 4) Japanese measures concerning its market for photographic film and paper as well as distribution services. And controversy surrounds the March 1996 passage and enactment of the Cuban Liberty and Democratic Solidarity (Helms-Burton) Act and the Iran and Libya Sanctions Act under which foreign firms and individuals doing business with these countries could face sanctions, including claims in US courts. This risks partner reprisals, with potentially important implications for multilateral trade.

There are also a number of other lingering bilateral trade disputes. A dispute with Japan over the 1952 civil aviation agreement remains unresolved. Negotiations are continuing in insurance, but the semiconductor issue was settled on 2 August 1996. A dialogue is underway concerning the implementation of the 1990 Wood Product Measures and progress has been made on most issues. In April 1996 the United States announced that the measures taken pursuant to the 1995 US-Japan automobile talks had produced significant results in all areas covered; the first annual review of the measures is being held in mid-September. The United States and EU announced at their 3 December 1995 summit the New Transatlantic Agenda. The NTA is a blueprint for expanded bilateral co-operation on a range of political and economic issues, including the pursuit of an

Information Technology Agreement that would dramatically reduce barriers to trade in high technology products. Also in December 1995, the United States and EU reached agreement (signed on 22 July 1996) on compensation owed to the United States under GATT Article XXIV:6 resulting from the enlargement of the EU by the association of Austria, Finland and Sweden. There has been a succession of bilateral open-skies agreements on passenger air transport with various European partners, but no overarching agreement with the EU, although such negotiations look set to get underway. In February, Canada committed to reduce its softwood lumber exports to the United States in exchange for a US commitment to refrain from trade action in this sector. Important issues with Mexico and NAFTA implementation are also outstanding: among these is the delay in implementing the partial liberalisation in cross-border trucking late last year. Finally, in June 1996 the United States reached agreement with China requiring it to enforce a February 1995 intellectual property rights agreement.

After the failure of comprehensive **health care** reform in 1994, a limited reform bill was passed during this session of Congress. It requires group insurance plans to disregard pre-existing conditions and guarantee policy renewals and policy continuations for workers who leave their jobs in order to improve ''portability''. It also sets up a pilot programme for four years as from 1 January 1997 permitting the creation of roughly 750 000 medical savings accounts (MSAs).[27] Some have argued that MSAs will attract those with the best health risks, leaving others to face much higher premiums. The bill also included provisions to increase the tax deductibility of health insurance premiums for the self-employed and to make premiums on long-term care insurance generally tax deductible. These revenue losses are offset by eliminating over five years the corporate tax deductibility of interest on loans secured by firms' taking out life insurance on their employees, and by cutting waste and fraud in federal health care programmes by stiffening penalties. Dropped at the last stage was a controversial provision which would have limited medical malpractice awards; according to some recent research, the latter might reduce the practice of ''defensive medicine'', thereby saving up to 5 to 9 per cent of medical expenditures (Kessler and McClellan, 1996).

In the area of **environmental policies**, extended discussion has taken place in Congress to reform environmental laws and regulations and streamline the Environment Protection Agency, but progress so far has been uneven. Legislation to re-authorise the Safe Drinking Water Act with a view to streamlining regulation of public water systems was signed in August 1996. It provides a $7.6 billion fund to assist local water systems to upgrade their facilities, gives regulators more flexibility in setting health standards, and requires annual reports on contaminants to customers. However, little progress has been made in Congress on overhauling the so-called "Superfund" (hazardous waste) law (necessary because the taxes which fund the programme, bringing in some $700 million per year, expired at the end of 1995, and the programme will run out of money around FY 2000; there is also a desire to eliminate "retroactive liability" whereby business can be held responsible for waste dumped before the 1980 passage of the legislation). There has, likewise, been no success in revising the Clean Water Act (where the problem is how to handle non-point-source emissions such as farms). In addition, the Senate recently voted by a narrow margin to overhaul the rules for grazing livestock on public lands, but the Administration has threatened to veto the bill.

The Environmental Protection Agency has introduced new approaches to achieve greater cost efficiency by allowing regional flexibility in emissions objectives, selecting quantified targets, using economic instruments and seeking the support of the regulated communities in the form of voluntary agreements and developing partnerships at all levels of society. Tradeable pollution permits, launched in 1993, have been judged a success: the target reduction in sulphur dioxide has been achieved at around half the cost that the traditional regulatory regime would have imposed, a saving of $2.5 billion; the permit price per tonne has fallen from $1 500 in 1993 to $68 most recently. The Environmental Protection Agency is now considering similar plans for other pollutants such as nitrous oxides and mercury. This would prove especially useful for nitrous oxides, as the Federal Energy Regulatory Commission has ruled that electric utilities must now open their transmission lines to competitors, another step towards the separation of transmission from generation, and it is expected that the resulting interregional trade will lead to an increase in the share of coal-generated power. Electricity futures prices began trading in March 1996.

At the end of March 1996 Congress passed a **line-item veto** bill that had been much discussed in recent years. As from 1997 and for a period of eight years the President will have enhanced rescissions authority, which means that he will be able to remove individual items in spending bills, new or expanded entitlement programmes and any tax change that benefits fewer than 100 taxpayers. To overrule the President the Congress would have to pass a new bill authorising the item(s); this could of course in turn be vetoed and would have to be overruled by a two-thirds majority in both houses. This will clearly shift the balance of power in the US system and will probably be challenged before the courts by those believing that it cannot be undertaken without modifying the Constitution. It may not, however, succeed in reducing the overall level of spending, as experience at the state level shows (Carter and Schap, 1990).

There are a number of other areas where major efforts have been made to undertake reform, but without success. Attempts to pass a major **financial services reform** were finally abandoned in June. Two House committees had passed legislation which would have repealed the Glass-Steagall Act (which separates commercial and investment banking) last spring. But it would not have allowed affiliations between banks and insurance companies nor between banks and non-bank commercial firms. New financial services holding companies would have been able to provide a full range of banking and securities underwriting and sales functions with oversight by the Federal Reserve. But recent Supreme Court decisions have given banks the right to sell annuities and insurance (the latter only from branches in small towns). And the Federal Reserve has asked for comments on its proposal to lift the revenue ceiling for "ineligible activities" (essentially underwriting and trading of corporate securities) of what are known as "Section 20 subsidiaries" (banks' securities operations) from 10 to 25 per cent. This could trigger a wave of mergers between banks and stock brokers. In a related matter, legislation is moving through Congress which would revamp the regulation of securities firms with a view to the elimination of duplication between the state and federal levels. Finally, at the end of 1995 the Resolution Trust Corporation was shut down after it had recouped $395 billion from the $456 billion (86 per cent) in book value of assets it had inherited in the form of failing savings and loan institutions. Some 25 per cent of the pre-crisis "thrifts" were closed at an overall taxpayer cost estimated to be around $145 billion, well below earlier worst-case projections. Remaining "thrifts" are now in better financial shape, with record 1995 earnings of $5.4 billion. But no provisions for further capitalising their deposit insurance fund have been passed, and the 23 basis point difference in premiums compared to commercial banks remains.

Legislation with a view to **liability reform** was passed by the Congress but vetoed by the President this spring. Its main feature was to cap jury awards of punitive damages in product liability lawsuits at the greater of $250 000 or twice compensatory damages or the lesser of the two for businesses with fewer than 25 employees.[28] The Administration opposed the bill, claiming that it is unfair to consumers (who are not the source of the recent increase in litigation), but it did indicate its support for reform in general. In a related matter, the Supreme Court ruled in May 1996 that product liability awards may be grossly excessive and, therefore, unconstitutional.

Finally, there are some additional areas where reform efforts are just getting underway. One is the longer-term problem with retirement income. On the basis of present arrangements, the **Social Security** trust fund would be expected to start running deficits in 2020 and to be bankrupt in 2029. An Advisory Council on its future is expected to propose imminently that it invest some of its proceeds in equities, rather than only in government debt. In April the Administration announced its proposed Retirement Savings and Security Act which would ease job-related pension portability, guarantee more rapid vesting and remove ceilings on tax benefits for retirement savings.

In the area of **competition policy**, in June 1996 the staff of the Federal Trade Commission issued a report which contained a variety of proposals for keeping competition policy up to date with changes in the increasingly high-tech, global marketplace. Among other things, the report suggested that the 1992 Horizontal Merger Guidelines be revised to specify better how the federal competition agencies (Department of Justice and Federal Trade Commission) analyse efficiencies likely to be achieved through mergers. A joint Department of Justice and Federal Trade Commission Task Force has now been established to consider whether the Guidelines' approach to efficiencies should be changed or more fully explained. The report also advocates that the Federal Trade Commission should continue to examine, with care, whether a merger or acquisition is likely substantially to lessen competition in new product development and thereby harm consumers.

Tax policy continues to be hotly debated, especially in view of the apparent widespread willingness to make major changes. For example, the report of a commission appointed by the Republican Congressional leadership calls for a single low tax rate on individual income (there are currently five), with a generous personal exemption, broadening of the tax base (although it did not clearly support the elimination of deductions for mortgage interest or charitable donations and did call for full deduction for payroll taxes for Social Security and Medicare), the elimination of double taxation of dividends and other disincentives to saving and investment, the abolition of estate taxation and the institution of a two-thirds majority requirement before tax rates can be raised.

III. Implementing the OECD Jobs Strategy

Introduction

Over the past several decades US labour markets have experienced rising rates of labour force participation and employment-to-population ratios. The unemployment rate has exhibited little secular movement, as, for the most part, variations have reflected cyclical factors rather than structural changes (Figure 17). Indeed, many estimates of the structural unemployment rate suggest that the rate has risen only modestly – perhaps by less than a percentage point since the 1960s – unlike the experience in many European economies. The narrow range for estimates of the structural unemployment rate and its relatively low level reflect the flexibility inherent in the labour and product markets as well as the structure of taxes and transfers. On balance, the broad policy settings influencing labour market performance have been little changed since the early 1970s, with somewhat higher tax rates perhaps dampening labour market performance, while falling real minimum wages and unionisation rates may have increased flexibility.

While US labour markets have generated ample job growth, the quality of the jobs created has been questioned in many quarters. Concern has been voiced for many years about the slow growth in productivity and real compensation that began in the early 1970s. Some have asserted that too much of the job growth has been concentrated in low-pay/low-skill jobs, of uncertain durability and providing few benefits. However, the data indicate that job growth has in fact been concentrated among the higher-paying occupations. And while the probability of layoff among white-collar workers has risen, the overall probability has not changed much. In recent years there has been growing interest in developments in the income distribution; while there is clear evidence that it has widened, the causes are still hotly debated. This chapter follows up the OECD Jobs Study in a US context (Box 4). First, key features and developments of the US labour

Figure 17. **KEY FEATURES OF THE LABOUR MARKET**

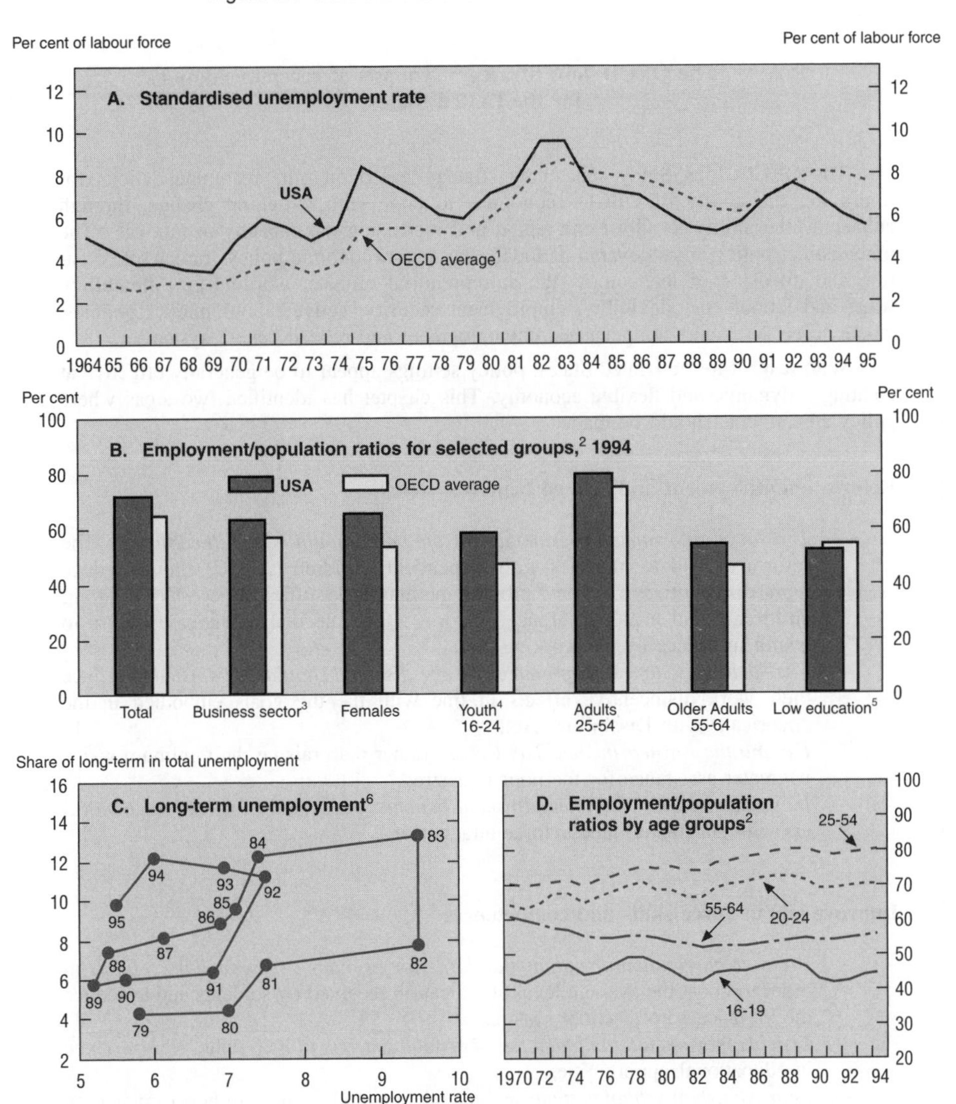

1. Excludes Austria, the Czech Republic, Denmark, Greece, Iceland, Luxembourg, Mexico, Turkey and Hungary.
2. Defined as the percentage of each population group that is employed.
3. Business sector employment divided by working-age population.
4. The minimum age for youth differs across countries (either 14,15 or 16).
5. In 1992. Completed less than upper secondary education.
6. Long-term unemployment is defined as individuals looking for work for one year or more.

Source: OECD, *Employment Outlook*.

Box 4. The OECD Jobs Strategy: synopsis of recommendations for the United States

The OECD Jobs Study sets out a strategy based on nine recommendations for improving the ability of OECD economies to cope with structural change, through enhancing the ability to adjust and adapt, and increasing the capacity to innovate. The nine distinct policy areas covered included: the macroeconomic policy framework, creation and diffusion of technology, the entreprenurial climate, working-time flexibility, wage and labour cost flexibility, employment security, active labour market policies, labour force skills and competences, unemployment and related benefit systems.

With respect to the United States, policy settings appear to be generally effective at creating a dynamic and flexible economy. This chapter has identified two areas where policy adjustments should be made.

Reform unemployment and related benefit systems

- *The social assistance programmes for the poor should be modified further.* The reform of Aid to Families with Dependent Children (AFDC) should reduce work disincentives. The new programme may lack sufficient access to training, child care and health insurance. Reform is also needed to increase access to health insurance by the working poor.
- *The social assistance programmes for the disabled should be adjusted* to reduce their work disincentive effects in line with the the goals embodied in the Americans with Disabilities Act.
- *Expand the Earned Income Tax Credit*, rather than raising the minimum wage, if greater assistance for the poor is desired.
- *Increase eligibility for unemployment benefits*, particularly for low-wage workers with substantial labour force attachment.

Improve labour force skills and competences

- *Promote curriculum or output standards for primary and secondary schools* in order to boost the average level of education received by students and to reduce the variance across school systems.
- *Provide more equitable financing of school districts* to help reduce the variance in educational opportunities.
- *Improve urban school systems* and attendant social services to boost graduation rates and quality of education received by vulnerable populations.
- *Increase information about the quality of programmes provided by community colleges and technical institutes* so that prospective students and employers may make better informed decisions.

market are described. Next, important characteristics of the policy and institutional environment are examined with respect to their effects on the ability of labour markets to adjust and adapt and on the efficiency and productive capacity of the economy. Finally, recent policy initiatives are outlined, and the scope for further action is presented.

Labour market and employment performance

Labour supply developments

In recent decades the US labour force has consistently grown faster than the working-age population, because the rise in participation by women has outweighed the gradual decrease experienced by men (Figure 18). Male labour force participation rates have fallen in nearly all OECD countries, but the decline has been much more limited in the United States than in most other countries (Table 12).[29]

Several factors have contributed to the decline in male participation: increased availability and use of both early retirement and disability benefits, increased time spent in school, and a sharp drop in labour market attachment among the least educated, perhaps reflecting lower real wages among the least skilled. All told, these factors have reduced labour force participation significantly for those 55 and above, but much less so among younger age groups (Figure 18). While these same factors have also tended to reduce female participation rates, they have been overwhelmed by other sociological and economic considerations, such as lower fertility and marriage rates, higher divorce rates and increased human capital which have contributed to rising female participation.[30] In recent years, growth in female labour force participation has slowed. Rates for young women and young men are currently very close. However, some future increase in overall female participation may still be expected due to cohort effects as the baby boom generation ages and its greater labour force attachment causes older-worker participation rates to rise. Most OECD countries have very similar labour force participation rates for prime-age men, but large international differences are found among the participation rates for other groups: the young, elderly and women (Table 13).

Figure 18. **US LABOUR FORCE PARTICIPATION**
By sex and age, 16 and over

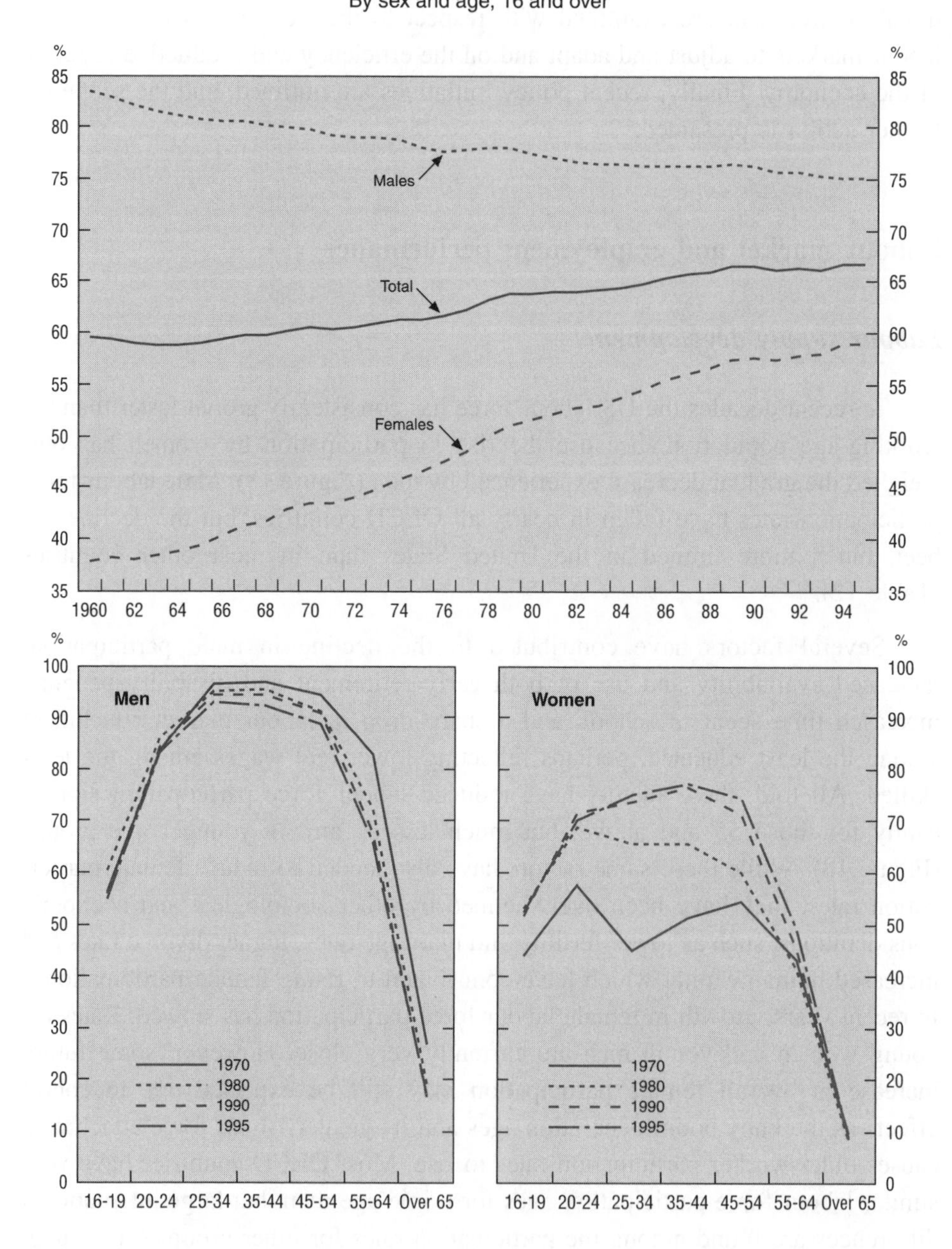

Source: Department of Labor.

Table 12. **Labour force participation rates in the OECD**[1]

Per cent of working age population (15-64)

	Men			Women		
	1970	1994	Change	1970	1994	Change
Australia	93.1	85.0[2]	–8.1	46.1	62.3[2]	16.2
Austria	86.5	81.0	–5.5	49.9	62.1	12.2
Belgium	84.4	72.6[3]	–11.8	39.8	54.1[3]	14.3
Canada	85.7	82.6	–3.1	43.2	67.8	24.6
Denmark	91.8	84.2	–7.6	58.0	73.8	15.8
Finland	83.2	77.1	–6.1	61.3	69.9	8.6
France	86.9	74.5[2]	–12.4	48.5	59.0[2]	10.5
Germany	92.6	80.8	–11.8	48.0	61.8	13.8
Greece	85.1	74.0[2]	–11.1	31.9	43.8[2]	11.9
Ireland	96.4	78.6[2]	–17.8	34.3	46.1[2]	11.8
Iceland	91.8	88.5	–3.3	45.8	80.0	34.2
Italy	86.8	74.8[2]	–12.0	33.5	43.3[2]	9.8
Japan	89.4	90.6	1.2	55.4	62.1	6.7
Mexico	87.3	91.9	4.6	21.3	40.0	18.7
Netherlands	90.2	79.1	–11.1	28.0	57.4	29.4
Norway	89.0	82.0[2]	–7.0	38.8	70.8[2]	32.0
New Zealand	91.9	83.9	–8.0	37.5	65.0	27.5
Portugal	106.9	81.1	–25.8	32.0	62.2	30.2
Spain	96.4	74.0	–22.4	28.4	44.1	15.7
Sweden	88.8	78.1	–10.7	59.4	74.4	15.0
United Kingdom	94.4	84.0[2]	–10.4	50.7	65.3[2]	14.6
United States	85.4	85.3	–0.1	48.9	70.5	21.6

1. OECD definition, which differs from US definition used in Figure 18.
2. 1993.
3. 1992.

Source: OECD, *Labour Force Statistics*.

Looking at other demographic groups, labour force participation rates are now about equal for white and black females, whereas black female participation rates were once much higher. Among men, labour force participation has fallen more rapidly for blacks than for whites, and black male participation rates are now 7 percentage points lower than those of whites. Labour force participation is also much lower for less-educated workers. In addition, changes in labour force participation over time have varied by education level. While the overall male participation rate (aged 25 to 64) has dropped about 4 percentage points over the past 25 years, it has fallen only 2 percentage points among those with four or more years of college, high school graduates' rates have dropped 7 percentage points, and participation by those who have not graduated from high school has

Table 13. **Labour force participation by age and sex**

Per cent of working age population

	Ages 15 to 24				Ages 25 to 54				Ages 55 to 64			
	Men		Women		Men		Women		Men		Women	
	1973	1993	1973	1993	1973	1993	1973	1993	1973	1993	1973	1993
Australia	75.4	70.0	58.5	63.5	96.7	92.0	47.5	67.1	82.6	58.9	24.5	25.9
Canada	66.0	65.5	50.7	61.5	96.2	91.6	44.0	76.0	81.3	61.0	31.0	36.4
Finland	67.1	53.3	53.8	42.9	92.2	91.0	75.6	84.5	67.6	44.0	44.6	40.2
France	57.0	35.1	45.5	29.3	96.8	94.9	54.1	76.0	72.1	43.5	37.2	30.4
West Germany	69.4	57.5	62.3	55.0	96.1	88.0	51.1	66.8	75.4	57.2	25.8	29.8
Italy [1]	47.3	43.5	33.6	36.1	93.8	88.9	29.5	49.1	42.0	32.9	8.7	11.8
Japan	55.5	47.6	50.1	46.7	97.7	97.7	54.3	65.2	86.8	85.4	44.7	48.6
Netherlands	59.0	62.0	50.9	60.9	94.8	92.2	25.7	69.3	77.2	41.5	14.8	17.0
Norway	51.8	58.1	46.1	52.7	93.5	90.2	53.4	79.3	83.9	71.5	41.7	53.5
Spain	73.0	48.7	54.9	43.2	96.6	92.8	27.9	52.2	82.7	59.0	24.8	20.2
Sweden	67.9	52.0	60.1	52.2	94.3	91.3	68.9	87.6	82.7	70.5	46.3	63.4
United States [2]	72.9	70.0	54.9	62.2	95.0	92.6	52.3	74.7	78.2	66.5	41.1	47.3

1. The figures for the 25 to 54 age group use data for 25 to 59 and the figures for 55 to 64 use data for ages 60 to 64.
2. The figures for the 15 to 24 age group use data for ages 16 to 24.

Source: OECD, *Labour Force Statistics*, Part III.

dropped 13 percentage points. For women a similar story holds: the largest gains in participation have been registered by those with the most education. A portion of the difference may be due to different average ages of each education group, but the shift in relative earnings may also have played a role. Discouraged workers, however, make up a smaller portion of non-participation than earlier (OECD, 1995*d*).

The effective size of the labour force has also been affected by the growing incidence of part-time employment, particularly among the young and less so for men aged 20 and over; the share of women with part-time employment has held steady (Table 14). Over 80 per cent of those working part-time do so voluntarily and that is the group that has grown over time. The share of workers holding

Table 14. **Part-time employment and multiple jobholders**

	Part-time work [1]			
	1968-69	1978-79	1988-89	1995
All employees	15.2	17.6	18.3	19.0
Voluntary	12.7	13.9	13.8	15.3
Involuntary	2.6	3.7	4.5	3.7
Employees 16 to 19 years old	51.7	54.4	64.1	68.1
Voluntary	45.7	45.7	54.2	61.2
Involuntary	6.0	8.7	9.9	6.9
Men, 20 years and older	5.4	6.9	8.5	8.8
Voluntary	3.8	4.5	5.1	5.7
Involuntary	1.7	2.4	3.4	3.1
Women, 20 years and older	23.5	24.7	23.8	23.9
Voluntary	20.2	20.1	18.7	19.9
Involuntary	3.2	4.5	5.1	4.0
	Multiple jobholders [2]			
	1970	1979	1989	1995
Total	5.2	4.9	6.2	6.2
Men	7.0	5.8	6.4	6.1
Women	2.2	3.8	5.9	6.2
Women as a share of total	15.7	29.8	43.0	46.2

1. As a share of total non-agricultural employment among those at work.
2. As a share of total employment.
Source: Bureau of Labor Statistics.

Table 15. **Employed foreign born and natives in the US civilian labour force**

Skill level	Employed labour force (thousands)				Change 1980 to 1990			Foreign born share of skill level	
	1980		1990		Per cent			Per cent	
	Foreign born	Native	Foreign born	Native	Foreign born	Native	Total	1980	1990
Less than high-school	2 445	19 804	3 011	12 121	23.2	–38.8	–32.0	11.0	19.9
High-school graduates	1 635	33 556	2 624	35 585	60.5	6.0	8.6	4.6	6.9
Some college	918	15 941	1 969	26 401	114.6	65.6	68.3	5.4	6.9
College graduates	1 179	15 317	2 293	21 843	94.5	42.6	46.3	7.1	9.5
Total	6 177	84 618	9 897	95 949	60.2	13.4	16.6	6.8	9.4

Source: Jaeger (1995).

multiple jobs has increased slightly, although this has leveled off in recent years. Historically, most holders of multiple jobs were men with a second job to supplement income from a full-time job. The source of the increase has been women who are now as likely as men to be multiple jobholders, but frequently with multiple part-time jobs.

Besides natural population growth and increased participation rates, the labour force has been augmented to an increasing degree by net immigration (Table 15). For example, the rising share of foreign born in the work force boosted the work force by 2¾ per cent between 1980 and 1990. Foreign born workers are just as likely as others to have college educations, but they are more likely to have not graduated from high school. Although the share of foreign born workers with less than a high-school education out of all foreign born workers declined from 40 per cent in 1980 to 30 per cent in 1990, their share of all workers with less than a high-school education rose from 11 to 20 per cent.

The educational attainment of the labour force has advanced quite rapidly (Figure 19), particularly in the 1960s and 1970s.[31] Over the past 15 to 20 years the relative demand for more educated workers has outstripped their growing relative supply, and accordingly their relative earnings have risen (in terms of higher hourly wage rates and lower rates of unemployment). The rise in the returns to college education, in turn, has encouraged more high-school graduates to enter college; this has worked to reduce earnings differentials (Bishop, 1996).

Figure 19. **DISTRIBUTION OF EDUCATIONAL ATTAINMENT AMONG MALE WORKERS**[1]

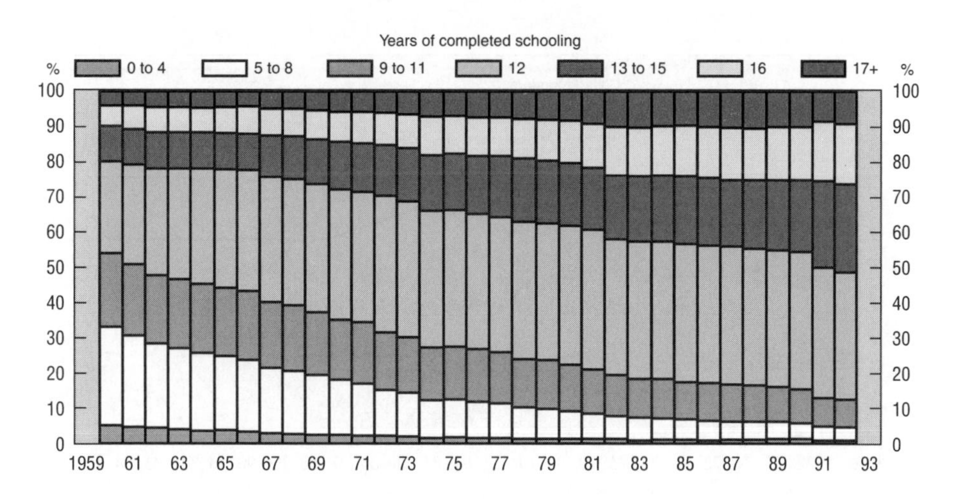

1. Private business, weighted by hours worked.
Source: Department of Labor.

Structure of unemployment

The unemployment rate has not drifted up in the United States as it has in most European countries. As a result, while the United States consistently registered higher unemployment rates than the vast majority of OECD countries in the 1960s, it now has one of the lowest rates. Part of the current difference is cyclical (because the United States is roughly at full employment, while many other OECD countries have significant output gaps), but much is structural (Figure 20). Structural unemployment rates must be interpreted with caution, because they are estimated with a significant degree of imprecision, but they do provide a useful judgement on the extent of cyclical factors in current unemployment rates. Unemployment rates for women are now quite similar to those of men, reflecting the greater labour market attachment of women as compared with several decades ago. Unemployment rates for blacks, especially those of teenagers, are much higher than those of whites. Looking across geographic regions, unemployment rates have tended to converge over time, reflecting wage flexibility and migration. Indeed, some studies indicate that net migration rates across states are heavily

Figure 20. **ESTIMATED STRUCTURAL UNEMPLOYMENT RATES AMONG THE MAJOR SEVEN OECD COUNTRIES**[1]

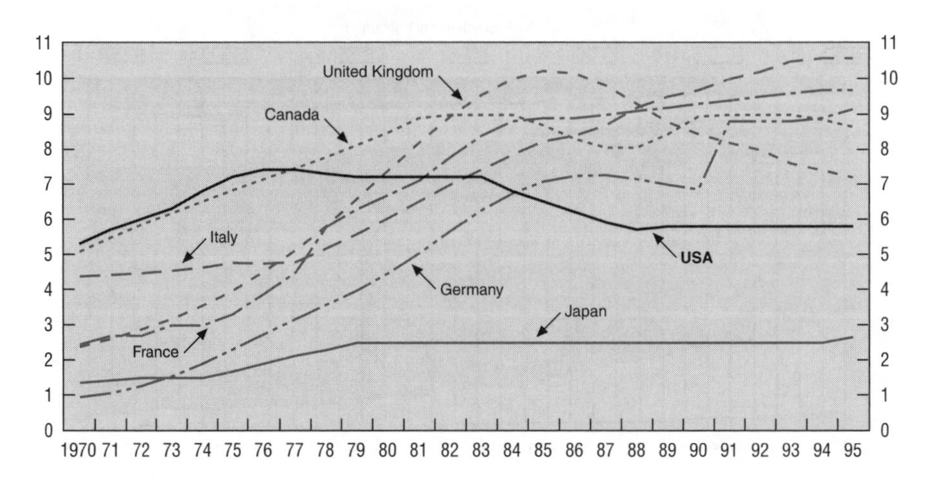

1. Structural unemployment rates are measured with considerable uncertainty over time and at a point in time.
Source: OECD.

influenced by unemployment differentials and only somewhat by wage differentials.[32]

Compared with other OECD countries, the incidence of long-term unemployment as a share of total unemployment (and especially as a share of the population) is quite low. In many OECD countries the share of unemployed for 12 months or longer is above 50 per cent of the unemployed, whereas it has ranged from 4 to 14 per cent in the United States (Figure 17). As indicated by the relatively short duration of unemployment for US workers, flows into and out of unemployment are much higher than in many other OECD countries. However, since the last recession, the duration of unemployment has not shortened as much as is typically the case for a given reduction in the unemployment rate, although changes in the survey methodology make the post-1993 figures not strictly comparable (Figure 21). The reasons for this are not well understood. It may reflect, in part, changes in the composition of those experiencing unemployment. Currently the unemployment rolls are more heavily weighted towards groups that

Figure 21. **DURATION OF UNEMPLOYMENT SPELLS**[1]

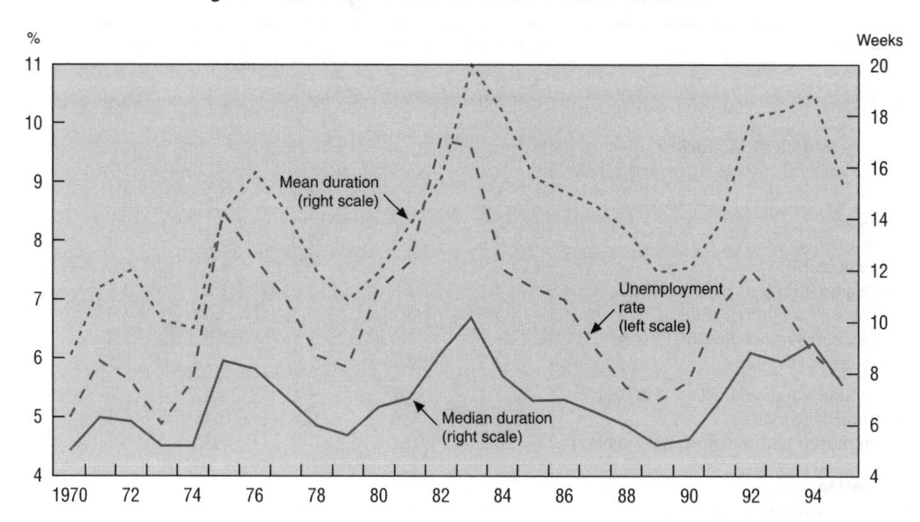

1. Data for 1994 are not strictly comparable to earlier years.
Source: Bureau of Labor Statistics.

typically have longer spells of unemployment – prime-age workers, managers, professionals and job losers not on temporary layoff.

According to some labour market indicators, displaced workers may have become an increasingly important phenomenon. Indeed, the displacement rate (measured by those with long tenures who lose jobs) was as high in the 1991-92 period as it was in the 1981-82 period even though the most recent recession was much milder (Table 16).[33] Although the most common categories of workers displaced continue to be blue-collar workers and those in manufacturing, white-collar workers and service-sector workers are becoming increasingly subject to displacement. However, broader measures of displaced workers that include all job losers indicate that displacement rates have not risen. Of particular note is the lack of any significant change in layoffs as a share of the labour force in recent years compared with earlier periods with low unemployment, despite many press reports to the contrary (Council of Economic Advisers, 1996).[34] The above mentioned displacement rate may understate the prevalence of layoffs, particularly during the deep 1981-82 recession, as it does not record multiple

Table 16. **The evolution of the displacement rate**[1]

Characteristic	1981-82	1983-84	1985-86	1987-88	1989-90	1991-92
Total	3.9	3.1	3.1	2.4	3.1	3.8
Industry and class of worker						
Non-agricultural private wage and salary workers	5.3	4.2	4.3	3.2	4.1	5.2
Mining	13.6	9.2	17.8	6.1	10.0	7.6
Construction	7.6	5.5	7.0	4.2	5.9	7.9
Manufacturing	8.2	6.5	5.2	3.9	5.0	6.9
Transportation and public utilities	4.1	3.8	3.1	1.8	3.6	4.1
Wholesale and retail trade	3.7	3.1	4.3	3.6	3.9	4.5
Finance, insurance and real estate	1.4	1.3	3.5	2.8	3.5	5.6
Services	2.3	2.1	2.3	1.7	2.1	2.8
Agricultural wage and salary workers	5.4	9.7	4.1	2.5	3.2	4.0
Government workers	1.2	0.6	0.4	0.4	0.4	1.1
Self-employed and unpaid family workers	0.2	0.1	–	0.3	0.2	–
Occupation						
White-collar occupations	2.6	2.1	2.6	2.1	2.7	3.6
Managerial and professional specialty	2.1	1.8	2.1	1.8	2.3	3.5
Technical, sales and administrative support	3.0	2.4	3.1	2.5	3.1	3.7
Service occupations	2.0	1.8	1.9	1.5	1.6	2.1
Blue-collar occupations	7.3	5.7	4.7	3.3	4.5	5.2
Precision production, craft and repair	6.2	4.5	3.9	2.7	4.2	5.1
Operators, fabricators and labourers	8.2	6.7	5.5	3.8	4.8	5.3
Farming, forestry and fishing	0.9	2.1	1.6	0.8	1.5	1.4
Age						
25–34	5.0	3.9	3.5	2.5	3.1	3.8
35–44	3.8	3.1	3.3	2.7	3.2	3.9
45–54	3.0	2.6	3.0	2.2	3.1	3.8
55–64	3.8	3.1	3.0	2.3	3.3	4.5

1. The displacement rate is the number of job losers with 3 years or more of job tenure during the 2-year period divided by the average number of workers in the category (including those with less than 3 years experience). The annual rate is half the reported figure.

Source: Gardner (1995).

layoffs over a short period of time because of its focus on workers with long tenures.

Displaced workers are particularly important because they appear to face discouraging labour market prospects. About three-quarters of those displaced during the 1991-92 period were employed in February 1994. Of the remainder, half were unemployed and half had left the labour force. About 40 per cent had exhausted their unemployment benefits before they found work. In a recent study, earnings in the year following displacement were estimated to fall by 25 per cent on average, and hourly wages by 12 per cent.[35] Moreover, even six years after displacement, annual earnings and wages remained approximately 9 per cent below the pre-displacement average. But, average earnings six years after a displacement are lower only for those that subsequently are displaced again. Earnings six years after a worker's most recent job loss are nearly equal to their expected level (the pre-loss level plus typical growth), had displacement not occurred. Also displaced workers who are re-employed in the same industries experience rapid recovery in earnings, while those displaced from their industries suffer large long-term reductions. However, many workers experience multiple displacements.

Structure of employment

Overall, the composition of employment has shifted from goods-producing sectors, particularly manufacturing, to service-producing sectors and from low-skilled occupations towards those demanding higher skills.[36] Similar shifts have occurred in most OECD countries. The recent period has often been incorrectly characterised as one of creating primarily low-skill jobs in the United States. The evidence frequently cited is the shift from manufacturing (where earnings are generally higher than average) to services where earnings are lower (Table 17).[37] Yet industries have both high- and low-skill jobs, and thus it is instructive to look at job growth by occupation. Employment growth has been most rapid in occupations that pay higher than average salaries (Table 18). The four highest paying occupations were among the top five occupations in employment growth. Despite the high relative growth, relative demand appears to have grown even faster, as these occupations generally recorded the largest real wage increases. Within industries, shifts in staffing towards higher paying occupations boosted earnings in all industries except in wholesale trade, where shifts reduced average earnings and in mining, retail trade and personal services, where they remained flat (US Department of Labor, 1994).

Virtually all service-producing industries have registered double-digit gains in employment over the past 25 years. The fastest growing sectors have been business services, social services, legal services and health services which have all doubled or tripled employment levels. Among business services (6 million

Table 17. **Change in payroll employment by industry**

Industry	Number		Annual rate of change	Share of work force	
	1969	1995		1969	1995
Total	70 384	116 600	2.0	100.0	100.0
Goods producing	24 361	24 229	0.0	34.6	20.8
Mining	619	579	–0.3	0.9	0.5
Construction	3 575	5 245	1.5	5.1	4.5
Manufacturing	20 167	18 405	–0.4	28.7	15.8
Service producing	46 023	92 371	2.7	65.4	79.2
Transportation and public utilities	4 442	6 193	1.3	6.3	5.3
Wholesale trade	3 919	6 322	1.9	5.6	5.4
Retail trade	10 785	20 836	2.6	15.3	17.9
Finance, insurance and real estate	3 512	6 948	2.7	5.0	6.0
Services	11 169	32 794	4.2	15.9	28.1
Business	1 328	6 640	6.4	1.9	5.7
Health	2 862	9 268	4.6	4.1	7.9
Government	12 195	19 279	1.8	17.3	16.5
Federal	2 758	2 820	0.1	3.9	2.4
State and local	9 437	16 459	2.2	13.4	14.1

Source: Bureau of Labor Statistics, *Employment and Earnings*.

Table 18. **Employment shares and real earnings by occupation**

Occupation	Employment share		Percentage point change	Earnings[1]		Per cent change
	1979	1992		1979	1992	
Executive, administrative and managerial	11.6	12.9	1.3	43 872	43 441	–1.0
Professional specialty	14.1	15.1	1.0	38 176	40 577	6.3
Precision production, craft and repair	13.6	11.0	–2.6	34 330	30 799	–10.3
Sales	7.3	9.6	2.3	32 994	34 015	3.1
Technicians	3.0	3.9	0.9	32 991	32 701	–0.9
Protective service	1.7	2.0	0.3	32 565	32 543	–0.1
Transportation and material moving equipment	5.1	4.5	–0.6	31 567	27 762	–12.1
Machine operators	9.6	7.5	–2.1	26 147	22 948	–12.2
Handlers, cleaners, helpers and labourers	4.3	3.7	–0.6	24 515	20 812	–15.1
Administrative support	18.0	16.8	–1.2	23 847	23 996	0.6
Farming, forestry and fishing	1.4	1.7	0.3	19 914	16 864	–15.3
Other service	9.4	10.6	1.2	18 029	16 530	–8.3
Private household	0.9	0.7	–0.2	8 734	12 256	40.3

1. Real earnings in 1992 CPI-U-X1 adjusted dollars of full-time year-round workers, aged 25-64.
Source: Bureau of Labor Statistics.

employees), temporary help agencies have grown very rapidly, from 400 000 at the end of 1982 to 1.3 million in 1990 and 2.1 million in 1995. Temporary help and outsourcing adds flexibility in staffing levels and also allows firms to utilise specialised skills efficiently.

Income and earnings inequality

The media and the research community have focused on changes in the distribution of income. As a result, there now exists broad agreement that the income distribution has widened and has been widening for many years, although the turning point is still subject to dispute. It is also accepted that labour market phenomena – the distributions of hours of work and wages – directly account for only a portion of the widening of family income, indeed perhaps only half (Burtless, 1995).

The issue of income inequality has been examined from many vantage points: families, households, individuals, total income before and after taxes and wage income. All of theses measures tell similar stories, that income inequality has risen, but the extent, timing and sources vary with each measure. To the extent that income inequality is concerned with living standards one of the better measures is family income (Figure 22). The share of aggregate income received by the bottom quintile of families has eroded significantly since the late 1960s. Indeed, there has been a shift from each of the four lowest quintiles into the top 5 per cent of the distribution. Despite the fact that the share of income going to the lowest quintile has declined in recent years, the poverty rate has begun to fall, from 15.1 per cent in 1993 to 13.8 per cent in 1995.

Family income, however, is a flawed measure because it fails to account for the changing composition and size of families. Some researchers have adjusted family income statistics by including single individuals (who are normally excluded from families by definition), adjusting income needs by family size and weighting families by their size. With this adjusted data Karoly (1996) shows that income inequality increased over the entire 1973-93 period, with real adjusted income falling 21 per cent for those at the 10th percentile from the bottom, rising 5 per cent at the 50th percentile and growing 22 per cent at the 90th percentile.[38] According to her calculations, the age distribution and the distribution of education both should have slightly attenuated inequality (Table 19). The change in family structures was an important factor in the growth of inequality among

Figure 22. **DISTRIBUTION OF FAMILY INCOME**[1]
Per cent of aggregate family income

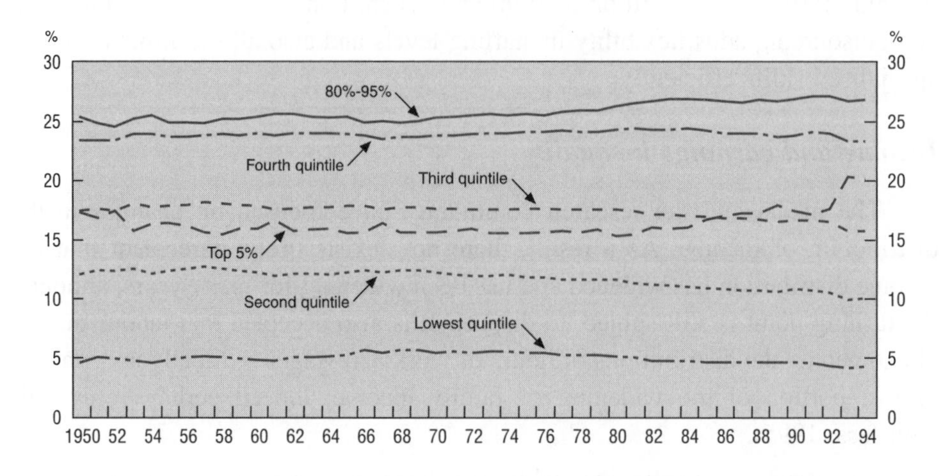

1. A portion of the jump in the share of income for the top 5% in 1993 reflects improved data collection.
Source: Bureau of the Census.

families, accounting for one-quarter of the increase. Performing similar calculations, Burtless (1995) finds that about one-quarter of the rise in the Gini coefficient[39] between 1969 and 1993 was from changes in non-labour income (capital income, transfers, retirement income). Thus, while educational attainment rates, capital income and family formation may be indirectly affected by labour markets, only half of the rise in inequality can probably be attributed directly to labour income (Burtless, 1995), and some of that may not be due to markets, but to changing attitudes towards work, etc.

Labour earnings differentials have widened essentially as a result of two phenomena: reduced labour force attachment of people with the least amount of skill as measured by education, and increased earnings differentials of those who work full time. The first factor has been at work for several decades for men, as the relative unemployment rates for high-school dropouts and high-school graduates have risen relative to those of college graduates, and the labour force participation rate has dropped for less-educated men. Among women, the rise in employment rates has been much sharper for those with more education. The

Table 19. **Distribution of individuals across selected segments of family income distribution**

Groups defined by	Overall group share		Odds ratio for subgroup share in distribution segment[1]			
	Per cent		Bottom 10%		Top 10%	
	1973	1993	1973	1993	1973	1993
Education of head						
8 years or less	21.3	8.9	2.00	1.88	0.41	0.11
9-11 years	16.2	9.9	1.52	2.56	0.52	0.18
12 years	31.7	33.6	0.66	1.06	0.83	0.48
13-15 years	15.1	24.4	0.56	0.71	1.20	0.83
16-17 years	10.6	14.7	0.25	0.26	2.15	2.04
18 years or more	4.9	8.5	0.15	0.15	3.21	3.65
Family headship						
Senior head/spouse	12.2	14.5	1.47	0.52	0.79	0.81
Single individual	5.5	10.9	1.98	1.48	0.90	0.72
Single headed family						
Male with children	0.8	1.8	1.20	1.68	0.43	0.37
Female with children	7.6	11.1	4.42	3.98	0.08	0.06
Other	2.2	3.1	0.68	0.56	1.63	0.78
Married couple family						
With children	55.4	42.2	0.55	0.57	0.64	0.80
Other	16.3	16.4	0.29	0.21	2.79	2.62

1. Odds ratio is calculated as group percentage share in distribution segment divided by group percentage share in total population.

Source: Karoly (1995).

causes for reduced participation among less-educated men may include the shift towards disability, lower real wages and changing attitudes towards work. Indeed, Juhn (1992) has presented considerable evidence that falling real wage rates have led to the decline in the labour force participation of low-skilled men. The share of discouraged workers has remained low probably because overall unemployment levels have not changed much. Weak labour force attachment is critical for explaining incomes of the least well-off, as a full-time minimum-wage job would generate enough income to escape the lowest decile.

Studies on the earnings of full-time workers indicate several stylised facts about wage developments in the 1970s and 1980s (Levy and Murnane, 1992). The returns to education fell in the 1970s and rose in the 1980s, more than

Figure 23. **REAL HOURLY WAGE RATES BY EDUCATION LEVEL AND YEARS OF EXPERIENCE**

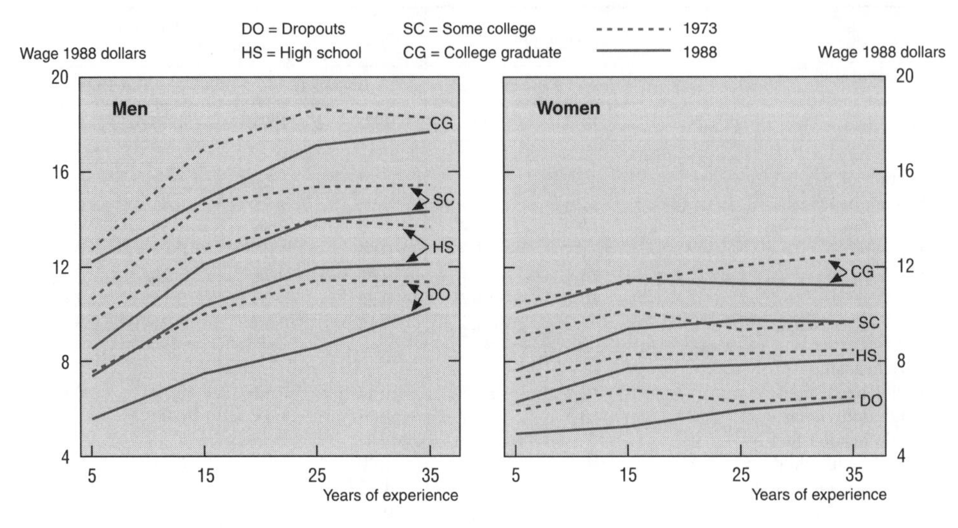

Source: Bound and Johnson (1992).

reversing the earlier decline (Figure 23). The returns to experience (proxied by age) rose in both decades. The wage differential between men and women narrowed in the 1980s. The wage differential between white and black men, with similar years of schooling, narrowed significantly in the 1960s and 1970s, but made no further gains in the 1980s.[40] Among women, the black/white differential had disappeared by the end of the 1970s. The dispersion of wages among similar age/education groups has widened since the early 1970s; this is quite important, as age, education, and sex only explain about one-third of the variance in earnings for full-time workers. There has been some hollowing out of the middle class as the earnings distribution for men flattened out. Using the CPI or other similar price measures, real hourly pay of non-college graduates fell in the 1980s, though, as discussed in Box 2 above, these price measures may have significant upward biases.

There is some indication that a portion of the increase in income inequality is the result of higher variance of income over time, rather than higher permanent income differentials. Moffitt and Gottschalk (1994) conclude that one-third of the rise in earnings inequality for men in the 1980s was due to the increased importance of income fluctuations which were particularly concentrated among those with the fewest years of schooling. This is consistent with the higher relative unemployment rates experienced by these workers. The authors find that much of the increase is due to increases in job-changing rates, but this finding is not consistent with other research which shows little change in mean tenure.[41]

Many observers have stressed that, from a policy perspective, inequality in lifetime income is more important than inequality at a point in time if individuals can borrow against future income and thus smooth consumption. Indeed, studies indicate that consumption is more equally distributed than income. Studies on income mobility show that many people are in the lowest deciles for a only short period of time, but many of those who leave poverty fall back into it later; thus, the high exit rates may be a misleading guide to the persistence of poverty.[42] But the increase in inequality has not been offset by greater rates of mobility (Gittleman and Joyce, 1995).

It is often remarked that US labour markets generate much more income inequality than those in continental Europe. Work by Atkinson (1996) indicates that based on disposable household income – *i.e.* including the effects of transfers and taxes but not transfers-in-kind or employee benefits – the United States had distinctly higher income inequality than found in countries in western Europe, with the difference largely arising at the bottom of the distribution. The Atkinson study, however, does not address the issue of labour earnings inequality. The ratio of the earnings of college graduates to those of high-school graduates is similar on both continents, but the earnings differential between high-school dropouts and high-school graduates is much larger in the United States than in almost all European countries (OECD, 1995*h*). This is similar to the disposable income results reported by Atkinson; however, earnings differentials among different skill groups only explain a portion of earnings dispersion. While earnings inequality among the full-time employed is undoubtedly higher in the United States, work by the OECD calls into question the extent to which labour earnings are distributed less equally in the United States than in Europe. Ongoing research indicates that labour earnings tend to be more evenly distributed in the United States than in Europe largely because hours of work are much more evenly distributed, reflecting the higher labour force participation rate and lower unemployment rate in the United States (OECD, 1996*e*).

Policy requirements

Enhancing the ability to adjust and adapt

The wage formation system

On average, wages and salaries (net of employer but gross of employee social security taxes) accounted for 71 per cent of total compensation in 1995. Non-wage benefits reflect tax-law considerations, legal requirements and a response to certain features of insurance markets.[43] Many of these benefits are relatively fixed costs per worker, because they have little connection with wages or hours worked – for example medical and other insurance coverage, defined-benefit pension programmes (since they are related more to years of service than to wage rates or hours worked except in final years), and unemployment insurance taxes (due to their low ceiling). Of the 29 per cent of compensation that is paid in the form of benefits, 9 percentage points are for legally required benefits (Social Security, unemployment and workers' compensation – *i.e.* insurance for work-related illness and injuries) and the rest for insurance (mainly health), paid leave, retirement programmes and supplemental pay (bonuses, premium pay) (Table 20). All of these non-wage payments by the firm provide some benefit to the worker. The wedge between wages and compensation is often cited as an impediment to employment because the worker is viewed as receiving less than what the firm must pay. However, this is true only to the extent that the worker values the non-wage benefits less than their cost. This is probably true only for Social Security contributions, because many people expect that they will receive less than they put in. There is only a loose connection between a particular year's contributions and eventual benefits, and most workers' planning horizons may be fairly short.[44] For non-mandatory benefits there is presumably a close relation between the firm's cost and the workers' benefits, as they are the result of bargaining; this is particularly the case for those benefits that the individual worker can select.

Wage formation in the United States is very decentralised. Unions play a much smaller role than earlier and are dominant only in the state and local government portion of the public sector, transportation, construction, and in some manufacturing industries (Figure 24). The union wage premium has declined, and work stoppages are much rarer. Anecdotal evidence points to greater use of

Table 20. **Employee compensation in 1995**

Compensation component	Costs [1]		Per cent of employees participating in plan in 1990	
	$ per hour	Per cent of compensation	Medium and large firms	Small firms
Total compensation	18.38	100.0	n.a.	n.a.
Wages and salaries	13.12	71.4	n.a.	n.a.
Total benefits	5.26	28.6	n.a.	n.a.
Paid leave	1.22	6.6	n.a.	n.a.
Vacations	0.55	3.0	96.0	88.0
Holidays	0.41	2.3	92.0	84.0
Sick leave	0.19	1.0	67.0	47.0
Other leave	0.06	0.4	n.a.	n.a.
Supplemental pay	0.42	2.3	n.a.	n.a.
Premium pay	0.17	0.9	n.a.	n.a.
Shift pay	0.05	0.3	n.a.	n.a.
Non-production bonuses	0.20	1.1	n.a.	n.a.
Insurance	1.29	7.0	n.a.	n.a.
Life insurance	0.05	0.2	94.0	64.0
Health insurance	1.21	6.6	83.0	69.0
Sickness and accident insurance	0.04	0.2	45.0	26.0
Retirement and savings	0.71	3.9	n.a.	n.a.
Defined benefit pension	n.a.	n.a.	59.0	20.0
Defined contribution pension	n.a.	n.a.	48.0	31.0
Legally required benefits [2]	1.59	8.7	100.0	100.0
Social Security	1.06	5.8	100.0	100.0
Federal unemployment	0.03	0.1	100.0	100.0
State unemployment	0.11	0.6	100.0	100.0
Workers' compensation	0.38	2.1	100.0	100.0
Other benefits [3]	0.03	0.2	n.a.	n.a.

1. Reflects the cost of the benefit and the frequency of participation.
2. Includes railroad retirement and supplemental retirement, railroad unemployment insurance, and other legally required benefits in addition to those shown.
3. Includes severance pay and supplemental unemployment benefits.

Source: US Department of Labor.

performance-based pay over time. This is particularly true in some highly visible areas such as compensation of top management, securities traders, and the sports and entertainment business, but it may be much more widespread (Frank and Cook, 1995). Nominal wages do not seem to display much downward rigidity, implying that the lower inflation environment does not hinder changes in relative wages that are necessary to reallocate resources when product and labour markets

Figure 24. **CHANGES IN WAGE-SETTING INSTITUTIONS**

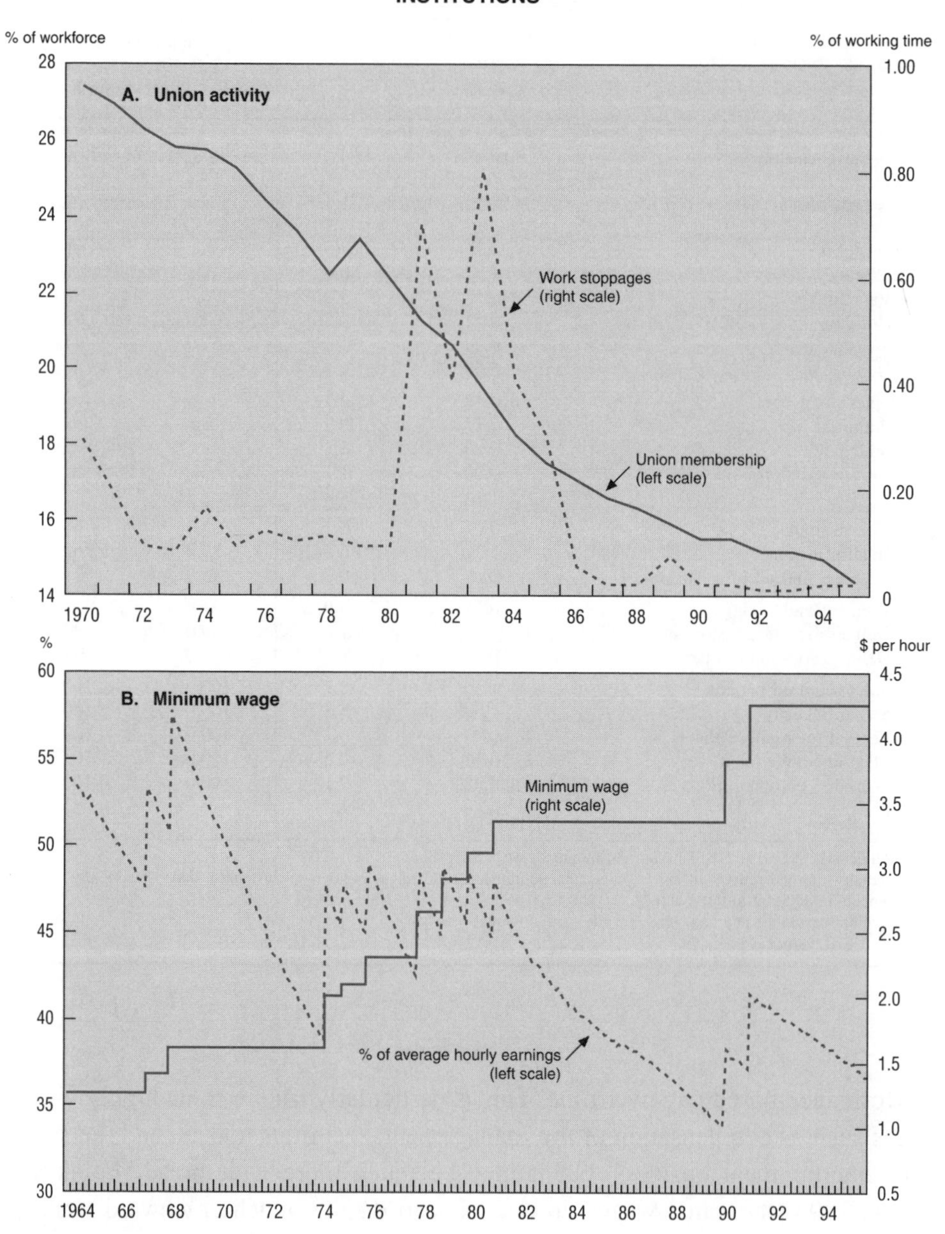

Source: Visser (1966); Bureau of Labor Statistics.

are flexible (Lebow, Stockton and Wascher, 1995).[45] Studies using macroeconomic models suggest that aggregate real wage flexibility, that is the response of wages to changes in the output gap, is relatively high in the United States. The statutory minimum wage has declined in real terms over the past two decades and thus plays a smaller role in wage determination. In 1995, about 3 per cent of workers earned the minimum wage or less; many of them are part-time workers and teenagers. The 1996-97 rises in the minimum wage will affect about 10 million workers. Given falling real wages at the bottom of the distribution, some reduction in the real minimum wage was necessary to prevent it from affecting an increasing share of workers over time.

The causes of the increased dispersion of wage rates are still not well understood. The potential factors may be grouped into those pertaining to the supply side, the demand side and the institutional setting. The supply-side factors have consistently worked to reduce the differentials among the college-educated, high-school graduates and dropouts. In the 1970s, the rise in the relative supply of college graduates was sufficient to reduce the college premium, but in the 1980s the relative supply rose less swiftly and was overwhelmed by other factors. Increased immigration dampened the relative decline in the supply of the least educated.

There has been considerable interest in the effects of immigration on wages and the wage distribution.[46] Immigration probably has had very little effect on average compensation. As noted earlier, rising immigration flows boosted the work force by about 2¾ per cent by 1990. These exceptional levels of immigration in the 1980s may have lowered the 1990 average wage level by up to 1 per cent.[47] But, it is likely that additional investment was induced by the larger labour force, and this may well have completely offset the effect of greater labour supply on average wages.[48]

While increased immigration probably had only a negligible impact on the average level of wages, it may well have been a factor in the increase in earnings inequality between those who did not complete high school and college-educated workers and between high-school graduates and those with college education. Immigration has boosted the relative supply of those without a high-school education. This increase in the relative supply should have decreased relative wages and perhaps induced some low-skilled native workers to drop out of the labour force. The extent to which this happened depends critically upon the degree of substitution between different types of labour. Reasonable estimates indicate that the relative supply shift from increased immigration may have been responsible for one-quarter of the change in the wage differential between high-school dropouts and college-educated workers and one-tenth of the widening differential between high-school graduates and the college-educated.[49] This relative supply shift may have been offset to some extent by firms choosing technologies to take advantage of the lower priced labour. As well, the shift in relative wages may have led people to obtain more schooling.

Among demand-side factors the most heavily investigated are the influences of trade and foreign investment.[50] Some studies show that a substantial portion of rising inequality can be explained by changes in trade and investment patterns. Some observers have mistakenly associated the trade deficit with job loss. Trade and trade deficits affect the mix of jobs, but not necessarily the level of employment.[51] That said, increasing trade with countries with abundant low-skilled labour should tend to depress the wages of the least skilled and thereby encourage firms to shift production techniques in order to hire these workers. But, in fact, firms – in both traded and non-traded goods and services industries – have shifted employment towards more highly skilled workers. This implies that changing production techniques or biased technological change (see below) has probably been a much more important factor. Its role is extremely difficult to quantify because of the difficulty of measuring technological change.

The significant changes to the institutional setting include the declines in real minimum wage, lower unionisation and changing tax structure. Changes in the tax structure have probably had only marginal effects. Lowering the top marginal tax rates on labour income may have boosted labour force participation by highly educated married women, but it is difficult to disentangle the tax effect from other factors that have increased women's participation rates (Bosworth and Burtless, 1992). The change in the structure of taxes also may have shifted the recording of income towards wages, particularly among the highly paid. The expansion of the Earned Income Tax Credit (EITC) is not captured in most studies on earnings inequality because they look at before-tax income. It has probably provided an important offset in recent years to the rise in pre-tax inequality by boosting after-tax incomes for families in the lower tail of the earned income distribution; the Census Bureau's measure of the poverty rates for 1995 drops 1½ percentage point when the EITC is included in income.

The decline of unionisation and the erosion of the real minimum wage may have made small contributions to the widening of the earnings distribution, but their effects on the income distribution would be muted because of the positive employment effects. Blackburn *et al.* (1990) estimate that the real decline in the minimum wage over the 1979-87 period was responsible for 1 percentage point and the decline in unionisation for 3 percentage points of the 13 percentage points change in relative wages between those with less than 12 years of education and college graduates (aged 25 to 64). The drop in the real minimum wage had no effect on the fortunes of high-school graduates because so few high-school graduates above age 25 received wages in the range between the actual minimum wage and the constant real minimum wage. The decline in union membership had a small effect on high-school graduates, responsible for 1 percentage point decline in their wage relative to the college-educated overall, but a 4 percentage point decline for those aged 25 to 34.

Increasing the flexibility of employment and working time

There is very little formal regulation regarding labour contracts in the United States compared with many other OECD countries.[52] Federal law sets a minimum wage which covers most employment (although some states have higher minimum wages), there are requirements for overtime pay for hourly employees after 40 hours of work and work during public holidays, and there is extensive legislation regarding union representation and bargaining. But there are no legislated severance pay and notice requirements, except that firms with more than 100 workers affected by a plant closing must give 60 days' notice; however, many firms do give notice and severance pay.[53] Reflecting the light degree of regulation, there is evidence that the adjustment of labour input to output fluctuations relies more on adjusting the number of persons in the United States, whereas in Germany more of the adjustment falls on hours per person. Average tenure tends to be shorter in the United States than in many other OECD countries. Experience rating of unemployment insurance (UI) taxes does impose some additional burdens on firms and industries that have records of a greater probability of layoff. As reported in the 1993 *Survey*, the concern about wrongful-dismissal suits against employers may have reduced employment at establishments in states which adopted stricter standards in the 1980s.

Taxes and transfers

Constructing the tax and transfer system in such a way as to provide adequate revenue to finance government operations and income support for the least fortunate, while minimising work and saving disincentives, is a challenge facing all governments, with the tradeoff between efficiency and equity proving particularly difficult. The United States has struck a balance by providing lower benefits with shorter durations and thus a lower tax burden than most OECD countries. The overall tax wedge on labour – the difference between the cost to employers and the consumption which can be supported from that wage – is lower in the United States than in most other OECD countries (OECD, 1996*a*). From the mid-1960s to the late 1970s average and marginal income tax and Social Security tax rates rose. Over the 1980s, average and marginal income tax rates edged back, while social insurance taxes continued to rise.[54] Transfer programmes, which expanded in the 1960s and 1970s, were trimmed in the 1980s, but total spending rose as a share of GDP, reflecting the ageing of the population and rising medical care costs.

- Taxes, benefits and the retirement decision

There are many factors that influence the retirement decision: health and life expectancy, the relative enjoyment of work versus leisure and potential retirement income. Many workers phase in retirement by leaving a career job and then working part time. Thus, aged families may receive income from many sources: Social Security, defined benefit pension plans, defined contribution pension plans, and personal savings and part-time or even full-time work (Table 21). Although Social Security benefits replace only 40 per cent of wages for the typical worker, much less than in European systems (OECD, 1995*i*), they still provide a large share of post-retirement income. In addition, government-provided health insurance coverage is available at age 65, and many large firms offer health insurance to their retirees.

The Social Security system has tended to discourage labour force participation of the elderly through two features: 1) the earnings test reduces benefits by one-third of earnings over a certain limit; and 2) the benefit formula gives little or no weight to working an additional year. The earnings threshold is now scheduled to be raised significantly in coming years. As there has been a bunching of workers who have earnings near the limit, its increase should boost earnings by

Table 21. **Sources of income for the elderly, 1993**

Type of money income received during year	Aged family units: Individuals aged 65 or older living alone or with non-relatives only			Multiperson families with householder aged 65 or older		
	Total	Non-poor	Poor[1]	Total	Non-poor	Poor[1]
Number of aged families and unrelated individuals (millions)	10.0	7.6	2.4	11.2	10.4	0.8
	Per cent receiving income of specified type					
Earnings	13	15	4	43	44	22
Public programme payments						
Social Security	92	95	85	93	94	81
Supplemental Security	8	4	20	5	4	20
Other public assistance	4	4	3	6	6	10
Other programmes	5	6	3	11	11	5
Other sources						
Dividends, interest, rent	65	74	36	77	79	27
Employment-related pensions, alimony, annuities, etc.	41	52	9	56	59	12
	Percentage distribution of income, by type					
Total per cent	100	100	100	100	100	100
Earnings	10	11	1	30	30	7
Public programme payments						
Social Security	46	43	82	32	32	71
Supplemental Security	1	1	9	1	1	9
Other public assistance	1	1	1	1	1	5
Other programmes	2	2	1	2	2	1
Other sources						
Dividends, interest, rent	20	21	3	16	16	3
Employment-related pensions, alimony, annuities, etc.	21	22	4	19	20	5
Median income	10 724	13 283	5 388	25 819	27 344	6 994

1. Poverty status based on money income of all family members after receipt of OASDI and any other cash transfer payments. In 1993 the poverty threshold was $6 970 for single persons and $9 430 for couples.

Source: Social Security Administration.

these workers.[55] The empirical importance of the benefit formula's effect on labour supply is open to question, as careful empirical and simulation studies indicate that little is known about retirement decisions. For example, while features of Social Security, health and pension programmes encourage clustering of retirement around the ages of 62 and 65, the prevalence of retirement at ages 62 and 65 is much greater than can be explained by these features (Lumsdaine *et al.*, 1995). That said, studies tend to show only small effects on retirement from rather large changes in benefits: for example, a 10 per cent reduction in Social Security benefits may delay retirement by about a month.[56] These sorts of estimates would indicate that the scheduled increase in the regular retirement age from 65 to 67 (while maintaining the current early retirement age) will have only a small effect on labour supply. However, if the spike in retirement at age 65 shifts out owing to a change in ''social custom'' induced by the change in rules, then a much larger response may occur.

Private defined-benefit pension plans have a more complex effect on labour supply. Because there is typically a strong relation between tenure and benefits, these plans reduce job turnover and increase labour market attachment for younger ages and decrease attachment at later ages (Ruhm, 1994). Firms have sometimes instituted special incentive plans to increase retirement of special groups of workers when restructuring. Defined-contribution pension plans are much more prevalent now than 20 years ago. These plans increase job flexibility and may provide more reliable pension coverage because there is no vesting requirement and they are more portable. However, the investment return risk is shifted to the worker, and some experts fear that young workers too frequently do not roll over their accounts when they change jobs and have temporary access to the funds.

- Unemployment benefits

The unemployment insurance system is designed as a federal-state partnership. Federal law presents a broad framework from which states develop programme-specific parameters, such as eligibility requirements, tax structure and benefit amounts. The programme covers virtually all wage and salary workers and about 90 per cent of employed persons overall, with the self-employed being the principal excluded group. It is financed by a tax on payrolls: the tax rate and benefits vary by state; the tax rate is incompletely experience rated; and the tax base is at least the first $7 000 paid annually to each employee.[57] Benefits are based primarily on wages in the prior job and are from 50 to 70 per cent of pre-tax wages up to a state-determined maximum; OECD estimates that benefits for most US workers fall in the range of 20 to 40 per cent of prior wages

(OECD, 1996*a*). Eligibility is based on several criteria: 1) duration of recent employment and level of earnings; 2) ability and willingness to seek and accept suitable employment; and 3) certain disqualifications related to the claimant's reason for job separation or job refusal. The employment test is a requirement to have been employed in two of the four preceding quarters with total earnings of typically at least $1 000 to $2 000.[58] A claimant with four quarters of earnings is entitled to up to 26 weeks of benefits and up to an additional 13 weeks when unemployment rates are unusually high.[59] Only about 40 per cent of the unemployed receive unemployment benefits, with the share rising during recessions. The low take-up rate is partly attributable to the fact that some eligible individuals do not apply, but it mostly reflects disqualification due to the eligibility requirements, in particular the work experience criterion. The average benefit duration is about 15 weeks, but substantial numbers exhaust their entitlements, particularly at the end of recessions.[60]

Unemployment benefits are provided to "alleviate the hazards of ... unemployment"[61] by assisting in the maintenance of consumption levels. Although benefit levels in the United States are low compared with other OECD countries, research by Hamermesh and Slesnick (1995) indicates that the unemployment insurance programme is quite effective at maintaining the well-being of benefit recipients.[62] Their research does not address the question of benefit adequacy for those who have exhausted their benefits[63] or others disqualified from receiving benefits.

A large body of research indicates that the size of the unemployment benefit has only minor effects on the duration of unemployment, but that the potential duration of benefits has a larger impact. Reducing replacement rates by 10 per cent may shorten unemployment spells by about 1 week, and reducing the potential duration by 1 week may cut spells by 0.1 to 0.2 weeks.[64] But not all of the change would result in increased work. As stressed by Atkinson and Micklewright (1991), some of the reduction in unemployment is the result of exit from the labour force. Indeed, there are many ways through which unemployment benefits may increase labour market attachment and improve job search though, at the same time, their financing may weaken these efforts.[65] An important dimension of benefits is their influence on layoffs, largely because of incomplete experience rating in the United States. Some estimates indicate that unemployment benefits have little effect on quits or permanent layoffs, but have a significant impact on the probability of temporary layoffs.[66]

- Taxes, benefits and labour supply by the poor

The US transfer programmes for working-age individuals are more limited than in most other OECD countries. They are not universal and leave a significant number of individuals uncovered. The major programmes are Aid to Families with Dependent Children (AFDC) [which is being replaced by Temporary Assistance for Needy Families (TANF)], Disability Insurance (DI) and Supplemental Security Income (SSI) for the disabled (see below), subsidised housing and Food Stamps for the poor, unemployment benefits, Medicaid (a health care programme for all those on AFDC and SSI) and Workers' Compensation for occupational injuries (OECD, 1994*a* and 1995*f*). In addition, the Earned Income Tax Credit (EITC) provides substantial aid to low-income workers. Because of the income restrictions and claw-back clauses (that reduce benefits as income rises) included in many of these programmes, there may be substantial disincentives to work or take on additional work. However other provisions, such as income disregards, mitigate these effects. All told, marginal effective tax rates of the order of magnitude of 70 per cent may apply to workers earning 60 to 70 per cent of the income of the average production worker (OECD, 1996*a*). This is feared to have large disincentive effects because high marginal tax rates may adversely influence the decision to work additional hours. However, the decision to enter the labour force is affected by marginal tax rates at low levels of income, which may be negative.

The EITC in-work benefits programme has been greatly expanded in recent years and is now on par with with AFDC and Food Stamps in the amount of aid given, but it affects far more families. Under the 1996 rate schedule, a single individual with two or more children would receive a credit of 40 per cent of earnings up to $9 000 ($3 600 maximum); the credit remains at the maximum as earnings rise from $9 000 to $12 000, and is then phased out at a 20 per cent rate over the range of $12 000 to $29 000 of earnings.[67] Simulation analyses indicate that the EITC boosts participation rates somewhat by increasing the after-tax earnings from holding a low-earning job, but slightly reduces hours worked of those already working because most workers receiving the EITC face higher marginal tax rates.[68] On balance, the effect is quite small which implies that the

EITC is quite effective at boosting income without distorting labour markets. In a life-time framework, the effects of the EITC may well be even smaller, as many recipients would expect to qualify only for a few years. For example, workers who see the need to gain work experience in order to accumulate valuable human capital and ultimately enjoy higher pay would greatly de-emphasise the temporarily elevated marginal tax rate.

The Food Stamp and AFDC programmes have provided a benefit guarantee and effectively impose a tax rate on earned income.[69] Studies show that the guarantee aspect provides a significant work disincentive. Empirical work also indicates that the discentive effects of the benefits reduction rate (which is roughly 24 per cent for Food Stamps and ranges from 67 per cent to 100 per cent for AFDC) may be small,[70] and, thus, adjustments of these rates may have little impact. Under the new law, able-bodied Food Stamp recipients between the ages of 18 and 50 who do not have dependents will have to work 20 hours per week or participate in state-approved training programmes to remain eligible. Otherwise, they will be eligible to receive no more than three months of benefits every three years.

The AFDC programme is being replaced by TANF over the coming year. The new law delegates much of the programme design to the states. The major features are that the benefit guarantee will be limited to five years, and adults receiving benefits will be required to begin ''work'' within two years of receiving aid. ''Work'' includes work, community service and attendance in educational or training programmes. Grants to states will be reduced if they do not have a certain percentage of their caseload in work programmes : at least 25 per cent in 1997 rising to 50 per cent in 2002. Many recipients already spend only a short period of time receiving AFDC, and the changes should have little effect on them. But a substantial portion of the caseload is composed of long-term beneficiaries with little education or work experience. The challenge will be to improve their employability. Two hurdles to increased labour efforts by AFDC recipients have been the lack of affordable day care and health insurance (as Medicaid eligibility runs out one year after leaving AFDC for work). The recent changes do little to confront these problems. The lack of access to health insurance is probably the most significant, because the US system does not have public health programmes for the unemployed nor for those working in firms that do not provide health insurance.

- Disability benefits

The United States has several programmes for disabled individuals. The SSI programme gives benefits to disabled individuals based on need; it is federally administered, but most states supplement the Federal SSI benefit. The Disability Insurance portion of the Social Security system gives benefits based on prior earnings history. The number of beneficiaries and outlays have been growing extremely rapidly in the 1990s (Figure 25). Both of these benefits are integrated with the Food Stamp, Medicare and Medicaid programmes. Benefit levels are adjusted for receipt of multiple benefits. More importantly, SSI benefits are adjusted for earned income and DI benefits are denied to those who are engaged in substantial gainful work. Thus, there are potentially large disincentives to work, which runs counter to the logic inherent in other government policies such as the 1990 Americans with Disabilities Act. The empirical literature is inconclusive as to the link between disability benefits and declining labour force participation because of estimation problems, but the effect may be modest (OECD, 1995*i*).[71]

Figure 25. **PERSONS RECEIVING DISABILITY PAYMENTS**

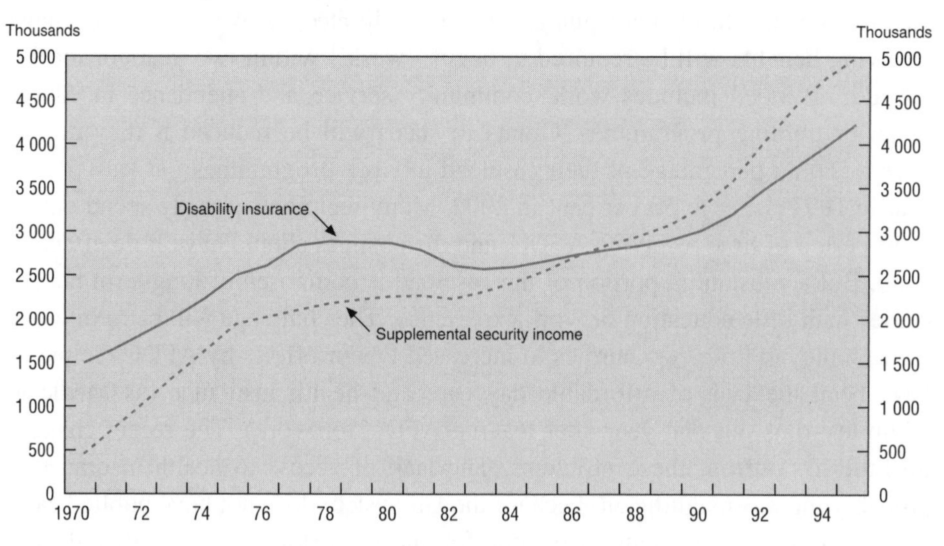

Source: Social Security Administration, *Social Security Bulletin.*

Active labour market policies

Active labour market policies comprise a variety of programmes, including placement and counselling of the unemployed, training, direct job creation and employment subsidies. They currently play only a small role in the US labour market, in part reflecting the low level of long-term unemployment (Figure 26). Expenditures as a per cent of GDP are among the lowest in the OECD. As described in last year's *Survey*, the main programmes provide training primarily to targeted groups such as disadvantaged youth and dislocated workers (including those who lose their jobs as a result of lowering trade barriers). In general, these programmes use the federal-state partnership model where the federal government provides the lion's share of the financing and broad guidelines, while the states design and implement the programmes. The results of these efforts appear to be mixed, with some of the least expensive services such as job placement assistance having relatively high benefit/cost ratios. The more ambitious programmes, particularly those targeting disadvantaged adults, appear to have had lower returns (US Department of Labor, 1995).

Figure 26. **FEDERAL GOVERNMENT OUTLAYS ON TRAINING AND EMPLOYMENT**

Per cent of GDP

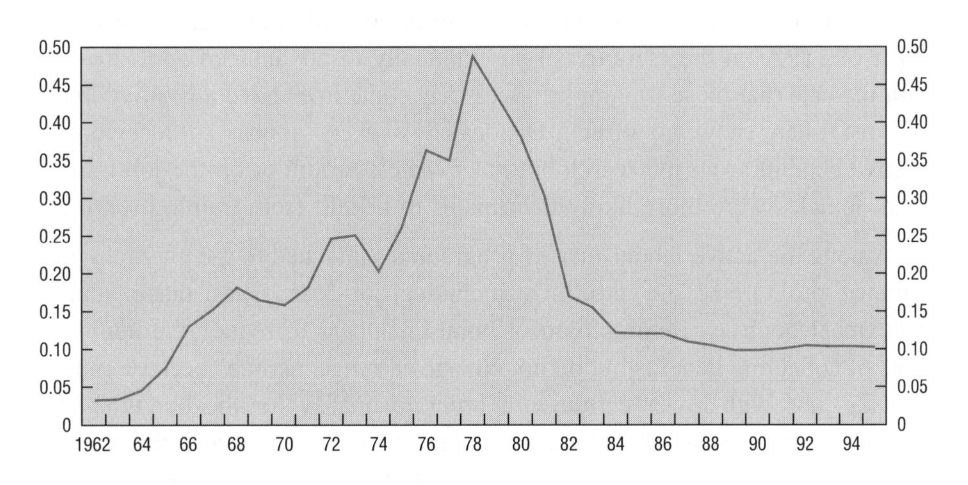

Source: Budget of the United States Government.

The two most important training programmes are Job Corps – which targets disadvantaged youth – and the Job Training Partnership Act (JTPA) which is designed for both economically disadvantaged persons and dislocated workers.[72] Job Corps serves about 60 000 young people per year, at a cost of $20 000 per person. It provides remedial education and jobs skills training in residential centres. It has not been subject to much rigorous evaluation, but some research indicates that it lifts earnings for male youths by $1 600 per year and females by $800 per year (summarised in Lalonde, 1995).

Participants in JTPA receive one or more of four services: job search, classroom training, on-the-job training (wage subsidies for private sector jobs) and work experience (a short-term job in the public or non-profit sector). The types of training typically received varies by demographic group. Adults participating in classroom training are more likely to be women taking vocation-related courses, while youths tend to be enrolled in remedial education. Those receiving on-the-job training are more likely to be adult men, while those in the work experience programme are more likely to be adult women or youth. Among dislocated workers, one-quarter receive job search assistance and half are enrolled in classroom training.

The evaluations of the JTPA programme for the economically disadvantaged show mixed results. For adult women, job search services are effective, but the results for classroom or on-the-job training have been ambiguous, with job-specific training showing more promise than basic skills training. Studies of the impact of JTPA on the earnings of economically disadvantaged adult men and youth indicate that these training services may sometimes have a positive impact but most often show no effect. Dislocated workers appear to receive cost-effective benefits from job search but not from classroom or on-the-job training. Again, females were more likely than males to benefit from training services.

Among the active labour market programmes attached to the unemployment insurance programme are profiling, including job-search assistance, and re-employment bonuses. Re-employment bonuses appear to reduce the number of weeks of collecting benefits but do not change earnings, perhaps because individuals take jobs with lower earnings in order to qualify for the bonus (Meyer, 1995). Profiling consists of screening claimants to see if they match the profile of those at risk for prolonged unemployment and, therefore, in need of more intensive services. All states have implemented worker profiling, which requires that individuals found to be at risk through a profiling system must participate in re-employment services, such as job search assistance early in their unemployment spells, in order to receive unemployment benefits.

Increasing the knowledge base, efficiency and innovative capacity of the economy

Much concern has been expressed in the United States about the low level of labour productivity growth over the past two decades, and the resulting small rates of increase in real compensation. Over time labour productivity can be increased by improving the quality of labour through education and training, augmenting amount of physical capital per worker, and improving production processes by incorporating new technology and management systems.

Upgrading skills and competences

The education and training "system" in the United States is a unique amalgamation of public and private efforts with a strong role for market mechanisms and little systematic oversight by industry or by the federal government. The previous two US Surveys (OECD, 1994*a* and 1995*a*) examined this system in depth. Primary and secondary education are run principally by local school districts and funded largely from state and local coffers, with a small amount of support from the federal government.[73] State governments usually provide some guidance on curriculum and the length of the school year. By tradition and by law, states and localities have responsibility over primary and secondary education. Therefore the federal role (including curriculum or other input or output standards) has always been controversial. The Goals 2000 agenda has been developed by the Federal government to improve educational standards by encouraging states and localities to adopt higher standards on a voluntary basis (OECD, 1994*a*). Because of the importance of local funding, there are considerable differences in spending levels both within and across states.[74] A modicum of choice and market discipline is provided by the public/private option and the ability of parents to select school systems by choosing their place of residence. Average expenditure per student is at the high end of the range of OECD countries' outcomes.

After high school many graduates go on to four-year universities, two-year community colleges or vocational schools run by either public or private entities.

Community colleges increasingly provide technical training tailored to the needs of local firms. Tuition and fees cover a growing share of costs in public tertiary education institutions. Low-and moderate-income students may receive financial aid (either grants or loans) from the government or the institution. Frequently, those going on to college and university also enter the labour market. Among 1995 high-school graduates, over 60 per cent were enrolled in colleges or universities that fall, of which nearly half were simultaneously in the labour force. Of the nearly 40 per cent of graduates that did not immediately enrol in further education, 80 per cent entered the labour market. In general, there is little formal connection between secondary school systems and industry such as in the German apprenticeship programme. Rather, the typical high-school graduate moves through several jobs looking for the right match.

Information about in-firm training is scarce. Formal training incidence and expenditures appear to be low by international standards, especially for low-tenure and low-skill workers and workers in small firms.[75] To the extent that skill needs become standardised some of this training may shift from firms to the tertiary education sector. Informal training and learning-by-doing is probably substantial.[76] In-firm training is potentially complicated by labour turnover and wage constraints. The cost of training needs to be recouped during the training period or the time that the worker is expected to be with the firm through compensation that is lower than productivity. Workers may have an incentive to switch firms if compensation is much below productivity after training is completed. Thus, firms have incentives to either try to recoup all of the costs during the training period, which may be difficult because of minimum wage laws or household liquidity constraints which may prevent the worker from accepting a low training wage, or to create compensation plans such as defined benefit pensions that link compensation with tenure. Recent survey evidence suggests that fear of losing the investments put into employee training is not an important determinant of the firm's training decision. Only 3 per cent of firms that do not offer formal job skills training stated that they feared losing newly trained employees to other firms, while over 50 per cent of the firms that did offer training stated that training was a way to retain valuable employees (Frazis *et al.*, 1995).

The results of this system of human capital development appear to be uneven. The primary and secondary school system's record is spotty, but the tertiary system and in-firm training appear to work fairly well. The success of the secondary system in preparing students for work may be measured in terms of graduation rates and achievement of graduates. High-school completion rates have risen over time, and the difference between blacks and whites has narrowed, but dropout rates are still disturbingly high for blacks and Hispanics. While completion rates are similar for suburban and rural areas, they are much lower in urban districts. The achievement of graduates is reflected in their level of preparation for tertiary education or work. One set of measures are scores on international achievement tests. By these measures, American children score well on tests of reading, in the middle of the pack on science and at the lower end in mathematics, despite the aforementioned high expenditure levels. Moreover, one-quarter of college freshmen enrol in at least one remedial course. The college and university system performs much better. Despite substantial tuition and fees, access to higher education is quite high by international standards, although there may be some difficulties for blacks.[77] There are no good measures of achievement at this level, but one indirect indicator is that US universities continue to attract significant and increasing numbers of foreign students.[78] On the other hand, a recently completed adult literacy survey of seven countries indicated that the United States tended to have higher shares of low attainment levels, even among those with university education (OECD and Statistics Canada, 1995). The poorer performance among university graduates may reflect greater access to university education, but that greater access does not appear to raise levels of literacy for the total population.

Another indicator of performance of the school and adult education and training systems is labour market outcomes. On this measure, US secondary schools perform better, and the lack of formal apprentice and in-firm training programmes does not appear to pose major problems. In a study by Harhoff and Kane (1996) comparing the United States with Germany, it was shown that: 1) returns to an additional year of schooling were the same in the two countries; 2) the share of youth who are both unemployed and out of school is similar;[79] 3) age-earnings profiles for US high-school graduates and German apprentices are virtually identical, even though US job tenure is much shorter; and 4) the wage difference between college graduates and high-school graduates/apprentices is similar. While unemployment rates, age-earnings profiles and earnings differentials are determined by many factors, their similarity across two very different training systems may indicate that the two systems work equally well.

Product market competition

The degree of product market competition may influence adoption of new technology, efficiency of production and relative prices of goods and services. Its effects on labour markets are quite complex. Typically a lack of product market competition is associated with rents which are shared by labour and capital. While workers and owners within the industry receive excess returns, the economy as a whole suffers from inefficient production, and thus average real wages economy-wide are lower. Industries with little internal competition often exhibit narrower wage distributions, perhaps reflecting a higher degree of unionisation.[80] A lack of product market competition shifts the industry composition of employment but may have little effect on the level unless it lifts the level of structural unemployment. This is less likely when labour markets are flexible although wage premia may lengthen search time, lead to queuing, and, thus, raise structural unemployment rates.

In the United States there was a wave of product market deregulation at the end of the 1970s and the beginning of the 1980s (Winston, 1993). This may have had some stimulative effect on sectoral employment in some cases. Airlines have increased employment much more rapidly than the overall economy, as deregulation led to lower prices and much higher volumes which overwhelmed cost-cutting efforts. Similarly, trucking has experienced noticeable gains in employment. On the other hand, employment has fallen in the telecommunications industry since partial deregulation. This may reflect gains in productivity driven by new technologies outstripping the demand increases from lower prices. The United States being a very large country, most competition is provided by domestic sources, but foreign trade and investment policies also contribute to a competitive environment. The economy is quite open to foreign trade and investment, and anti-competitive practices are heavily penalised by competition policy authorities.

Technology and innovation

Production of goods and services has evolved as a result of new technology and adoption of new work practices such as problem-solving teams and flexible job assignments. These changes have resulted in the upskilling of some production processes, as repetitive tasks by low-skilled workers have been replaced by new technologies, and in the deskilling of other production processes where skill requirements have been reduced. Thus, new technologies may either be complements or substitutes for skilled workers. Numerous studies of the United States as well as other OECD countries indicate that, in general, technological change in recent decades has had a positive skill bias, that is, technology and worker skills are complementary.[81]

Because technological change has been skill biased it raises the relative demand for skilled workers, but its ultimate impact on relative wages depends upon the substitutability between skilled and unskilled labour, the substitutability between goods with high and low skill content and the efficiency and flexibility of labour and product markets. It appears that in the United States the balance of these factors has led to a rise in the relative wage of skilled workers and a small increase in the relative unemployment rate of workers with low levels of education, while much of continental Europe, which has less flexible labour markets, has experienced a much sharper rise in unemployment and less change in relative wages (OECD, 1996*b*).

Evidence indicates that the upskilling of employment in the OECD area since the 1980s has been greatest in those countries and sectors which have a high rate of R&D intensity in production (OECD, 1996*b*). Total R&D spending in the United States accounted for 2.5 per cent of GDP in 1994, one of the highest intensities in the OECD area. The increased R&D intensity of the US manufacturing sector has led to greater demand for higher skilled workers to undertake more varied and sophisticated tasks. Over the last two decades the share of low-technology manufacturing employment has continued to decline, while high-technology jobs now account for approximately 21 per cent of manufacturing jobs. Despite this growing but small share, high-technology jobs have been the source of nearly all gains in manufacturing employment.

The services sector has also seen strong increases in high-skilled employment, particularly in the financial, insurance, real estate and business services. Concurrent with upskilling of services, the services sector has emerged as a large user and provider of technology. The share of R&D performed in the services sector accounted for about 26 per cent of R&D performed in the US business sector in 1993.

The government's spending on R&D has declined in real terms over the past decade, reflecting a decline in defence R&D. Besides its own R&D activities the government actively promotes private initiatives through provisions in the tax code and its role as catalyst in the development and diffusion of technology through various ''partnership'' initiatives with industry and by promoting best practices. Research and experimentation (R&E) expenditures can be expensed and increases in R&E expenditures are subject to a tax credit of 20 per cent of qualified expenditures over a base amount. This provision expired in July 1995, but has been extended through May 1997. In addition, the rate of innovation and diffusion of new technologies is aided by the high degree of product market competition and protection of intellectual property rights found in the United States.

Partnership initiatives account for only a very small share of government-funded support but represent an important link between industry and government, allowing them to share knowledge and leverage financial resources in developing pre-competitive technologies. The *Advanced Technology Program* is an industry-led partnership based on sharing costs for developing high-risk advanced technologies that private firms would not otherwise undertake. Over the past two years, the *Manufacturing Extension Partnership* (MEP), which links universities, communities, and government through a nation-wide network of technology extension centres to help SMEs adopt appropriate manufacturing technologies, has expanded from 7 to 44 centres. The *Cooperative Research Development Agreements* (CRADAs) provide firms with access to research from federal government laboratories (*i.e.* NASA, DoE, DoA). The development of an information infrastructure, remains a high priority for the US government. The *National Information Infrastructure* (NII) initiative is a federal strategy to promote private investment in high performance computing and communications networks through the use of tax incentives and regulatory policies, as well as matching grants to state and local governments and non-profit entities for funding networking pilot projects.

Recent actions

In the United States, the policy formation process is often slow and complex because of the system of checks and balances between the Administration and the legislature. Despite this, major changes have been made over the past year to low-income support programmes (see above) and to the minimum wage. The minimum wage had been $4.25 an hour. It is now scheduled to rise to $4.75 on

1 October and to $5.15 on 1 September 1997. These increases will reverse the real erosion that has occurred since it was last raised in 1991. A training wage of $4.25 will be available for workers under age of 20 during their first 90 calendar days of employment.

The Administration continues to promote the Goals 2000 agenda, but with limited success, and the House of Representative has again proposed to deny it funding.[82] While nearly all states now participate in the programme, efforts to create curriculum standards have floundered. The Administration has also had difficulty revamping the grants programmes for elementary and secondary education to target the funds where needs are greatest, although some progress has been made. Funding for Head Start, a pre-school programme that has been shown to be effective in improving early school performance, has been expanded. The School-to-Work Opportunities Act of 1994 and related efforts to establish occupational skills standards attempt to develop programmes and standards for vocational studies.

Significant changes in product market regulation have been enacted over the past year in telecommunications, electricity and agriculture (Chapter II). In recent years the US government has made changes in federal anti-trust legislation to allow closer research co-operation between firms. The Department of Justice and the FTC have issued new anti-trust guidelines for intellectual property that generally permit collective licensing agreements if the parties each account for not more than 20 per cent of market share.

Assessment and scope for further action

In summary, the macro and microeconomic climate in the United States has fostered a relatively high level of labour utilisation and has allowed the efficient redistribution of labour across sectors and occupations over time. The high level of productivity indicates that workers on average are well trained, equipped with adequate physical capital and have good management practices. The flexibilities of the system result in little long-term unemployment which, as a share of the unemployed, is among the lowest in the OECD. Although job tenure is shorter in the United States than in many other countries, this does not appear to have dampened earnings growth. This suggests that much of the human capital gained at firms is either general or industry-specific, rather than firm-specific, and thus may carry less risk of being lost with job changes.

However, there is still ample scope for improvement. The elementary and secondary education system leaves too many inadequately prepared for work or further education. This is particularly true in the inner cities. Efforts should be redoubled to raise high-school graduation rates and improve the quality of education. Setting curriculum standards is one method to provide information that may prompt local officials to improve their schools. In addition, funding inequities may also contribute to the variance in outcomes. The cost of school failure is much more than a labour market problem, because of the attendant costs in the form of crime, drug- and alcohol-abuse, and in the domain of citizenship. The Goals 2000 programme, redirection of grants towards the communities most in need, expansion of Head Start and the encouragement of magnet schools and other experiments could be useful steps in the right direction. The use of standards as a means to improve results is a potentially effective approach, but the implementation of such standards may require further innovation as indicated by the experience of Goals 2000. However, with regard to Head Start, some of the gain appears to be lost subsequently (Currie and Thomas, 1995), and the role played by elementary and secondary schools in maintaining those early gains needs to be clarified.

The adult education system works well for much of the population. Several reforms, however, would be welcome. The government should help to improve information about the quality of vocational schools. The highest default rates on student loans are by students attending proprietary schools, often because the programme fails to deliver on the education or job opportunities that were expected. Again, the past two Administrations have made progress by disqualifying institutions whose students have high default rates. But there remain some information problems which do not exist for the university sector, in part because the small scale of these operations makes it unprofitable for private firms to collect and sell the information.

The economic fortunes of black Americans continue to lag that of whites. Although the wage gap between white and black males of similar years of schooling has narrowed and it has disappeared among females, blacks on average have lower annual labour earnings than whites, in part because of higher rates of unemployment and lower college and university graduation rates. Moreover, the poverty rate is much higher among black families, and blacks are much more likely to be crime victims or convicted of criminal activity. Many of the problems facing the black community are of a social nature; for example, the high rate of poverty reflects the much higher rate of female headship among black families. That said, certain areas where the United States should make progress, such as improving the quality of urban school systems, may have a disproportionate impact on blacks.

The tax-transfer system does not appear to have created major disincentives to work for the vast majority of the population. There are several areas of concern, however. The disability programmes have been growing quite quickly, and for a person once receiving benefits there are strong disincentives to work. Further efforts may be possible which would encourage more self-reliance; however, as these changes may also boost eligibility, they must be made with care that the right balance is struck. The Advisory Council on Unemployment Compensation has recommended that unemployment insurance eligibility be eased to allow a greater share of lower-wage workers to qualify for benefits. In general, the work disincentives for the poor due to the interaction between the tax system and means-tested transfers do not appear too high except for one target population: single mothers. AFDC and Medicaid have created an unemployment trap for many low-skilled women, in part because of the potential need for child care and the loss of health insurance when leaving welfare for work. The changes that have been enacted, particularly the time limits, should reduce this unemployment trap, and continued experimentation at the state level should generate valuable insights about work and training programmes. But fundamental health insurance reform at the federal level is probably necessary to reduce that element of the unemployment trap. Moreover, the time limits placed on the Food Stamp and TANF programmes will further shrink the safety net for the non-aged, non-disabled poor.

The income distribution has widened over the past twenty years or so. Much of the widening has come from changes in demographics and the distribution of non-labour income. On the labour market side, participation rates have fallen and unemployment rates have risen for the least-educated, and the wage differentials between education levels have widened. As the Administration has stated, the principal actions by the government should be in training and improving job search: increasing high-school graduation rates, Skill grants and One-Stop Job

Centers will help. If the resulting distribution of income is unsatisfactory with respect to the degree of equality of outcomes desired by society, then redistribution of income through a further expansion of the EITC or other programmes may be warranted.

The government has addressed the rise in inequality by boosting the federal minimum wage to $5.15. It is generally agreed that an increase of this magnitude will probably result in only a small amount of job loss among minimum wage workers and that this will redistribute income towards minimum-wage workers, of which about one-half are under 25 and one-third are teenagers (OECD, 1996*a*). Job loss should be largest for the least skilled among minimum-wage workers. Indeed, some research suggests that a rise in the minimum wage may cause a shift in time from school to employment, and those crowded out tend not to return to school. Thus, these least-skilled workers may acquire less human capital through the combination of school and work when the minimum wage is raised. The problem confronting policy-makers is whether the benefits of imposing a higher minimum wage outweigh the associated costs and whether other policies are more efficient. The Secretariat believes that the minimum wage is too blunt an instrument, with too many of the benefits going to teenagers and second earners in higher-income families, who are not the target group, and with much of the cost – in terms of foregone income and human capital – borne by the least skilled.

IV. US corporate governance: the market as monitor

Nearly all economic activity in modern societies is conducted through organisations. All but the simplest organisations, and firms to be sure, face a conflict between their goals and the differing objectives of the various agents who play a role in their operation. Given that the resolution of these conflicts entails transactions costs, that is that complete comprehensive contracts among the various agents cannot be conceivably written, residual rights of decision-making and control over firms' nonhuman assets must be allocated (Hart, 1995). How this is done – the institutional and legal framework[83] – is, in essence, the subject of business or, more usually, corporate governance.[84] It is increasingly recognised to be a significant determinant of economic performance.

Corporate governance is a field of economics which has experienced rapid growth in recent years. Far from being the exclusive domain of economists, it has received equally close attention from academics in law, political science and business and finance. There has been much more research on the US system, the paragon of market-based or ''outsider'' systems in the OECD, than on any other. Nonetheless, experts' views differ widely. Should the emphasis be on alleged short-termism and unjustified ''downsizing'', with the resulting high cost of capital, financial excesses and speculation? Or is a more apt characterisation one of arguably the world's most dynamic and competitive set of firms in an environment conditioned by transparency, disclosure, market-based discipline and agency-cost minimisation? Divergent opinions are the norm, not only with respect to an overall assessment of its systemic performance, but even with respect to many of its particular traits. For example, are seven-figure executive compensation levels grotesque examples of managerial immoderation, or are they legitimate rewards for the achievement of shareholder value maximisation? The public policy issues follow from the answers to these questions: if the system is not functioning efficiently, then there may be grounds for invervention in the form of more active use of taxation policy and increased securities and labour market regulation, for example.

This chapter will begin by briefly relating the historical development of the US financial system and the positions of its major players in the corporate governance process. It will then describe the key objective of corporate governance in the orthodox model: the control of agency costs. The major ways in which managers can be shown to have and exploit discretion are enumerated before the mechanisms by which they are disciplined are detailed. An alternative "stakeholder" view of the corporation is then briefly discussed. An overview of the current policy debate is presented before the implications for overall economic performance are examined. An overview of this chapter is provided in Box 5.

Historical development of the US corporate governance system

The twentieth century has seen several sea changes in business ownership and control. At its outset the business sector was dominated by the "captains of industry" who as individuals or families both managed and controlled giant firms in a variety of sectors. But as these entrepreneurial owners aged and eventually disappeared, they left behind them a legacy of non-owner professional managers, hired by the firms' increasingly dispersed owners – represented by the board of directors – to run them for a salary. And this gave rise to the problem of having ownership and therefore risk-bearing separated from control,[85] first identified by Berle and Means (1932)[86] and later recognised as just one example of more general "principal-agent problems". The era of what has been termed "managerial capitalism" came to a peak in the 1960s, by which time ownership had become fragmented,[87] and exemplary economic performance had provided management with substantial political and popular support. But with the more severe supply side shocks of the last 25 years and the resulting need to restructure, management's position of primacy in governing US corporations has gradually been eroded: sometimes *via* the resurgence of owner-managers, reminiscent of their earlier forebears, in the wake of management buy-outs; but more often *via* a shift to joint governance along with a fairly small number of increasingly activist institutional owners. US financial institutions are, however, subject to legal

Box 5. **US corporate governance: an overview**

Corporate governance is the subject of how and to what extent the interests of the various agents involved in a corporation are reconciled. Views differ widely, both as to the advantages of the overall system in the United States as well as the effects of its many component parts. Perhaps the greatest single reason for recent interest in the subject is the charge that the system is not working well because corporations continue to engage in downsizing even though the economy is expanding, while at the same time executive compensation is rising swiftly. Heightened concern over the rush to lay off employees has led to calls for greater social responsibility by corporations and for the abandonment of shareholder value maximisation as their sole objective in favour of a broadly defined ''stakeholder'' approach. But downsizing is not evidence that there is anything fundamentally wrong with the system. Rather it is the manifestation of the dynamism of the business sector, the acuity of competition in product markets and the deregulated nature of labour markets, all of which are great sources of competitive strength and mitigate the social and human costs of such job destruction.

Stakeholder models of various kinds are present in many other OECD countries. They promote greater trust, loyalty and commitment among the various parties, thereby allowing greater investment in firm-specific assets. But they tend to reduce the focus on profit maximisation and to slow adjustment to external shocks. Even so, it would be helpful in a number of respects if non-owner stakeholders did have a greater voice in US governance fora. Banks could be allowed to own equities so that they could derive clearer benefits from the success of their corporate clients and would do more monitoring. And, given the fact that so few US workers are represented by trade unions, employees could be given a greater say in the running of the corporation in order that their firm-specific human capital be adequately safeguarded; this could be done, for example, by having more employee compensation provided in the form of equity.

The other long-standing subject of debate in this field is whether the existing set of institutions, laws and regulations do a good job in minimising the agency costs which result from the separation of ownership from control. These costs are several. Managers may use their discretion to maximise the firm's size rather than its profits; to hoard cash flow rather than pay it out to shareholders in the form of dividends; to choose low-risk/low-return strategies because they cannot diversify their income risk as easily as shareholders; to pay themselves excessively; and to entrench themselves rather than be exposed to the various mechanisms which exist to replace them.

These costs can be reduced by appropriate managerial shareholding, executive compensation packages and capital structures and by monitoring. Most US financial institutions are constrained by long-standing regulatory limits on their behaviour; and boards of directors have only recently come to have sufficient independence from management to provide much oversight. But some fiduciaries, especially pension funds, have become increasingly activist in recent years. By taking on a greater monitoring role, they have brought into better balance the monitoring and disciplinary responsibilities of shareholders or their fiduciaries and the markets. Yet markets continue to bear the largest monitoring role in the United States. Highly competitive product markets are an impor-

(continued on next page)

(continued)

tant disciplinary device, but one which acts rather slowly in comparison with the ''market for corporate control'', *i.e.* takeovers. While this process is costly and many takeovers are undertaken for empire-building, tax minimisation and rent-seeking motives, the mechanism is nevertheless effective and should not be inhibited. For the case that US markets suffer from ''short-termism'' is unconvincing. US firms have been regaining competitive ground in the 1990s: they are export leaders; they have a strong network of overseas subsidiaries; they generate substantial income in the form of royalties and licence fees based on their stock of research and development capital; and they manage fixed capital so well that they can afford to invest less than most of their rivals. Thus, the system of corporate governance appears to function at least as well as any other.

fiduciary standards of prudence and care insofar as they are entrusted to exercise ownership rights on behalf of their beneficiaries. Thus, they too are agents for the ultimate principals – the owners. This most recent stage of development has, therefore, been labelled ''fiduciary capitalism'' (Hawley and Williams, 1996), even though these institutions' monitoring activities remain circumscribed by regulatory and legal constraints.

These developments have occurred partly in response to economic and technological forces, but to a substantial extent corporate governance is also a political question of determining the allocation of entitlements, rather than merely an economic question of optimally designing contracts and institutions in order to minimise transactions and agency costs (Grundfest, 1990). Indeed, the evolution of the US financial sector and of corporate law[88] has been heavily influenced by the rules of the game as set by state and federal governments and as interpreted by the courts over time (Roe, 1990 and 1994). In particular, already in 1863 the National Bank Act had prevented national banks from owning equities. Then a whole series of Depression-era federal legislation, passed in response to popular distrust of concentrated power and perceived abuses in the issuance and trading of securities, sought to limit the scale, scope and strength of financial institutions and directed the system toward one based on market-driven rather than bank-centred governance,[89] backed up with complete and timely disclosure of relevant information. US financial institutions have long faced tougher legal and regulatory constraints than their equivalents in other OECD countries (Table 22). The

Table 22. **Important portfolio restrictions on large financial institutions**

A. United States

Institution	Assets year-end 1994	Restriction	Source
Banks	$4.2 trillion	Stock ownership prohibited.	Glass-Steagall National Bank Act.
Bank holding companies	$411 billion	No more than 5 per cent of the voting stock of any non-bank.	Bank Holding Company Act of 1956.
Bank trust funds	$656 billion	1. No more than 10 per cent of assets in any one company.	Comptroller regulations.
		2. Active bank control could trigger bank liability to controlled company.	Bankruptcy case law.
Insurers (total)	$2.6 trillion	No more than 2 per cent of assets can go into a single company, no more than 20 per cent of assets can go into stock.	New York Insurance Law (for insurers doing business in New York).
Life insurers	$1.9 trillion		
Property and casualty insurers	$670 billion	No control of non-insurer.	
Open-end mutual funds	$1.3 trillion	1. For half of portfolio: No more than 5 per cent of fund's assets can go into stock of any one issuer and fund may not purchase more than 10 per cent stock of any company, otherwise tax penalties apply.	Investment Company Act of 1940; subchapter M of the Internal Revenue Code.
		2. Must get SEC approval prior to joint action with affiliate, *i.e.* a fund needs SEC approval before acting jointly to control a firm of which it and its partner own more than 5 per cent.	Investment Company Act of 1940.
Private pension funds	$2.4 trillion	1. Must diversify unless clearly sensible not to.	ERISA.
		2. Enhanced duty of care to beneficiaries probably retained if pension fund designee sits on portfolio company board (directors usually subject only to low-level business judgement rule).	ERISA.
State and local pension funds	$1.2 trillion	Economic control of private pension funds usually held by operating company managers.	Structural.

Table 22. **Important portfolio restrictions on large financial institutions** *(cont.)*

B. Other major OECD countries

Institution	Germany	United Kingdom	Japan	Italy
Commercial banks	No restrictions, apart from prudential rules: sum of shareholdings not to exceed 60 per cent of bank's own capital; no single share-holdings to exceed 15 per cent of own capital.	Bank of England may discourage ownership on prudential grounds. Capital adequacy rules discourage large stakes.	Prior to 1987 banks could hold up to 10 per cent of a firm's stock. After 1987 can hold up to 5 per cent.	Priori to 1993, stock ownership was prohibited or required prior approval (in special cases) by the Bank of Italy; proxy voting is still prohibited, while the presence of banks' employees on non-financial firms boards has been allowed since 1992.
Life insurance companies	Can hold up to 20 per cent of total assets in equities.	Self-imposed limits on fund assets invested in any one company stemming from fiduciary requirement of liquidity.	Can hold up to 10 per cent of a firm's stock.	Can hold up to 5 per cent of a firm's stock.
Mutual funds	No more than 5 per cent of fund assets in one company; no more than 10 per cent of the total voting rights from the stock of the same issuer.	Cannot take large stakes in firms.		No more than 5 per cent of a listed firm's stock (10 per cent if unlisted). Proxy voting prohibited.
Pension funds		Self-imposed limits on fund assets invested in one company stemming from fiduciary requirement of liquidity.		Limits on fund assets invested in one company (5 per cent if quoted, 10 per cent otherwise) and in the sponsoring company and its subsidiaries (20 per cent).
General	Regulatory notification required for ownership in listed companies from 5 per cent and upwards.	Insider trading laws discourage large stakeholders from exerting control. Regulatory notification required for 3 per cent ownership.		Consob[1] notification required for 2 per cent ownership in listed firms and 10 per cent ownership in unlisted firms by listed ones.

1. Stock exchange commission.
Source: Roe (1990) and OECD.

result is a fragmented financial services sector in comparison with most of its leading competitors (Jacobs, 1991), although this gap has been reduced to some extent by deregulation in the intervening years.

Banks, which today hold over 12 per cent of the nation's financial assets, have been especially constrained by legal and regulatory barriers.[90] The Glass-Steagall Banking Act of 1933 denied all commercial banks the right to deal in or own corporate equities (except, under the terms of the 1956 Bank Holding Company Act, through a holding company whose actions are severely circumscribed), thereby splitting commercial from investment banking to this day. Possibly even more constraining is the legal doctrine of ''equitable subordination'': if it can be shown that a bank had any significant influence over a client firm's business decisions, then it might face subordination of its claims in the event of bankruptcy. Thus, although banks' trust holdings are sizeable, their direct holdings of corporate equities are minuscule[91] (Table 23), and they are prevented from capitalising on their knowledge of the borrower by taking an ownership position which they might otherwise have sought in order to gain thereby an upside investment return risk.[92] The result is that banks do little monitoring and have little incentive to see borrowers achieve anything better than adequate success.

Insurance companies are also generally constrained as to their ownership and control of non-financial firms by state law (Table 22), and their behaviour is accordingly fairly passive. They too are subject to subordination of claims if they are deemed to have exercised control. Their share of equity ownership has been fairly steady over the past few decades, but with an uptrend visible in recent years (Figure 27).

Likewise, the portfolios of open-end *mutual funds* (unit trusts) have been restricted by 1930s legislation: in 1935, 56 investment companies had controlling interests in 187 corporations (Roe, 1993), but tax changes in 1936 and the passage of the 1940 Investment Company Act deliberately ended the monitoring role they were developing through what amounted effectively to forced diversification (Roe, 1993; Blair, 1995). Any possible willingness to become more active investors from a corporate governance point of view also became subject to notification requirements under the 1976 Hart-Scott-Rodino Act which attempted to distinguish stock purchases for portfolio purposes from those made with the intent to secure competitive information or aid in a potential takeover.

Table 23. **Holdings of corporate equities by type of owner**

Percentage shares, end of year

	Holdings at market value $ billion	Households	Foreign	Financial groups										
				Total	Commercial banks	Savings institutions	Life insurance companies	Other insurance companies	Private pension funds	State, local pension funds	Mutual funds	Closed-end funds	Brokers and dealers	Bank personal trusts
1952	170.1	89.7	2.2	8.2	0.0	0.2	1.4	1.9	1.1	0.0	2.0	1.2	0.4	0.0
1955	294.2	88.6	2.2	9.2	0.0	0.3	1.2	1.8	2.1	0.1	2.4	1.0	0.3	0.0
1960	424.9	85.8	2.2	12.1	0.0	0.3	1.2	1.8	3.9	0.1	3.5	1.2	0.1	0.0
1965	734.9	83.8	2.0	14.2	0.0	0.3	1.2	1.6	5.5	0.3	4.2	0.8	0.2	0.0
1970	841.4	68.0	3.2	28.7	0.0	0.3	1.7	1.6	8.0	1.2	4.7	0.5	0.2	10.4
1975	800.2	56.7	4.2	39.2	0.0	0.5	3.4	1.8	13.5	3.0	4.2	0.7	0.4	11.5
1980	1 534.7	60.2	4.9	34.9	0.0	0.3	3.0	2.1	14.6	2.9	2.8	0.3	0.2	8.8
1985	2 360.0	48.9	5.8	45.3	0.0	0.2	3.1	2.4	21.6	5.1	4.8	0.2	0.6	7.3
1990	3 530.2	49.9	6.9	43.2	0.1	0.2	2.8	2.3	16.8	8.4	6.6	0.5	0.3	5.4
1991	4 863.6	54.5	6.1	39.3	0.1	0.2	3.1	1.9	14.1	7.9	6.4	0.4	0.3	4.8
1992	5 462.9	53.4	6.0	40.5	0.1	0.2	3.2	1.8	15.0	8.2	7.3	0.4	0.3	4.0
1993	6 278.5	52.3	5.9	41.7	0.1	0.2	3.6	1.6	14.7	8.1	9.7	0.4	0.4	2.9
1994	6 293.4	50.8	5.4	43.8	0.0	0.2	4.4	1.8	14.6	8.1	11.3	0.5	0.3	2.6
1995	8 345.4	51.4	4.2	44.5	0.1	0.2	4.2	1.8	13.8	8.4	12.5	0.5	0.4	2.7

Source: Blair (1995), updated from Board of Governors of the Federal Reserve System, *Flow of Funds Accounts, Flows and Outstandings*, Washington.

Figure 27. **WHO HOLDS US CORPORATE EQUITIES?**

Per cent of total, year-end

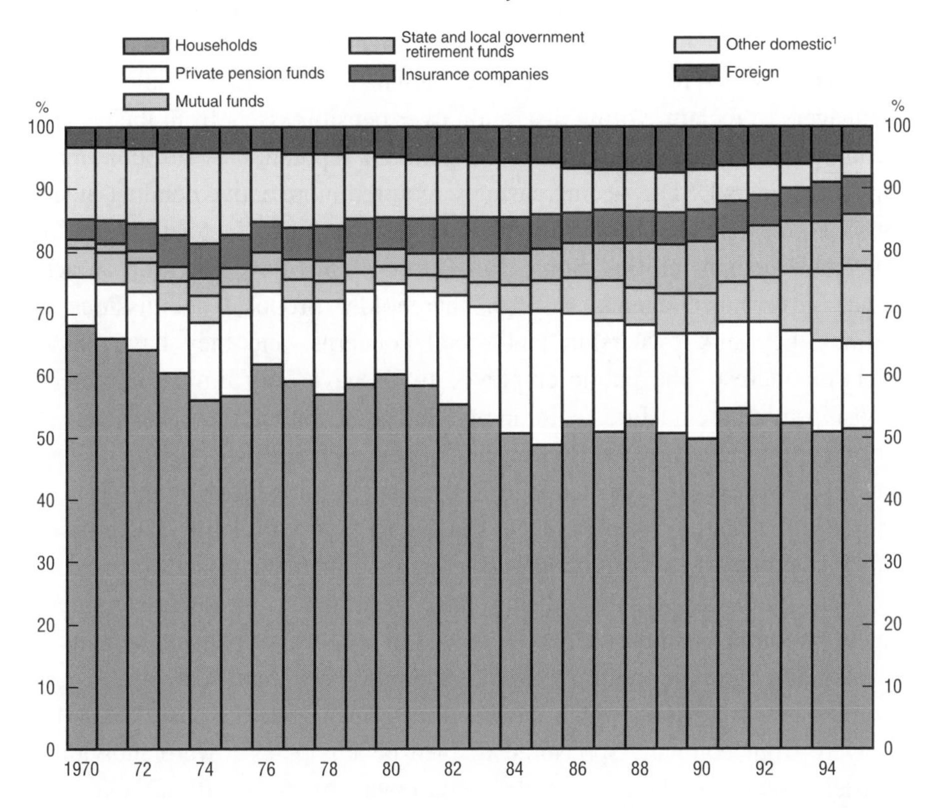

1. Includes commercial banks, savings institutions, closed-end funds, brokers and dealers, and bank personal trusts.

Source: Board of Governors of the Federal Reserve System, *Flow of Funds Accounts.*

Nevertheless, with the good stock-market performance over the past 15 years or so and with the advantages of liquidity, convenience, diversification and professional management, stock market mutual funds have become increasingly popular, especially in recent years. This year, for example, inflows have averaged about $20 billion per month, an annualised growth rate of over 25 per cent.

Finally, *pension funds* are of three types: company-sponsored funds covering private-sector employees which are regulated by the Employee Retirement Income Savings Act (ERISA) of 1974, union-sponsored plans which are dealt with under the Taft-Hartley Act of 1947 (both administered by the Department of Labor – USDL) and those covering the employees of state and local governments which are regulated by state law.[93] The employer-sponsored plans have fairly obvious incentives to remain passive on governance issues: ERISA allows corporate managers to reclaim voting discretion over pension assets from their managers, leading fund managers to try to avoid getting a reputation as a trouble-maker. But in recent years USDL has increasingly required more active conduct in terms of proxy voting and monitoring for them to discharge satisfactorily their "prudent-person" responsibilities. Some Taft-Hartley funds have taken up an active corporate governance agenda through shareholder proposal submissions, but sometimes they mix ownership and social concerns, and they have obvious conflicts of interest. The public employee funds have only limited commercial relationships with the business community, and some among them (especially the California Public Employees Retirement System – CalPERS – with assets of around $100 billion, and the College Retirement Equity Fund of the Teachers Insurance and Annuity Association – TIAA-CREF – with some $70 billion in equities) have been the most vociferous actors on governance issues (see below). The private funds are larger, and they have benefited from the favourable tax treatment of compensation given and received in the form of pension benefits and from socio-demographic trends, as well as the relatively small scale of the public pension system. But their growth has been restrained over the past decade by a trend away from company-sponsored defined-benefit plans toward individually administered plans known as Individual Retirement Accounts (IRAs) and 401(k) plans which are not subject to prudential regulations; these are recorded either under direct household holdings or under holdings of mutual funds. The state and local government plans, on the other hand, are all defined-contribution plans, and, with rapid employment growth, they have therefore maintained their relative shares in recent years.

Overall, much has been made of the growing importance of institutional investors in OECD countries (OECD, 1996*c*)[94] and the increased institutionalisation of equity holdings in the United States (CPC, 1995; Hawley and Williams, 1996) – and indeed total institutional holdings rose from less than 10 per cent of all equities in the 1950s to nearly 45 per cent most recently. In fact, though, this process seems to have come to an end in the mid-1980s (Figure 27), and direct household ownership has again rebounded above 50 per cent of total holdings of corporate equities. Nevertheless, institutional investors are powerful actors on the corporate scene, given their 57 per cent ownership share for the top 1 000 corporations (Table 24). In comparison with other major OECD Member countries US households still hold easily the greatest share of listed corporate equities. But unlike other countries (except the United Kingdom) cross-shareholding among non-financial corporations is limited. Among financial institutions it is only US insurance firms and pension and mutual funds which are comparatively important shareholders; in particular, banks' holdings are especially small (Table 25).

Table 24. **Institutional investor concentration of ownership, 1987-94**

	Average institutional holdings Per cent					Percentage point change:	
	1987	1990	1992	1993	1994	1993-94	1987-94
Top 50	48.7	50.1	52.1	47.2	52.7	5.5	4.0
Top 100	53.6	54.8	55.5	55.6	58.5	2.9	4.9
Top 250	52.8	54.8	55.6	58.0	59.5	1.5	6.7
Top 500	51.8	52.9	55.3	57.8	58.8	1.0	7.0
Top 750	49.6	51.1	53.6	57.1	58.7	1.6	9.1
Top 1 000	46.6	49.5	52.8	55.8	57.1	1.3	10.5

Source: Hawley and Williams (1996) from *The Brancato Report on Institutional Investment*, September 1995.

Table 25. **Ownership of exchange-listed firms: an international comparison**

Per cent

	United States	Japan	Germany	France	United Kingdom
Financial institutions	31.2	48.0	22.0	6.5	58.8
Banks	0.3	26.7	10.0	4.3	0.9
Insurance firms	23.9[1]	17.2	12.0[1]	2.2	18.4
Other	7.0	4.1	..	1.9	39.5
Non-financial institutions	68.8	52.0	78.0	93.5	41.2
Households	48.1	22.6	17.0	20.7	21.3
Non-financial enterprises	14.1	24.8	42.0	54.5	3.6
Public authorities	..	0.7	5.0	4.5	3.9
Non-residents	6.6	3.9	14.0	11.9	12.4

1. Including pension funds.
Source: OECD (1995*a*).

Securities market regulation at the national level also began in the 1930s with the 1933 Securities Act and the 1934 Securities Exchange Act which led to the foundation of the Securities and Exchange Commission (SEC). Ever since then, the accent has been on ensuring that markets have the maximum access to information and that all trading is transparent. Initially, the SEC imposed only minimal trading disclosure requirements and a prohibition against fraud, but in 1956 the SEC amended its proxy rules to encompass all communication among shareholders, thereby deterring shareholder initiatives and inhibiting the development of a private market for information about voting issues (Pound, 1991). It has been only in recent years that a reversal of some of these regulations has taken place (see below).

Managerial discretion: types and control mechanisms

The mainstream academic view in the United States is that corporations exist solely to maximise shareholder wealth, as opposed to a broader ''stakeholder'' approach, discussed below. The core governance problem under shareholder wealth maximisation is the divorce of ownership from control and the resulting informational asymmetries. The key question is, therefore, how to overcome or at least minimise these ''agency costs'' by making managers more responsive to shareholder interests. Even if blatant expropriation of shareholder capital is rare, managerial discretion is substantial, given the ''business judgement rule'' which is accepted by law. The likelihood of rent-seeking behaviour reduces the willingness of arms-length investors to provide capital to the corporation and may lead to a less efficient outcome than if the firm were organised in a non-corporate form. While explicit contracts with strong incentive mechanisms can be imagined, overt bargaining cannot take place, because it would imply contravention of management's fiduciary duty (the ''duty of loyalty'' in legal parlance); thus, in practice contracting remains largely implicit, and in the main residual control rights are necessarily allocated to management. With small and dispersed shareholders, and therefore a ''free-rider'' problem, monitoring responsibilities are delegated to the board of directors, but, as will be argued below, this is, in most cases, inadequate, and monitoring will generally be under-provided. Thus, it may be more of a puzzle to explain managerial discipline than discretion (Edlin and Stiglitz, 1995).

How may managers use their discretion and behave opportunistically? A number of ideas will be touched on here (more details are given in Annex I):

- they may choose to "build empires" by maximising sales or growth, rather than profits and by pursuing acquisitions which result in few synergies;
- they may adopt investment strategies with excessively low risk because they cannot diversify their income risks as easily as shareholders can;
- they may avoid returning capital to shareholders, preferring to dissipate free cash flows on unproductive activities including wasteful takeovers and other investments;
- they may arrange to have themselves paid excessively[95] (Figure 28), or consume excessive amounts of perquisites, through their dominance of the board of directors;
- they may engage in inefficient asset sales; and/or
- they may attempt to entrench themselves by weakening the mechanisms which exist in order to discipline or replace them (the takeover

Figure 28. **MANAGERIAL COMPENSATION**[1]
In 1990 US dollars

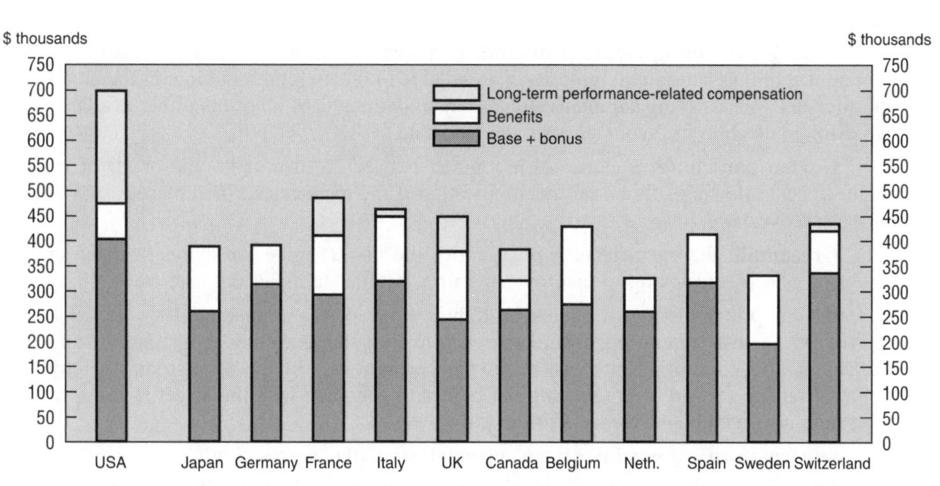

1. Compensation of Chief Executive Officers in 1992.
Source: Abowd and Bognanno (1993).

mechanism) through adopting ''poison pills'' (see Box 6), increasing leverage, choosing an organisational structure which makes them indispensable or investing in projects which are either specific to themselves or which they can manage better than their rivals.

But there exist numerous mechanisms to control management's incentives to behave opportunistically.

Box 6. **A lexicon for corporate governance**

There follows a simple definition of some of the most popular terms specific to the corporate governance domain.

Business combination law: an anti-takeover law which delays acquisitions typically for three to five years, effectively allowing management a moratorium on hostile takeovers.

Control share law: an anti-takeover law which allows firms to disenfranchise all shares beyond a certain threshold unless other shareholders vote to restore those voting rights in a special election that must be held within a short period after a hostile takeover attempt gets underway.

Cumulative voting rights provision: a charter provision permitting a method of voting that allows substantial minority shareholders to obtain representation on the board of directors. When voting cumulatively, a shareholder may cast all of his or her available votes in an election in favour of a single candidate.

Golden parachute: a clause in a contract between a firm and some or all of its management allowing substantial indemnification if the management is replaced following a takeover.

Greenmail: the payment of a price above the market price for shares held by an investor who is threatening to take over the firm in order to avoid the takeover.

Poison pill: an issue of shares or rights, never put to a shareholder vote, as a protection against an unwanted takeover. By creating burdensome obligations to any purchaser of a controlling block, it raises the potential cost of the acquisition, thereby either deterring the bid or compelling the bidder to negotiate with the target in order to persuade it to withdraw (''redeem'') the pill.

Supermajority amendment: an amendment to the corporation's charter which specifies that changes in control of the firm must be approved by more than half – usually two-thirds but sometimes as much as nine-tenths – of outstanding shares.

Managerial shareholding

When corporations perform badly, the reaction of financial investors is known as the "Wall Street Walk": they exit by selling their shares, thereby bidding down the equity price and boosting the firm's cost of capital. This has a negative impact on managers' reputation and, potentially, compensation. Thus, perhaps the most fundamental way in which managers are persuaded to act in owners' interests, other than the risk to their reputations, is if the two roles are combined through heavy managerial shareholding. This can occur in the domain of corporations or through other organisational forms: traditional and limited liability partnerships, venture capital funds and LBO associations, for example.

Optimal executive compensation packages

Providing management with the appropriate incentives to act on shareholders' behalf is most often undertaken through the design of executive compensation packages.[96] Granting management and especially CEOs stock and/or stock options rather than straight cash compensation at least puts their financial wealth at risk, and providing even apparently small incentives may boost effort and firm value (Haubrich, 1994).

But it is unclear whether varying the sensitivity of CEO pay to share price outcomes has any bearing on performance (Stiglitz, 1985; Jacobs, 1991). There is little impact of changing share values on CEO wealth, both through a weak impact on compensation and because of the limited sensitivity of the probability of dismissal with respect to poor performance.[97] A heavy dose of equity-based compensation does lead to an obvious diversification problem for executives (it would effectively tie much of their financial as well as their human wealth to the firm's financial results), and depending on their tolerance for income swings, the result may be behaviour biased toward risk avoidance. Using stock options rather than equity may have the opposite effect, as managers do not share in downside risks. But boosting executive compensation in the form of stock options leads to distorted decisions favouring greater profit retention, since options do not receive dividends. CEOs have a fair degree of influence over their own pay levels, and, despite the inapplicability of the "business judgement rule" as a protective screen for management in legal cases resulting from executive compensation, having pay too sensitive to share price performance can open up the possibility of managerial self-dealing (Shleifer and Vishny, 1996). In any case, the very limited prevalence of high-powered incentive contracts for executives may also be attributable to the need to avoid severe price-cutting behaviour in oligopolistic industries (Aggarwal and Samwick, 1996).

Capital structure

Many specialists in corporate finance have also argued that the firm's capital structure is related to its governance.[98] Besides being a signalling device for firm prospects, leverage has implications for managerial discretion. Debt reduces the agency costs of free cash flow by compelling its disbursement in the form of interest and principal payments, thereby reducing the funds available for unwise investments (Jensen, 1986; Hart and Moore, 1995); it may also constrain management's avoidance of efficient layoffs (Sharpe, 1994) and trigger renegotiation or bankruptcy if assets can be better redeployed.[99] As would be expected, debt constrains investment only where the markets think that opportunities are poor (Lang *et al.*, 1996): high leverage is associated with lower future realised growth only for firms with low Tobin's Q.[100] According to this view then, increased debt should be efficiency-enhancing, and evidence from the effects of leveraged buyouts (LBOs) and other restructuring transactions is at least partly supportive (see Annex I).

The disciplinary attractions of debt to shareholders should reflect the effectiveness of the other agency cost-reduction mechanisms available. Higher institutional ownership – and, therefore, a potential for greater monitoring (see below) – has been shown to substitute for greater leverage (Samuel, 1996). And with a stronger threat from takeovers in the 1980s, the need for debt should have eased; but debt is also a takeover deterrent and, thus, became more attractive to management (Novaes and Zingales, 1995). Partly as a result of this, partly because of the financial innovation popularly known as "junk bonds" and partly because of an increase in the tax bias in favour of debt in the 1980s (Gertler and Hubbard, 1993), there was a huge increase in leverage from 1983 to 1989, when measured using book values (Figure 29). Equity worth a cumulative $632 billion was withdrawn, and all corporate equity would have disappeared by the year 2003 if the trend had continued (Jensen, 1989). But the trend was probably related to the huge increase in the market value of equity as from 1982: indeed, more meaningful measures of leverage based on market values reveal that it reached a peak in 1984, only surpassed in the recession year 1974, before it

Figure 29. **THE RATIO OF DEBT TO EQUITY AND NET WORTH**

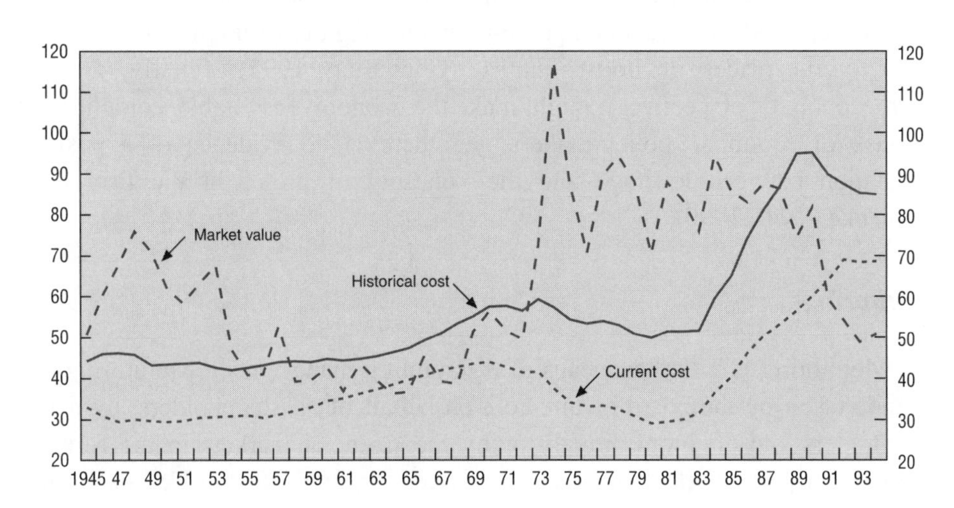

Source: Board of Governors of the Federal Reserve System, *Balance Sheets for the US Economy, 1945-94.*

began a steady decline, especially pronounced in recent years, thereby plumbing depths not seen since the early 1970s. Thus, a substantial rise in corporate borrowing in the 1980s was required merely to avoid deleveraging, and on a market value basis there seems to have been little change over the decade (Bernanke *et al.*, 1990).

But the impact of higher levels of debt on the performance of the firm is not uniquely favourable: the short-term cash flow needs can lead to an excessively short-term focus by management and can force actions not in the long-run interests of shareholders if the state of the world is disappointing. And increased leverage restrains not only inefficient investment when cash flow is high but profitable investment when cash flow is low because it limits management's ability to raise new capital (Stulz, 1990). The cumulation of such cases in a period of economic weakness leads to what has been termed "debt overhang" in the macroeconomic context. With a given bankruptcy law, debt may also force liquidation even when that course of action is inefficient; a bankruptcy law that shields management from creditors for a very long time (such as Chapter 11 in the United States – see below) may dull the disciplinary effectiveness of debt

(Hart, 1995). And there is some evidence from the supermarket industry that it may weaken product market competition by reducing the willingness or ability of firms to cut prices or boost quality (Chevalier, 1995). Finally, from a macroeconomic perspective, it might make the economy less stable, complicating the task of economic policy-makers; yet there is no evidence of a positive association between leverage and the volatility of profits at the firm level (Bernanke *et al.*, 1990).

Monitoring

Monitoring is a further means of disciplining management. Monitoring can be undertaken by the board of directors on behalf of all shareholders, by major shareholders and creditors directly or by the financial markets in the form of takeovers, a particularly blunt control device, especially in the US disclosure-based system.

...by the board of directors

The most immediate monitor of management is the board of directors. In principle, since World War Two the board has been appointed by shareholders to choose and then oversee the management and ensure satisfactory performance.[101] It has been its responsibility to replace management when the latter proves to be either incompetent, dishonest or engaged in excessive self-dealing. This would appear to be a low-cost governance mechanism (Fama, 1980). Should shareholders be dissatisfied with the board's conduct, then a proxy contest is the appropriate mechanism to change the board's composition.[102] Thus, in theory, if the market for managerial labour and the proxy mechanism are functioning well, directors' positions, like management's, are contestable.

Traditionally, however, the overwhelming majority of directors lacked the incentives to carry out these duties. Like management in many cases, boards too became entrenched, with only rare proxy contests and staggered terms preventing rapid restructuring. The board has often been surrounded by a "club ethos" (Coffee, 1991), a culture that has resulted from the fact that most directors have been named by the CEO, who is also, in the great majority of cases, its chairman, and have been comprised either of insiders (other senior management) or of other CEOs, often of major suppliers or clients and sometimes with very little if any equity in the business (see Annex I). As for management, compensation is generous by international standards: compared to the average wage of an employed male, directors' fees in the late 1980s were about 13.5 times as high, whereas in Japan the corresponding multiple in the early 1980s was only 4.8 (Kaplan, 1994). Board meetings were few and not overly long, minimal information was provided, and the agenda was entirely under management control (Jensen, 1993). In such a situation it is small wonder that the board was a largely ineffectual cog in the corporate governance mechanism, and management discretion was largely, even if not totally, unrestrained (Mace, 1971) (see Annex I).

But in recent years increasing global competition, faster technological change, greater institutional activism and more frequent and onerous shareholder litigation – but, notably, almost no government intervention – have changed the situation, even if the shift marks only a beginning. For the time being, however, doubts remain over whether the board is truly more independent of senior management (Neiva, 1995), and whether the change is material (Jensen, 1993). In setting corporate strategy, CEOs are relying more on their boards (whose members are being remunerated even more generously than previously) and are allowing them more access to information and the board agenda (NACD, 1995). It has also proved increasingly necessary over time, in order to attract and retain good directors, to protect them, along with management, against shareholder litigation through directors' and officers' liability insurance (now routinely provided by large firms) and state indemnification laws. Increasing numbers of directors are now apparently independent outsiders,[103] aware that they are putting their reputations on the line, especially among their peers. Thus, they spend more time on board matters and, therefore, restrict the number of boards on which they sit (see Annex I). As a result boards have become smaller: average membership has fallen from around 14 in 1987 to about 12 in 1992, and most firms seem intent on going below 10 (NACD, 1995); by way of comparison, Japanese boards average around 21 members. Downsizing the board and increasing the share of directors comprised of outsiders would appear to be good strategies, as there is fairly strong evidence of a negative correlation between both board size and outsider membership and various measures of corporate performance (see Annex I). That boards have become more assertive is exemplified by the ousting of some high-profile CEOs (though these coups occurred only after billions of dollars in share value had been wiped out), the separation of CEO and chairman positions[104] and the creation of audit committees with a majority of outside directors (as required by New York Stock Exchange-listed firms since 1978).

...by banks

In several other OECD Member countries monitoring is largely the responsibility of the firm's main bank. It is clear, for example, that banks have traditionally played a greater monitoring role in Japan, as do other corporate blockholders (Kaplan and Minton, 1994), and in Germany (OECD, 1995*e*; Cable, 1985), even if some movement away from such relationship-oriented banking seems to be underway. Supporters of this system point to the innate advantage that bank-based monitoring has in mitigating ''short-termism'' biases (see below). In addition, it may reduce the (information) costs of delegated monitoring in a multiple-principal setting (Diamond, 1984), although the relevant evidence is decidedly mixed (Mayer, 1996). In theory, banks have the same incentive to monitor as other holders of concentrated claims. As well, by lending short term, the borrower is forced to come back regularly to the bank for funds, whereas equity never has to be repaid. And, in addition, the incentive to monitor is enhanced to the extent that, because intermediated loans are less standardised than other debt, they are less liquid and likely to be held longer (Prowse, 1994). On the other hand, banks are to a large extent concerned only with default risks, implying that their interests may diverge sharply from those of shareholders.[105] Non-bank arm's-length finance is fostered in the United States by the heavy reliance on disclosure; and banks are also prevented from becoming concentrated claimants by the limitation that they provide no more than 15 per cent of their capital to any single borrower – while the corresponding limits are 30 per cent in Japan and 50 per cent in Germany. It is only in the bankruptcy process that US banks have much of a governance role.

...by shareholder voice

- Institutional monitors

Monitoring can also occur by shareholder voice. But the fundamental theoretical difficulty that then arises is the free-rider problem: any performance improvement brought about by effective monitoring must be shared with all other equity holders. Thus, effective voice can be exercised only by major institutional owners, for it is difficult for shareholders to exert their ownership rights and deter managerial self-dealing when they are small and dispersed. This is the logic behind the governance systems in several continental European countries:[106] concentrated shareholdings may be one of the most efficient ways of minimising agency problems (Prowse, 1994), although the interests of large shareholders may diverge from those of small holders, for example with respect to dividend policy (Shleifer and Vishny, 1986).[107]

In any case, the combination of the availability of liquid financial markets (in other words, ease of exit), and the many legal and regulatory constraints on institutions holding large blocks in individual corporations as well as the relatively good legal protections provided to investors and strong shareholders' rights in the United States (La Porta *et al.*, 1996) serve to limit the importance of concentrated ownership in the governance process, other than in the extreme case of a full-fledged takeover (see Annex I). For example, the attractiveness of institutional monitoring *via* blockholding is reduced by Section 16(b) of the Securities Exchange Act which requires that any holder of 10 per cent or more of any class of equity turn over to the company any profit earned on purchase/sale or sale/purchase sequences occurring within six months. Fragmented ownership is also promoted by preventing mutual funds from calling themselves diversified and from claiming tax-exempt status if they take large stakes; this forces investors wishing to do so to form private investment companies (such as venture capital, LBO associations and hedge funds), but these are limited to 100 participants and cannot issue public securities. The justification for such regulatory constraints cannot be the minimal amount of risk reduction achieved by the added diversification; in any case, modern financial theory shows investors how optimally to achieve a diversified portfolio, especially given the existence of more complete and deeper derivatives markets. The official defense of these constraints is that they provide investors with accurate disclosure of the nature of their investments. And the SEC points out that no law or regulation prohibits mutual funds from being active shareholders.

Yet, given fragmented ownership, are institutional or other investors capable of serving as an effective check on managerial discretion? If any agent can mitigate the free-rider problem, it would have to be institutional investors, only a few of whom would normally be required to agree in order to take collective action. There is some evidence that greater institutional holdings are associated with higher values of Tobin's Q (McConnell and Servaes, 1990), at least until such holdings reach about 50 per cent (Morck *et al.*, 1988; Samuel, 1996). Many observers believe that it is only overregulation which has prevented institutional investors from more effective monitoring. But there are a number of problems with potential institutional monitoring, not least of which is the question of who would monitor the monitor, given the agency problems within financial institutions themselves (see Annex I).

- Shareholder resolutions

Another method of disciplining management is *via* shareholder proposals or resolutions. In theory, they provide owners with the chance to make managerial and strategic changes at the corporation's annual meeting. However, this "voice" mechanism has been seldom used and rarely effective (see Annex I), in part because of the expense of challenging management through the proxy process and the lack of incentives to get involved, given the obvious free-rider problem (Stiglitz, 1985) and the low costs of exit.[108]

- Shareholder activism

In recent years, however, the costs of resorting to voice have declined, primarily as a result of greater ownership concentration (Coffee, 1991) and also SEC rule changes (see below). What is termed the "shareholder democracy movement" has sought easier shareholder access to the registry of shareholders, the elimination of barriers to communication among investor groups, enhanced access to the proxy statement, guarantees of confidential voting and the right of shareholders to vote on "poison pills", "golden parachutes", "greenmail" and other such practices (see Box 6).

Greater activism began with CalPERS, the New York State Employees Retirement Fund and TIAA-CREF in the mid-1980s. These funds increasingly came to the view that there was little to gain from trying to pick individual stocks for their portfolio (given the spreading belief in the efficient markets hypothesis), making indexing increasingly popular (even though by no means dominant) – in which case exit is not an option. They also recognised that they were growing so fast that, with constraints as to their individual holdings in particular firms, they were *de facto* required to hold the entire market. In either case the inescapable conclusion was that they would have to try to improve overall corporate performance in order to boost returns for their investors.[109] Initially, activist institutions were concerned about their minimal role in nominating directors and about adoption without shareholder approval of anti-takeover devices. They and other public funds began to put forward dozens of resolutions, even though only a small number were approved. Then, in 1987 CalPERS began to publish an annual target list of firms from whom it was seeking governance changes. As from 1993 so too did the Council of Institutional Investors (CII), an association of 100 mostly public pension funds with nearly a trillion dollars in assets. Initially, CalPERS' targets were chosen based on their governance practices, but after little success with that strategy, it began to emphasise corporate performance in 1989. The results have clearly been favourable (see Annex I).

In 1995, CalPERS decided to expand its corporate governance attentions beyond the largest US firms and to look at the performance of individual directors across different boards; and in 1996, it announced that it would develop a formal international corporate governance programme to be applied to the 16 per cent of its portfolio held abroad. Another recent trend in shareholder activism is the appearance of so-called "corporate governance funds". As transactions costs in the equities market have declined, it has become possible for this specialised class of active investors to amass a stake in an underperforming firm, seek a governance change, and, once achieved, exit with a substantial profit if the change is seen by the market as enhancing likely future performance. Although the evidence on whether governance arrangements affect share prices is unclear (see Annex I), Gordon and Pound (1993) have found the strategy to be successful, especially if the investment is non-negotiated at the outset and the initiative is clearly not for control (possibly because there is a reduced risk of self-dealing by the active investor in this case). The importance of such funds is set to grow, albeit from a small base: in June 1995 CalPERS decided to invest $200 million in a fund professing this strategy.

Shareholder activism has been given a boost in the 1990s by various regulatory changes. The most important of these was the decision in 1992 by the SEC to revise its proxy rules to permit easier communications among those shareholders not seeking control. This encouragement of voice may reduce exit, thereby lengthening holding periods and time horizons. However, stringent disclosure requirements remain for any action deemed to be a non-exempt proxy solicitation, and the litigation risk under Section 13(d) of the Securities Exchange Act in a takeover situation is still a concern (CPC, 1995). Nevertheless, the result of this deregulation is that companies appear to be more willing to talk to major investors, with the result that, despite a 1991 change easing the process of filing shareholder resolutions, there has been a marked decline in the number of resolutions sponsored by institutions (other than Taft-Hartley, *i.e.* union, pension funds[110]). The SEC has also tried to promote shareholder participation through its proposed Rule 14A-X of the Securities Act: it would allow substantial shareholders who have held stock for a prescribed period of time to have a short statement with their views on management quality mailed with the proxy statement.[111] Then in 1994 the Department of Labor formally advocated a "corporate activist" role for ERISA funds: all fiduciaries were thenceforth required to vote their proxies, even for foreign equities. Funds were also urged to provide their outside investment managers with written voting guidelines. But no such requirements have been imposed by other federal or state regulators on other institutions, despite the advantages in overcoming free-rider problems.

...by the markets

Finally, the functions of monitoring can be effectively undertaken by the markets – either by the product market or more clearly by the capital markets in general and the "market for corporate control" (a term coined by Manne, 1965) in particular. Ultimately, if no other disciplinary device operates effectively in securing the future of the corporation, and some (*e.g.* Jensen, 1993) believe this to be the case, then it falls to the markets to take up this role. Where markets are highly competitive and positions are contestable, some argue that the details of corporate governance may not be important to performance (Roe, 1994).

- Product market competition and bankruptcy

Product market competition can reduce the scope for managerial discretion if, for example, there is a common component to firms' costs: such competition would force all firms toward similar price levels and changes (Hart, 1983). Through the threat of liquidation, competitive pressures can also limit the exercise of managerial discretion by forcing the firm towards a clearly defined "best practice", where that exists. However, Hermalin (1992) and Schmidt (1996) argue that the effect of competition on managerial consumption of "agency goods" is theoretically ambiguous. And while product markets provide signals that assist in monitoring, they do not act very quickly to squeeze out managerial inefficiencies, at least relative to capital markets, because declining market share and sub-par profitability will force bankruptcy only slowly; it is the ultimate sanction for failure to compete successfully in product or input markets. Most shareholder value has been destroyed before the firm files for bankruptcy, and the bankruptcy process is long, drawn-out, relatively cumbersome and, therefore, costly: Weiss (1990) estimates the average direct costs for 37 bankruptcy filings from 1979-86 for listed firms at 3 per cent of the value of the firm (over 20 per cent of the value of its equity). Nonetheless, annual bankruptcy rates in the United States are much higher than in Japan and Germany, but somewhat lower than in Canada in recent years.

Termination of the life of the corporation is used only as a last resort due to the nature of the bankruptcy law (which dates back to 1978), its Chapter 11 in particular. The law strives to maintain the operation of the business, at least temporarily, by allowing existing management to retain control – although a specialised judge retains oversight authority and, according to Gilson (1990), more than half the directors are normally ousted – by protecting the company from the claims of its creditors, while it attempts to escape its financial distress. This right accorded to management – the ability to seek protection from creditors by unilaterally filing for reorganisation – gives US managers a powerful position compared with the situation in many other countries where creditors' consent is required or where existing management is replaced during the reorganisation process. The logic is that a going concern is worth more than its liquidation value, and the emphasis is on avoiding the high social costs of shutdown to the various "stakeholders", even at the risk of reducing the proceeds available for creditors (Franks and Torous, 1992). Thus, the courts effectively reprioritise the claims on the corporation in about three-quarters of all cases, and even when it is not efficient to do so according to Longhofer and Carlstrom (1995). While in such cases creditors – primarily those who are unsecured (Weiss, 1990) – at first glance lose out to stockholders, they, along with the courts, are often allocated an effective veto because they are either directly allotted equity[112] or at least begin to resemble shareholders in that their claims become residual. Although they benefit from reprioritisation by an average of 2.3 per cent of firm value (Franks and Torous, 1994), shareholders are assigned only a small decision-making role relative to management, as they are seen as having relatively poor incentives in bankruptcy situations: given that the value of their equity has in most cases been all but lost, they would normally have a greater willingness to pursue high-risk investment strategies in order to try to recover their bets.

The inefficiencies of the bankruptcy law are several. First, the possibility of creditor claims being downgraded in hierarchical terms, as well as the heavy direct costs of bankruptcy, may raise the supply price of debt capital (Weiss, 1990; Jenkinson and Mayer, 1992), exacerbate any credit-rationing problems and cause firms to shift their capital structures towards financial leases (which must continue to be paid in the event of entry into Chapter 11). Second, the system may be opened up to abuse, as Chapter 11 can be used to try to gain a competitive advantage over rivals by, for example, seeking new financing which can be granted priority over existing financing (Franks and Torous, 1992). This charge was levelled at firms in the airline industry in the 1980s. There is in fact some evidence that the announcement of bankruptcy causes a decline in competitors' share prices, especially in industries with high leverage and where the returns of the bankrupt firm and its rivals have been highly correlated (Lang and Stulz, 1992). Third, creditors go a long way to avoid the costs of formal reorganisation under Chapter 11; therefore, with informal reorganisations under so-called distressed exchanges, they grant even larger deviations from absolute priority (an average of 9.5 per cent of firm value, compared to the aforementioned figure of 2.3 per cent under Chapter 11) (Franks and Torous, 1994). This strategy pays off, for creditor recovery rates then average 80 per cent, compared to only 51 per cent under Chapter 11. The result is the effective privatisation of much of the bankruptcy process.[113] But a possibly more efficient system would allow contracts to be written with an explicit opt-out from formal bankruptcy procedures, thereby allowing agents to decide themselves whether to allow violations of absolute priority (Longhofer and Carlstrom, 1995); this might especially benefit small entrepreneurial firms with uncertain markets and unproven products.

- The market for corporate control

But the characteristic of the US system of corporate governance which sets it apart most clearly from others is the reliance on the market for corporate control or, more simply, takeovers as one of the primary disciplinary devices to force managers to seek good corporate performance. Merger waves occurred in the 1890s, when many giant monopolies were formed, during the 1920s, in the second half of the 1960s when conglomerates were popular, in the 1980s and most recently once again.[114] In the second half of the 1980s, for example, the value of US mergers totalled around one trillion dollars, an average of one-twelfth and a peak of nearly one-fifth of total market capitalisation per year, more

Table 26. **Completed domestic mergers and acquisitions, 1986-89**[1]

	United States	United Kingdom	Japan	Germany
Volume (in $ billion)	1 070.0	107.6	61.3	4.2
As percentage of total market capitalisation	41.1	18.7	3.1	2.3

1. Only those with disclosed values.
Source: Prowse (1994).

than twice the share for UK firms and about 15 times the modest levels seen in Japan and Germany (Prowse, 1994) (Table 26). In recent quarters US merger activity has represented more than half the worldwide total. In a longer-term perspective, in the years 1968 to 1995 there were some 83 000 merger and acquisition transactions in the United States (an average of more than eight every day of the year), worth some $3.9 trillion in 1995 prices (Table 27).

Besides the magnitude of this phenomenon, what was unique from a historical perspective was that for the first time some were undertaken without the approval of the target firm. Such unsolicited tender offers or proxy fights are almost unheard of in many other OECD Member countries. But the frequency of these hostile or contested takeover attempts should not be exaggerated: they numbered only 364 in the period 1985-89, and only 172 of them were successful. Nevertheless, the mere threat of such corporate control actions should in theory go some way toward the elimination of opportunistic managerial behaviour,[115] but where that is not sufficient, actual changes might be more successful, especially given the higher levels of debt that usually ensue (see below). Yet it must be admitted that many mergers and acquisitions do take place involving as targets firms whose performance is not substandard, but where various synergies are expected or where the correction is of a possible *ex ante* failure, that is where there is a prospect for superior performance through a different strategy. It is this difference of opinion which often leads to the opposition to a tender offer. Such synergistic factors are believed to be driving the current merger wave which got underway in 1993.

Most observers believe that these takeover transactions are efficiency-enhancing for the most part: besides improving management quality, they may

Table 27. **Number and value of merger and acquisition transactions, 1963-95**

$ billion

	Number of transactions	Value[1]	
		Nominal dollars	Constant[2] (1995) dollars
1963	1 361	n.a.	n.a.
1964	1 950	n.a.	n.a.
1965	2 125	n.a.	n.a.
1966	2 377	n.a.	n.a.
1967	2 975	n.a.	n.a.
1968	4 462	43.0	188.4
1969	6 107	23.7	98.5
1970	5 152	16.4	64.4
1971	4 608	12.6	47.4
1972	4 801	16.7	60.9
1973	4 040	16.7	57.3
1974	2 861	12.5	38.6
1975	2 297	11.8	33.4
1976	2 276	20.0	53.6
1977	2 224	21.9	55.1
1978	2 106	34.2	79.9
1979	2 128	43.5	91.3
1980	1 889	44.3	81.9
1981	2 395	82.6	138.4
1982	2 346	53.8	85.0
1983	2 533	73.1	111.8
1984	2 543	122.2	179.3
1985	3 001	179.8	254.7
1986	3 336	173.1	240.7
1987	2 032	163.7	219.5
1988	2 258	246.9	318.1
1989	2 366	221.1	271.8
1990	2 074	108.2	126.2
1991	1 877	71.2	79.7
1992	2 574	96.7	105.0
1993	2 663	176.4	186.1
1994	2 997	226.7	233.1
1995	3 510	356.0	356.0

1. Tabulations measure only publicly announced transactions and include transfers of ownership of 10 per cent or more of a company's assets or equity, provided that the value of the transaction is at least $500 000.
2. Using the consumer price index.

Source: Council of Economic Advisers (1985) and *1996 Mergerstat Review.*

reallocate capital to more efficient uses – either directly, or, if unsuccessful, through subsequent voluntary liquidation (Fleming and Moon, 1995) – and allow for synergistic production and distribution economies and technology transfer

(Council of Economic Advisers, 1985). However, some takeovers – especially, as mentioned above, leveraged buyouts – are driven by strong rent-seeking and -preserving motives. Yet the average takeover premium of 41 per cent is *prima facie* evidence of prior inefficiencies; indeed Jensen has argued that a minimum of $750 billion in additional wealth was created, assuming that bidders were not systematically overpaying for their targets.[116] The literature on the effects of mergers provides a number of signals that they boost efficiency (see Annex I). One of the inefficiencies being corrected is the excessive retention of free cash flow, avoidance of exit and resulting over-investment (Jensen, 1986 and 1993). Another, often cited, is overmanning. A third is excessive pay and related expenses and inefficiently designed management compensation contracts (Scharfstein, 1988). Finally, takeovers may result from a history of value-decreasing acquisitions (Mitchell and Lehn, 1990) or, similarly, an unwillingness of managers to undo earlier inefficient diversification; the breakup value of such conglomerates was higher than their market prices, allowing an average of 30 per cent of assets acquired in hostile takeovers to be subsequently sold, primarily to firms with other similar assets (Bhagat *et al.*, 1990). This return to corporate specialisation (''focus'') since the 1980s has been associated with better stock performance for the firm (Comment and Jarrell, 1995).

But others have pointed to a variety of other explanations for the ability and willingness of bidders to pay such premia, many of which have completely different normative implications (see Annex I): the prospect of exploiting product market power and achieving monopoly rents; taking advantage of tax minimisation possibilities; the opportunity of expropriating extramarginal wage premia and overfunded defined-benefit pension plans through ''reversion'' (termination) (Petersen, 1992; Pontiff *et al.*, 1990; Ippolito and James, 1992); taking actions prejudicial to bondholders (Asquith and Wizman, 1990); and cutting back on the firm's longer-term investment activities in both tangible and intangible forms.

Takeovers are a costly way of aligning investors' and managers' interests: legal, advisory and financing costs average about 4 per cent of the purchase price (Jacobs, 1991).[117] And they face considerable difficulties, because they too suffer from a free-rider problem: small shareholders have little incentive to tender their shares to a bidder, because if the bid is successful, the holder would stand to gain at least as much through the resulting productivity/profitability increase needed to justify the bid in the first place (Grossman and Hart, 1980). Bidders sometimes try to eliminate such free riding by subsequently merging the acquired firm with another they control on terms not favourable to minority shareholders; such dilutions are permitted under Delaware law, for example. Most often, however, successful bidders eliminate nontendering shareholders in a second stage, with a cash-out offer at the same price as the original tender offer.

State-level anti-takeover legislation and management-induced corporate changes may also play a important role in limiting the effectiveness of the corporate control market (Grundfest, 1990; Jensen, 1993). However, the strength of their deterrence effects may not be significant, even if such legal and corporate changes provide the target with added bargaining power (Comment and Schwert, 1995). The revival of the takeover boom in the last few years would also seem to put into question the importance of such constraints, although it would appear that fewer bids are now contested. At least 34 states have passed 65 anti-takeover laws since an important 1982 Supreme Court Decision that struck down a previous generation of 37 such laws.[118] And 25 states have passed multi-constituency laws defining management's fiduciary responsibility as being owed not just to shareholders but to other ''stakeholders'' as well (see below), thereby providing grounds for opposition to attractively priced takeover bids. Companies themselves – 1 500 according to Jacobs (1991) or 35 per cent of all listed firms by the early 1990s – have resorted to ''poison pills'' to ward off unwanted takeovers which would eliminate management's benefits of control. These have generally been allowed under the ''business judgement rule''.

Overall, 87 per cent of all listed firms are covered by at least one of these common anti-takeover measures (sometimes called ''shark repellents''), but only ''business combination laws'' (see Box 6) seem to have had any systematic negative effect on the probability of being taken over (Comment and Schwert, 1995). Other tactics used to deter takeovers are to pass corporate charter amendments (Bhagat and Jefferis, 1991), or to form an employee stock-ownership plan (ESOP): since employees normally support management, announcement of their formation depresses stock prices (Gordon and Pound, 1990; Beatty, 1995). The evidence is fairly strong that such takeover defenses lower stock prices by promoting entrenchment (Mahoney *et al.*, 1995), at least if the board of directors is dominated by insiders (Brickley *et al.*, 1994) and/or if share ownership by directors and officers is high (Jarrell and Poulsen, 1987; McWilliams, 1990) or if the CEO and the chairman of the board are the same person (Sundaramurthy *et al.*, 1995). But since the nature of takeovers has changed somewhat in the 1990s – with bidders in related sectors making better financed offers and apparently more persistent – it is possible that "poison pills" and other such provisions designed as delaying tactics are now less effective than they were in the 1980s.

The alternative "stakeholder" view

There are some commentators who criticise the very foundations of the orthodox view by disputing the fundamental goal of the corporation. Rather than being an institution designed to maximise solely shareholder wealth, these critics argue that corporations exist in order to promote overall societal wealth (Wallman, 1991), and that shareholders' interests and property rights should have no primacy over those of other "stakeholders" in the firm: workers, managers, creditors, suppliers, customers and other members of the community.[119] This is clearly recognised in most state laws, but only with respect to takeovers: what are termed "multi-constituency laws", which have been passed in at least 29 states, with similar jurisprudence in others, state explicitly that the fiduciary responsibilities of officers and directors are owed to the corporation as a whole, that is to all its "stakeholders".

The importance of this alternative view can be gauged by looking at some of the potential conflicts of interest that may arise. Shareholders and debtholders may be at odds because the latter do not want the firm to engage in high risk/high return projects which might lead to bankruptcy while they have no possibility of higher returns. This antagonism is mitigated to some extent in other countries by the custom of having debtholders (largely banks) own equity as well; this may allow a lower cost of debt capital (Prowse, 1990). Managers and owners may also clash with employees over a wide range of business decisions, but most especially over job security. As a result, employees may have inadequate incentives to invest in firm-specific human capital because of the risk that it might be effectively expropriated by the firm whose owners cannot make a credible commitment not to do so. Thus, where the need for such capital is great, there is a strong incentive to seek out alternative contractual arrangements such as partnerships in many of the professions. More generally, employers try to manage long-term employment relationships (that is, reduce turnover) by several possible incentive mechanisms: paying their workers above going market wages, seniority elements in compensation and pension-based ''bonding'' (Greenwald and Stiglitz, 1990). Corporations the world over try to control and co-ordinate the actions of different ''stakeholders'', and, conversely, ''stakeholders'' monitor one another to ensure their interests are respected. While in the US case there is a greater reliance on explicit contracting than in most European economies or in Japan, nevertheless there are important implicit contracts with employees, suppliers and customers which rely upon mutual trust for their efficacy (Kester, 1992; Fukuyama, 1995).

The most sophisticated exposition of the ''stakeholder'' view has been provided by Blair (1995). She points out that maximising shareholder wealth is equivalent to maximising social wealth only if shareholders truly receive the residual returns and bear the firm's residual risk. But unless labour contracts are complete, some residual risk is borne by long-tenured employees with firm-specific human capital, even if general skills predominate in the US labour market (see Chapter III). Increasingly in this service-producing world, and especially in high involvement workplaces (Levine, 1995), the firm is an institution which manages team production using more human than physical capital in the production process.[120] Putting it another way, since limited liability excuses shareholders from undertaking all the responsibilities facing owners of real property, then, one might argue, they should not benefit from all the rights either. Creditors too bear some of the residual risk, especially with the tendency to reprioritise claims in bankruptcy cases (see above). Indeed, all those contributing specialised inputs to the firm have a claim to control rights over the firm's assets. Only if all participants with firm-specific assets have the right incentives to work together without risk of ''hold-up'' (Milgrom and Roberts, 1992) will the firm succeed in minimising the costs of co-ordination and dispute resolution. Without mutual monitoring by such ''stakeholders'', there is a risk of what has been called ''co-operative shirking equilibrium''. The predominance of general skills in the US work force, the lack of relationship-specific investments by suppliers and customers and the possibly excessive zeal for downsizing in the 1990s may be some of the results of a lack of attention to the interests of non-owner ''stakeholders''.

The implications of this view are that firms should offer greater job security in order to elicit greater loyalty[121] and effort and that all ''stakeholders'' should hold equity in proportion to their firm-specific capital: concretely, workers would be paid a fixed wage for the opportunity cost of their general human capital and then in equity for their specific skills.[122] And all important constituencies could be represented on the board (Porter, 1992), despite the opposition of current directors (Neiva, 1995).

A common reaction to this view is that it ultimately makes little or no difference: only firms which are keeping their other ''stakeholders'' satisfied are maximising long-term shareholder wealth, and only those firms which are profitable can pay any attention to other constituencies. But, while this is true in general, in practice there are likely to be many instances of zero-sum games. Another response is that if management is not accountable to the shareholders, then it will be accountable to no one. But the greatest objection is that only the orthodox view safeguards the system from interference in the fundamental *de facto* objectives of the corporation: to seek to maximise profit.[123] For example, some senior members of the current Administration and of the Congress advocate using the tax system to encourage ''good corporate citizenship''. ''Socially responsible'' firms would avoid inefficient downsizing and excessive executive pay and refrain from breaking implicit contracts with their employees. The Administration has apparently wisely decided to pursue such goals in a non-interventionist fashion. For example, moral suasion is being used to urge firms to recognise the importance of worker ''employability'': given the perception of greater job precarity, there is some onus on employers to provide workers with the skills they need to find work elsewhere, should the need arise. But it is also incumbent upon workers to negotiate for training in general skills as part of their compensation packages, wherever that is desirable.

The current policy debate

Corporate governance reform has been on the agenda without interruption for decades. It seems that no observer finds the system at any moment in time entirely satisfactory. However, some urge complete overhaul (Porter, 1992), while others advocate more minor changes. One of the determinants of attitudes towards the urgency and scope of reform is one's faith in economic natural selection. In an ideal world, company founders have the incentive to choose an efficient corporate governance structure, because their claims can be sold in a competitive market. Thus, the case for public intervention in the form of governance rules rests on the existence of externalities and unforeseen contingencies (Hart, 1995). Yet, although it is clear that the corporate governance system is constantly evolving for reasons other than as a result of legal and regulatory changes, it remains much debated whether the evolution is constantly moving it towards greater economic efficiency – to what extent is economic natural selection operant? Some believe it holds only in a weak version: the fitter will survive, but not necessarily the fittest (Williamson, 1988). Others believe that, whatever natural tendency might exist in this direction, it is likely to be more than offset by policy interventions (Grundfest, 1990). If this is the case, then the *status quo* may very well be in need of improvement.

Many observers believe that the US system is in need of greater monitoring. Whoever is to undertake that role will need information on performance that is as clear and useful as possible. Even though US disclosure practices are widely regarded as at the leading edge and vital in the operation of the market-based corporate governance system (Lowenstein, 1996), current accounting data are seen by some as too backward-looking in nature and focusing excessively on actual outlays rather than their opportunity cost or the value thereby created (Johnson and Kaplan, 1991); and forward-looking information is rarely provided because of the risk of shareholder litigation (CPC, 1995)[124], another indication of the costly effects of litigiousness in US society. In any case, in order for monitors to do their job effectively and to make clearer the wealth created by the firm and its longer-term viability, accounting data could usefully be supplemented by information on intangible investments which are usually expensed (Myers, 1989; Millstein, 1995*a*).

Probably the most common recommendation is to strengthen the shareholder voice mechanism and allow the possibility of greater shareholder monitoring through the deregulation of voice, at least if some possibly self-imposed constraints are placed on shareholder liquidity (exit); this is, of course, aimed primarily at boosting institutional investor monitoring. Proponents feel that the landmark 1992 SEC liberalisation, while helpful, was insufficient (Black, 1992):

- shareholder communications could be further eased in situations where control is not being sought;
- access to the proxy process could be facilitated, at least for major shareholders (Jacobs, 1991);

– application of the Securities Exchange Act could be restricted, so a voting group of shareholders is not constituted so readily, thereby reducing the risk of private litigation (CPC, 1995);
– an exemption (''safe harbour'') could be allowed for at least some institutional investors from being considered controlling persons, should they try to monitor, for example, by electing a representative to the board (CPC, 1995);
– the 100-investor limit set out in the 1940 Investment Company Act could be relaxed to allow the formation of ''relational funds'' which could provide dedicated, long-term capital (Jacobs, 1991; CPC, 1993 and 1995);[125]
– a parallel proposal is for closed-end ''interval'' funds or pools, similar to European managerial strategic investment companies (Gilson and Kraakman, 1993), which could play the role of ''guardian shareholders'', if the 1940 Act and parts of the Internal Revenue Code were modified (to maintain pass-through tax status);
– investment companies could be exempted from the unrelated business income tax for owning up to say 25 per cent of a firm's equity for the purposes of monitoring;
– most institutional investors' holdings are diversified far beyond the point at which the bulk of gains are realised; the ERISA prudence requirement could be relaxed to allow more focused portfolios which could more easily be monitored (CPC, 1995); on the other hand, ERISA could be tightened up to say that merely hiring money managers is not sufficient to fulfil fiduciary duties;
– taxes on intercorporate dividends could be eliminated so as to eliminate the disincentive for supplier-customer cross-shareholding (Roe, 1994);
– finally, as recommended by the SEC itself in 1992, the Investment Advisers Act of 1940 could be amended to allow results-based compensation for money managers providing services to qualified institutions in order to strengthen performance incentives (Coffee, 1991; CPC, 1995).

Another policy change often proposed has been the overhaul of the Glass-Steagall Act in order to allow somewhat greater voice in the governance process by large financial institutions (Kester, 1992). Few advocate its entire elimination, however; rather, most believe that the prohibition of non-financial firms owning banks should be retained (Twentieth Century Fund, 1992). An alternative, less radical approach for the Federal Reserve is to ease the restrictions on banks' securities operations (see Chaper II). It is especially important to small firms that banks be allowed to underwrite their debt and equity offerings, a need not currently being well met (CPC, 1995). In any case, restrictions on joint ownership of equity and debt could be eliminated (Stiglitz, 1985; Porter, 1992).

Yet many scholars also view strengthened requirements to exercise voice as necessary. For example, the incentives for money managers to monitor may be too weak, given the competitive market for their services and the resulting thin margins they face. Accordingly, monitoring could be required at least indirectly through the relevant federal and state regulators following the Department of Labor's example with respect to ERISA and ordering all other fiduciaries, especially mutual funds, to vote their proxies prudently (Coffee, 1991; Monks and Minow, 1995; CPC, 1995); this would go hand in hand with the proposal to create a new market for proxy advisers, who would be exempt from the risk of being subjected to strict SEC proxy solicitation rules.

Proxy voting procedures and the workings of the board of directors have also come into the limelight under the heading ''corporate democracy''. For example, much debate has taken place over whether multiple classes of shares with differential voting rights should be permitted,[126] or whether in general disclosure is sufficient to protect the interests of shareholders (Rydqvist, 1992; Blair, 1995). Similarly, many oppose the practice whereby proxy votes are currently counted by assuming those not voted are in favour of management and would endorse efforts to limit management's ability to bundle issues on the proxy statement (Coffee, 1991). CPC (1995) also recommends that greater disclosure be required regarding the independence of the members sitting on the nominating and audit committees of the board and, as does Blair (1995), urges full voting rights for employee owners (be they through ESOPs, profit-sharing plans or other means). Staggered and/or longer director terms have been painted both as a mechanism to prevent hostile takeovers and, alternatively, as a way of assuring longer time horizons. In addition, director and executive compensation issues have been at the forefront, with many experts advocating greater performance-based compensation (Jacobs, 1991; Edlin and Stiglitz, 1995), and some defending the idea of paying directors solely in stock. Finally, there would seem to be fairly widespread support for expanding the list of corporate actions which require shareholder approval or which could be forced by a shareholder vote to include: re-incorporation in a different state,[127] issuance of a new class of stock with different voting rights, consideration of a hostile tender offer (not required under the 1968 Williams Act), and adoption of a "poison pill".

Some governance experts have also urged reforms which would further inhibit shareholder exit. The most extreme proposal, made by Lester Thurow (1988), is to link voting rights to holding periods. Less radical would be to set lower capital gains tax rates for longer-term holdings (Stiglitz, 1985; Porter, 1992; Twentieth Century Fund, 1992; CPC, 1995). Another similar proposal which would have the effect of lengthening holding periods is Tobin's (1984) idea to institute a small tax possibly on all financial market transactions.[128] Such a tax was in fact in effect from 1863 to 1965, but never with a rate in excess of 0.06 per cent. Keynes believed it should be made substantial "in order to mitigate the predominance of speculation over enterprise in the United States" (cited in Jacobs, 1991, p. 85). Thurow (1988) even proposed that quarterly profit reports be abolished in order that investors and managers focus on longer-term results. Finally, bankruptcy law reform – with a view to streamlining procedures so as to eliminate the attractions of privately bargained agreements by improving creditor protection – has also been called for (White, 1989).

A number of institutional changes have also been mooted. One of these is the idea of full-time professional directors to represent institutional investors (Gilson and Kraakman, 1991), similar to the British Promotion of Non-Executive Directors System (PRO-NED). While their effective independence might be questioned, and they may cause as many agency problems as they solve, they could help break down the allegedly clubby atmosphere in the boardroom. A further question which has been debated in the context of clarifying the appropriate fiduciary role of public pension funds in the corporate governance system has been their independence from state politicians. From time to time the latter have attempted to raid the funds in order to finance projects which cannot for one reason or another be financed on budget. So-called "economically targeted investments" are made at below-market rates of return; they recently amounted to an average of 4.6 per cent of the total assets of the 20 largest public funds, nearly $30 billion (Hawley and Williams, 1996).

The implications for performance

Ultimately, there are two issues that have to be addressed: first, whether the US system of corporate governance provides an efficient framework for new business startup, job creation and destruction, capital allocation, tangible and intangible investment and productivity performance; and, second, whether there exists the flexibility in legal and regulatory institutions to allow the system to develop in response to the changing environment. Unfortunately, the direct evidence on the first set of linkages is extremely limited, and it would be misleading to attribute, even in part, the US record to either the specifics or overall character of the corporate governance structure. For much of the evolution of public attitudes towards US corporate performance and the corporate governance system more generally can be explained by macroeconomic conditions: for example, US firms and the US system were most heavily criticised in the late 1980s when the effects of the earlier high real exchange rate were most pernicious; and they have been widely praised in recent years when that has been reversed, and when US macroeconomic performance has outpaced those of major trading partners. The remainder of this section will nevertheless try to answer these questions by discussing some of the specific issues that have been intensely debated in the United States in recent years. However, it does seem fair to say that the US governance system has, at the very least, not significantly inhibited recent corporate performance.

Has market-based monitoring led to short-termism?

Relying on the financial markets to achieve good corporate performance has been criticised by a number of experts on the grounds that they are excessively volatile, unduly concerned with short-term outcomes and subject to periodic speculative bubbles (Jacobs, 1991; Porter, 1992; Twentieth Century Fund, 1992); this, it is alleged, has led to a ''time horizon'' problem which has manifested itself in the form of low rates of both tangible and intangible investment and an excessive focus on projects with short-term payoffs. While US financial markets are undoubtedly the world's deepest and most efficient and may well rapidly reflect all available information, that information may be incomplete (as implied by the shortcomings of accounting data, described above), of poor quality or inefficiently transmitted (CPC, 1995).[129] The primary problem has been described as ''the distant relationship between providers of capital (shareholders and lenders) and users of capital (corporate managers)'' which has led to the ''commoditisation'' of corporate capital (Jacobs, 1991, p. 10). Others have referred to a lack of co-operation or even an outright conflict between owners and managers in combination with a low-trust market-based system as leading to short-termist behaviour and underinvestment (Dickerson *et al.*, 1995). It is largely because of this problem that proponents justify the anti-takeover legislation passed in the 1980s as well as the various proposals to institute transactions taxes or to make the capital gains tax rate a function of holding periods. Of course, if true, it would imply that in some sense managers were too sensitive to short-term shareholder interests rather than the contrary, as held in the orthodox model.

The evidence cited in favour of the hypothesis of ''short termism'' follows a number of tracks, but much is indirect and, overall, it is not entirely persuasive; indeed, many of the ''long-termist'' decisions made by foreign firms have proved to be ''goldplating'', that is have involved products or features which customers are unwilling to pay for (McKinsey Global Institute, 1996). One piece of evidence proponents of the ''short termism'' critique point to is that if the compensation of portfolio managers is based on performance at all, then it is most often on short-term results. But if the market is efficient, then it is unnecessary to lengthen the period over which to reward investment managers, as all relevant information will have been discounted in any case. Second, average holding periods have shortened noticeably over time: US stocks are now held an average of 500 days, down from seven years in 1960. This reflects the increasing institutional ownership of equity, described above. Mutual funds are especially accused of having short holding periods and time horizons, given their need for liquidity and pressures for performance, but what little evidence does exist indicates that non-indexed pension funds have equally short holding periods (Table 28). However, holding periods elsewhere are often no longer: in Germany, for example, average holding periods for the relatively few listed corporations are less than a year (Table 29).[130] And it is less than perfectly clear whether short investor holding periods imply short managerial time horizons. Nevertheless, the cost of all this trading is enormous: stock trading commissions amounted to one-sixth of total corporate profits in 1987 (Jacobs, 1991).

Third, some have charged that markets undervalue investments with longer-term payoffs, such as research and development: Malkiel (1992), for example,

Table 28. **Shareholdings and turnover by type of investor**

12 months ending 30 September 1990

	Equity holdings December 1989 ($ billion)	Per cent		Dollar turnover ($ billion)	Share of volume	Time horizon (years)
		Ownership	Turnover			
Pension funds	957	25.0	45	434	32.0	2.2
of which:						
Active	766	20.0	53	406	29.9	1.9
Passive (indexed)	191	5.0	14	28	2.0	7.1
Foundations/endowments	82	2.1	22	18	1.3	4.5
Households	2 055	53.7	22	447	33.0	4.5
of which:						
Self directed	1 723	45.0	21	361	20.0	4.8
Bank trust departments	332	8.7	26	86	6.4	3.8
Insurance companies	211	5.5	40	84	6.2	2.5
Mutual funds	240	6.3	53	127	9.4	1.9
Foreign	257	6.7	91	234	17.3	1.1
Other/unexplained	11	0.3	103	11	0.8	1.0
Total for non-members	3 813	99.6	36	1 356	100.0	2.8
Exchange member firms	14	0.4	3 211	449	24.9	0.03
Total	3 827	100.0	47	1 805	100.0	2.1

Source: Froot *et al.* (1992).

alleged that the stock market is myopic and that this myopia had worsened in the 1980s. Subsequent work by Hall and Hall (1993) confirmed the existence of an unexplained return-on-equity premium, but they went on to show that the unexplained premium shrank in the 1980s and possibly disappeared in the 1990s. Most importantly for the purposes of the present chapter they found that high-earnings and advertising-intensive firms face *higher* discount rates, while research-and-development-intensive firms and firms with high ratios of fixed investment to assets face *lower* discount rates (and, for the latter, increasingly so over time). Others too had found that markets do not systematically undervalue fixed investment (McConnell and Muscarella, 1985) nor research and development, at least for high-technology firms (Chan *et al.*, 1990).[131] Nevertheless, financial market efficiency does not imply that managers do not underinvest, as

Table 29. **Equity market turnover rates[1] across countries**

	1994	1993	1992	1991	1990	1989	1988	1987	1986
United States	72.1	70.2	58.9	n.a.	n.a.	n.a.	n.a.	n.a.	n.a.
New York	53.0	52.4	44.7	46.3	47.4	58.6	60.3	87.9	68.5
Japan (Tokyo)	25.6	27.9	17.4	28.8	37.7	61.1	70.2	80.6	67.2
Germany	114.3	135.0	120.3	118.0	144.2	113.6	155.3	158.8	61.9
France	43.0	41.0	33.3	36.6	35.6	38.8	35.8	52.4	45.0
Italy	69.6	47.7	18.6	17.7	26.4	27.2	26.0	25.3	46.2
United Kingdom	39.9	40.5	38.0	36.7	33.1	43.9	43.0	76.2	32.1
Canada (Toronto)	41.6	39.5	24.5	22.8	20.6	26.6	23.7	36.9	26.7
Australia	44.0	40.0	32.1	36.9	32.6	28.1	23.7	48.0	34.9
Austria	28.2	27.1	20.6	28.3	n.a.	n.a.	n.a.	n.a.	n.a.
Belgium	15.0	15.4	11.8	10.0	9.6	12.5	17.2	18.5	15.2
Denmark	54.1	55.9	40.7	24.2	28.8	42.4	22.3	10.7	11.8
Finland	43.0	45.1	16.7	8.9	14.5	25.1	28.7	39.4	21.6
Luxembourg	1.1	1.4	1.0	1.4	1.8	0.7	0.6	0.4	0.6
Mexico	44.5	36.8	37.0	43.9	56.7	56.6	42.3	138.0	105.1
Netherlands	35.4	33.2	33.6	30.1	27.0	37.2	33.3	46.8	42.3
New Zealand	26.8	32.6	20.9	24.2	6.4	7.2	7.5	13.4	16.1
Norway	54.0	75.7	49.5	52.8	54.5	63.7	35.6	80.7	16.6
Spain	54.3	n.a.	n.a.	n.a.	n.a.	n.a.	n.a.	n.a.	n.a.
Madrid	n.a.	39.0	30.3	31.9	30.5	32.1	26.9	52.0	37.1
Sweden	70.6	47.3	30.7	23.4	14.7	16.6	22.4	29.4	39.5
Switzerland (Zurich)	80.4	81.8	56.3	n.a.	n.a.	n.a.	n.a.	n.a.	n.a.
Turkey	94.2	80.9	68.8	n.a.	n.a.	n.a.	n.a.	n.a.	n.a.

1. Turnover during the year divided by the simple average of starting and ending domestic market capitalisation, all in local currencies. Foreign firms and investment funds are excluded.

Source: Fédération Internationale des Bourses de Valeur (FIBV), *Annual Report and Statistics, seriatim.*

some of their actions are not visible to the markets (Stein, 1989). Conversely, managers could still be making efficient decisions, even if the stock market does not value firms correctly.

Finally, there is a literature which has examined the question of whether the cost of capital is higher in the United States than elsewhere, Japan in particular, and, if so, for what reasons. McCauley and Zimmer (1989) were perhaps the first to point to the phenomenon of high US capital costs. Also, a 1990 survey of US CEOs showed that hurdle rates for US corporations, at about 12 per cent, are far higher than the average real rates of return on bonds and equities (perhaps around 7 per cent) and above corresponding hurdle rates of some 10 per cent in Japan (Poterba and Summers, 1995*a*), although the gap of hurdle rates over rates of return may be even higher in Japan. Possible explanations include a lack of trust (Jacobs, 1991) – something whose wider importance was recently stressed by Fukuyama (1995) – between owners and managers which might raise required rates of return. However, there is no evidence to show that US capital costs are boosted by the alleged excessive volatility of share prices (Froot *et al.*, 1992); indeed, greater institutional ownership, by enhancing turnover and liquidity, may have served to reduce share price volatility and to narrow bid-ask spreads, thereby lowering capital costs. And there has been some degree of international convergence in capital costs in the intervening years, lending doubt to the claim that US markets suffer from systematic agency-related inefficiencies (Frankel, 1991; McCauley and Zimmer, 1994).

The strengths of US corporations

Apart from possibly higher costs of capital, it is widely accepted that the US system has great comparative strength in a number of domains. For example, new businesses are formed extremely rapidly, thanks to the relatively easy availability of start-up finance (see Box 7) and low legal and regulatory barriers. And the initial public offering market is very deep: some estimates say that 3 000 US firms have availed themselves of it to raise more than $150 billion over the past four and a half years. This constant threat of entry spurs existing firms to improve performance. The latest figures show that new incorporations were running at an annual rate of 769 000 per year in the first half of 1995, up from 264 000 in 1970; from 1970 to 1991 the total number of business enterprises, therefore, rose from 9.1 million to 20.5 million.[132] Similarly, the rate of gross job creation in new establishments is possibly the highest of any OECD country, although such international comparisons are fragile at best (OECD, 1994*b*). However, gross job losses in closing firms are also high, as survival rates are rather low. Yet the willingness of capital markets to cut off inefficient firms from access to credit could, in fact, be seen rather as a strength. The bottom line is that firms are free to get started but free to fail as well: Schumpeterian ''creative destruction'' is alive and thriving in the United States.

US firms are also successful on the world scene. Besides their dominance in many export markets, they are the world's premier multinationals. Majority-owned foreign affiliates of US multinational companies generated some $356 billion in gross product (value added) in 1991, nearly one-third of what their US

Box 7. A brief primer on LBO and venture capital funds in the United States

One form of start-up finance is venture capital, usually provided through limited liability partnerships. The supply of such funds grew rapidly in the 1980s thanks to: the substantial cut in the maximum capital gains tax rate to 20 per cent in 1981; the 1980 change in the Investment Advisers Act which exempted private equity partnerships from ceilings in the number of contributing investors; and the 1979 Labor Department ruling allowing pension funds to participate – in 1994 they provided 47 per cent of total capital committed. After the 1987 stock-market crash, supply shrank rather noticeably. In recent years there has been something of a resurgence, however, with some $3.8 billion in annual funds raised and $2.7 billion in new investments. Cumulatively, some half a million US firms have benefited from such financing. Only the United Kingdom would seem to rival the United States in this respect.

LBO funds are similar to venture capital funds in some respects. They too receive most of their capital from institutional investors and are organised in limited liability partnership form. They have also declined in importance since the late 1980s when they raised nearly $100 billion in a single year; today's figure is around $18 billion, but they still control over $500 billion in business assets. Over the past decade there have been over 2 400 LBO deals. Their nature has changed in recent years, however: they now use less leverage and, therefore, take on less financial risk, but they tend to acquire a greater equity stake and, therefore, absorb more business risk.

For more details see Sahlman (1990*b*), Brophy (1995) and OECD (1996*d*).

parents produced and 2.5 per cent of non-US OECD GDP. And such operations are extremely profitable (see Table 4 in Chapter I).

US businesses are major builders of intangible capital by any standards. OECD data on business enterprise expenditure on research and development (R&D) as a percentage of domestic product show that the United States is surpassed only by Sweden, although once that which is government-financed is subtracted out it falls behind Japan and Germany as well. In any case, the result is a technology balance of payments in strong and rising surplus: in 1993 receipts of over $20 billion were more than four times corresponding payments. On the human capital side it has already been pointed out that the lack of long-term relationships and trust may lead to an insufficiency of firm-specific skills, but there is no indication that overall skill levels suffer from problems which are attributable to any failure of the employer-based training system: only new recruits get relatively little training (OECD, 1995*c*), and given heavy job turnover in US labour markets this is undoubtedly efficient.

While there are some difficulties associated with international comparisons, it is now widely accepted that the level of national saving and investment is low, and this has also been blamed on the US business sector in general and the US system of corporate governance in particular in some quarters. It is true that US firms do invest relatively little in fixed capital in relation to their production in comparison with other OECD countries (Table 30). However, the productivity of such capital investments appears to be higher than at least those made by Japanese and German firms, by some recent estimates 50 per cent higher, with

Table 30. **Business sector investment-output ratios**

Per cent

	Averages for all available years in the			
	1960s	1970s	1980s	1990s
United States	12.3	13.8	14.5	11.9
Japan	21.0	19.5	18.7	20.5
Germany	17.0	15.5	15.1	16.5
Western Germany	–	–	–	15.1
France	18.1	17.4	15.6	15.2
Italy	17.5	16.5	14.4	13.3
United Kingdom	10.5	12.2	14.6	14.4
Canada	17.1	17.7	17.1	14.5
Australia	19.9	18.6	21.1	16.8
Austria	20.9	22.4	19.7	21.6
Belgium	..	16.0	13.9	15.6
Denmark	17.4	16.6	17.0	16.1
Finland	20.7	21.5	20.3	16.0
France	18.1	17.4	15.6	15.2
Greece	11.3	14.3	13.8	14.8
Iceland	..	..	18.7	14.6
Ireland	15.7	20.1	17.6	13.4
Mexico	..	..	10.1	13.1
Netherlands	..	16.1	14.7	15.2
New Zealand	12.2	13.4	14.9	11.9
Norway	23.4	26.5	26.5	23.6
Spain	18.5	18.8	15.8	16.6
Sweden	16.8	17.6	17.6	14.5
Switzerland	16.7	13.5	14.1	14.1

Source: OECD.

the result that substantially greater new financial wealth per capita is created nonetheless (McKinsey Global Institute, 1996).

The higher capital productivity has allowed US firms to maintain high levels of profitability: real internal rates of return to corporate sector capital have averaged 9.1 per cent over the period 1974-93, well above corresponding German and Japanese rates (7.4 and 7.1 per cent, respectively) (McKinsey Global Institute, 1996). This is a strong indication of efficient capital allocation. Less product-market regulation, a virtual absence of public ownership and a single-minded managerial focus on profits which has possibly increased over time and is certainly high by international standards have boosted price-earnings ratios on US markets to levels unsurpassed elsewhere except in Japan. At the same time, the changing functional distribution of income – the rebound in the profit share in recent years (Figure 30) – has been controversial, given the meagre growth in real compensation and wage rates and the ''downsizing'' which has occurred over the same period. However, this shift should be seen in perspective: first, most wage earners are also shareholders, at least through their pension funds; and, second, the recent trend has no more than reversed the fall in the cyclically-adjusted profit share which had occurred in the second half of the 1970s – much of this merely reflects changing interest rates and therefore the distribution of capital returns among shareholders and debtholders. Also, there is every reason to expect a stabilisation in profit shares in the not-too-distant future: one of the longest-standing features of the US economy has been the long-run constancy of factor shares.

Furthermore, while ''downsizing'' is unfortunate for those involved, and it may well have been abused by some firms which got caught up in a sort of bandwagon effect, it is in fact the natural response of the market-based economy to a need to restructure as a result of changing patterns of demand and technological innovation, and its negative social and human costs of adjustment are relatively well handled by the flexibility and mobility features of US labour markets (see Chapter III). In some sense then, the tendency of US firms to downsize is a strength: avoidance of adjustment merely creates distortions, delays the inevitable and ties up the resources needed to enter new more dynamic markets. It is no wonder that large private firms in both Europe and Japan are beginning to show signs of engaging in the practice and of paying more attention to shareholder value in their business decisions.

Figure 30. **BEFORE-TAX PROFIT SHARE OF CORPORATE GDP**

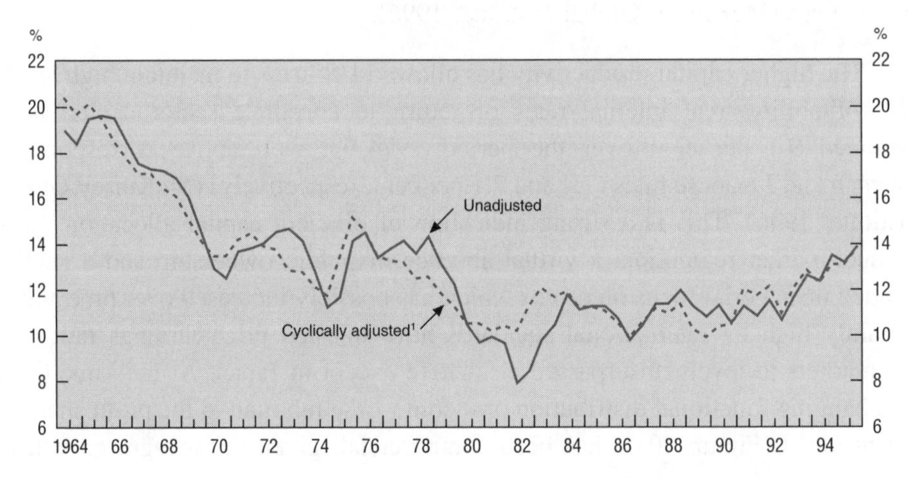

1. Cyclical adjustment derived by means of a regression against the output gap contained in the OECD's Interlink model.

Source: OECD.

The flexibility to meet future challenges to the system

Probably the most important structural change which can be foreseen for the next decade will be the effect of ageing populations – on product markets, labour markets, medical care requirements, public finances and financial markets. In anticipation of these new demands it is essential that OECD economies have the wherewithal to provide the baby boom generation with the appropriate savings incentives and vehicles to prepare adequately for retirement. At the same time, individual working careers may become much more varied than in the past, with the possible spread of human-capital-intensive ''holistic'' firms (Lindbeck and Snower, 1996)[133] and ''virtual'' corporations (which are established to meet some temporary market and then disband when the need has been met) and with the development of new technologies which sidestep entry barriers and eliminate scale economies. In such an environment job transitions will have to be made more ''seamless'', with greatly improved pension portability, for example. Individuals will also undoubtedly have to take on greater responsibilities than heretofore to save for their own old age. The United States, along with the United

Kingdom, would appear to be uniquely positioned, given the strength and experience of their private pension funds and the burgeoning size and variety of their mutual funds, to cope with these needs. The combination of active and competitive financial institutions, which are increasingly attentive to the performance of the companies in their portfolios and ready to correct managerial failures when discovered, and corporate governance structures which are appropriately focused on shareholder value looks the best bet for dealing with this test.

With its history of financial innovation the United States may also be well placed to try out new business financing forms. Equity has served the system well by providing stable capital to firms and diversification possibilities to investors. But with ever-deeper capital markets it may be that in future a new kind of liquid security may prove attractive: one that combines the characteristics of debt and equity but without control rights, leaving a new more stable form of equity to be held only by those willing to give up liquidity and risk-spreading in return for control rights and responsibilities. This would differ from preferred shares which do not participate in upward earnings surprises and growth.

It is only the market segmentation – especially the limits put on banks – which may possibly still handicap US fiduciaries excessively. But with ongoing deregulation, it now seems that the system is evolving so as to correct at least some of the weaknesses inherent in the market-based governance model and to allow new governance forms to emerge, as is shown with respect to changes brought about by shareholder activism, venture capital funds and LBO associations, for example. The one remaining difficulty would seem to be that of non-owner stakeholders. The interests of communities must necessarily be handled by their elected representatives, but it is debtholders and particularly employees who are ill represented at present in US governance fora, especially in view of the fact that fewer than one in eight private sector employees are represented by a union. It would seem logical that a more extensive use of equity-based compensation might be the best way of providing employees with voice and returns commensurate with their human capital input.[134] This may not be happening spontaneously to a greater degree because of the measurement and accounting problems involved. But otherwise there is little reason to believe that the information, monitoring and incentive problems of modern organisations and markets are not being dealt with at least as well in the United States as elsewhere.

Notes

1. Although state balanced budget restrictions often exclude investment activities, state governments tend to cut capital budgets when revenue growth weakens.
2. The improvement in the saving-investment balance (0.5 percentage point of GDP) far exceeded the improvement of the current account balance (0.1 percentage point of GDP); the difference is accounted for by the statistical discrepancy.
3. Using the establishment survey the growth in jobs is significantly stronger over the period; only a portion of the difference can be accounted for by differences in coverage and definition. For example, from the fourth quarter of 1994 to the fourth quarter of 1995 the establishment survey showed employment gains of 2.2 million, while the household survey recorded a gain of 0.9 million. Of the difference, only 0.4 million reflects differences in definitions (exclusion of self employment and agricultural employment from the establishment survey and increased number of multiple job holders, which appears as additional jobs in the establishment survey but not added employment in the household survey).
4. The ECI is a true wage index in that the weights of different types of employees, as distinguished by occupation and industry, are held constant over time. For this reason it is a superior measure of wage growth than average hourly earnings (AHE) which allows weights to shift with changing patterns of employment. However, the AHE has some advantages. For example, it picks up higher costs due to increased use of overtime which is missed by the ECI. Also, it is available on a more timely basis.
5. This figure refers to employment on the payrolls of manufacturing establishments. It may not fully reflect developments in the manufacturing sector to the extent that outsourcing and the related shift of jobs from manufacturing establishments to non-manufacturing establishments (such as legal, engineering or janitorial services) has increased.
6. Some evidence of this is that core consumer goods inflation has eased somewhat over the first half of 1996, while core services inflation has edged up. That said, the link between producer prices and consumer prices is not hard and fast.
7. The peak-to-peak growth rate was 1.1 per cent from 1973 to 1979, 1.0 per cent from 1979 to 1990 and 1.0 per cent from 1990 to 1995. Of course because of the cyclical nature of productivity growth very different patterns emerge when other periods are chosen.
8. It has been shown that the the productivity increases stemming from adoption of electric motors beginning in the late nineteenth century were not fully achieved until the 1920s when production processes were overhauled.

9. In 1995 the BLS modified its estimation procedures for food and owners equivalent rent, which BLS estimated to reduce CPI growth by 0.1 per cent. In mid-1996, they instituted procedures to reduce formula bias, see Box 2 (0.1 to 0.2 per cent). In 1997 they will modify procedures for medical services (0.1 per cent), and in 1998 the BLS is scheduled to update the market basket to reflect new spending patterns (0.2 per cent). According to the Administration, the largest potential biases – quality measurement and adjustments for new goods – will not be addressed by these changes (US Office of Management and Budget, 1996).
10. This draft legislation would, in essence, call on the Federal Reserve to define what constitutes price stability, maintain monetary policy in order to attain that goal and keep the Congress informed as to progress in meeting it. Opinions vary widely both among FOMC members and others as to the desirability of setting quantified official inflation targets as an alternative to the monetary aggregates for communicating its intended longer-run inflation path – see Haldane (1995) for a recent review. The question is whether such a course of action would enhance credibility, thereby shaving the costs of achieving price stability and allowing temporary responses to the development of economic slack without stimulating inflation concerns. In any case, a good track record itself is extremely valuable in achieving such credibility.
11. This is not merely an empirical question. The question of the theoretical and moral implications of comparing utility across different generations has been debated in the profession for decades.
12. Futures rates on federal funds do not reflect only expectations, as risk premia rise with the length of the time horizon.
13. Yet investors did not grow disheartened: this is exemplified by the persistent unusually wide gap between the rates on federal funds and on three-month Treasury bills.
14. There is by now a fair amount of experience with indexed bonds in other OECD Member countries. At least six now include them in their debt management arsenal: the United Kingdom, Canada, Australia, New Zealand, Sweden and Iceland. Recent interest rates vary from around 3¾ per cent in the UK case to about 5¾ to 6 per cent for New Zealand and Iceland. In general, returns to savers have been moderately lower than on conventional bonds, demonstrating the existence of the risk premium.
15. Admittedly, this figure is heavily influenced by the depreciation of the Mexican peso and would therefore be much smaller if adjusted for inflation differentials.
16. Such funds are reported to have taken advantage of the aforementioned short-term interest rate spread with Japan, which reached about 5 percentage points late in 1995, to borrow in yen and use the proceeds to buy medium- and long-term US Treasury notes, thereby strengthening the dollar against the yen and boosting Treasurys' prices (at least until mid-winter).
17. While no official data exist, it is also likely that US residents raised their share of total non-US public debt in 1995.
18. The principal changes in tax policy were raising marginal income tax rates for the highest income groups (expected to raise about $25 billion in FY 1995), removing the wage cap for the Medicare portion of social security contributions ($7 billion), reducing corporate tax expenditures ($8 billion) and boosting excise tax rates on some fuels ($6 billion).

19. More detail on the budget debate is provided in Annex II.

20. In addition, some of the bills were vetoed by the President, in part because of disagreements about non-budgetary clauses which were included in the bills.

21. The first shutdown occurred from 14 November through 17 November, idling an estimated 800 000 of the 2 million federal civilian employees. The second shutdown lasted from 16 December until 5 January 1996 during which time 280 000 were furloughed and another 476 000 ''emergency workers'' worked without pay. The second shutdown affected fewer workers because additional appropriations bills had been passed by that time. An estimate of the real output lost due to the shutdowns would be about $1 1/4 billion – reducing the fourth quarter's annual rate of growth by about 0.3 percentage point. The Bureau of Economic Analysis (BEA) estimated that real non-defence compensation fell $1.4 billion, while nominal spending fell only $0.2 billion in the fourth quarter, consistent with 28 000 lost employee-years at an average of $50 000 per person.

22. A rough breakdown of the improvement would be net saving of $10 to $15 billion from new spending legislation (principally lower discretionary spending and higher agricultural subsidies) which is partially offset by the expiration of the excise taxes, some $30 to $35 billion for the better economic outlook, especially for interest rates, and $35 to $40 billion of changes to technical assumptions about taxes and spending such as effective tax rates and medical care price inflation relative to overall inflation.

23. Capital gains realisations are not included in income; thus, increased taxable capital gains realisations appear as a rise in the effective tax rate and a reduction in disposable income. But, the result is that the capacity to consume has risen, not fallen.

24. The major proposals include a non-refundable tax credit for families with children under age 13 of $300 per child initially and rising to $500 beginning in 1999 (at a cost of $11 billion in FY 2000). The credit would be phased out for taxpayers with adjusted gross incomes between $60 000 and $75 000. The Administration proposes that the phase-out ranges for individual retirement accounts (IRAs) be doubled over time and that the $2 000 annual contribution limit be indexed to inflation (reducing revenues by $1 billion in FY 2000). To boost education and training, the Administration has proposed to create a deduction for expenditures on post-secondary education and training, amounting to $10 000 per tax filing unit ($8 billion in FY 2000). This too, would be phased out for high income families. Families could opt for a $1 500 refundable tax credit for the first two years of post-secondary schooling instead.

25. Specifically, if the deficit in 2000 is not at least $20 billion below the CBO's current estimate of the President's policies for that year then the tax cut will be reduced or rescinded and further discretionary spending cuts will be required. The CBO estimates that the deficit would be $105 billion in 2000 under the Administration's policies and, thus, a deficit higher than $85 billion would trigger the contingency plan.

26. The question is controversial in part because of the increase in both legal and illegal immigration in recent years: by 1994 8.7 per cent of Americans were foreign born, up from 6.2 per cent in 1980 and a twentieth century low of 5.4 per cent in 1960, but well below the figures of more than 13 per cent in the early years of the century. It has been argued that the recent wave of immigrants has fewer skills than its predecessors and that therefore they are

more likely to require government assistance (Borjas and Hilton, 1996) and more likely to drive down the relative wages of the unskilled (see Chapter III).

27. The idea would be to allow individuals with high-deductible (''catastrophic'') health insurance plans to accrue tax-deductible savings to be used solely for medical expenses.

28. By 1990 caps on punitive damages were in effect in 15 states, up from 5 in 1984. Such liability-decreasing reforms may boost the levels and growth rates of employment and productivity in a broad range of industries (Campbell *et al.*, 1995).

29. The OECD measure of labour force participation rates differs from the US Bureau of Labor Statistics measure because the US measure includes those over 64 in both numerator and denominator, while the OECD measure excludes them from the denominator.

30. The direction of causality between some of these factors and labour force participation may run both ways. For example, greater participation rates may reduce fertility rates and boost desired human capital.

31. The distributions for male and female workers are similar. The distribution among the labour force is also roughly similar to that among the employed, although the share of less than high-school graduates would be a bit higher, especially in recent years because of the evolution of relative unemployment rates. For example, in 1992 the share of those who have not graduated from high school would be about 13 per cent of the labour force, compared with 12 per cent of those employed.

32. For a recent example, see Gabriel, Mattey and Wascher (1995). Historically, black migration from the rural south to northern urban areas was also driven by employment opportunities.

33. Gardner (1995) calculates that the displacement rate in 1991-92 was 3.8 per cent. The displacement rate is defined as the number of workers who have held jobs for three or more years and who lose those jobs over a two-year period due to plant closures, insufficient work or abolition of positions or shifts, divided by the average level of employment during the period. Thus, the 3.8 per cent figure is the share that lost their job in either of the two years, and the average annual displacement rate would be half the rate shown in the table. A broader concept that includes all job losers regardless of tenure would be roughly twice that size.

34. Indeed, recent preliminary data on displaced workers show declining displacement rates. There were 4.4 million displaced workers over the 1991-93 period and 3.8 million over the 1993-95 period.

35. See Stevens (1995*a*) and the references therein. Farber (1996) also finds similar results.

36. The level of employment in the goods-producing sector has been relatively constant since the late 1960s. At the same time the distribution of employment within the sector has changed markedly. For example, employment levels in primary metals, apparel and other textile products, and leather and leather products have dropped substantially. Large gains have been registered by printing and publishing, rubber and miscellaneous plastics, and construction. The statistics for total goods-producing dependent employment increasingly understate employment dependent on goods production because of the spreading prevalence of contracting-out of service-type jobs within the sector such as janitorial work, data processing, engineering, etc. (which appear in business services and self-employment).

37. For example US Department of Labor (1994) shows that six of the ten fastest growing industries (by number of employees, not per cent change) had lower-than-average pay and seven of the ten slowest growing industries were above average in terms of pay levels.

38. The absolute changes are subject to criticism that the bias in the price index may understate growth substantially – by 30 to 40 percentage points, if the rise in the consumer price index is biased upwards by the 1.3 to 1.7 percentage points per year that many analysts believe (Diewert, 1996). The widening of the income distribution, though, is unaffected by deflation problems.

39. The Gini coefficient is one of the many measures of income inequality. It varies from zero to one; an increase represents greater inequality.

40. O'Neill (1990) presents evidence that wage differences in the 1980s can be explained by region of residence, years of schooling, age, Armed Forces Qualification Test scores, industry and occupation. This would suggest that wage rate discrimination has been eliminated, but this result is controversial and other researchers still find evidence of discrimination.

41. See for example, Diebold, Neumark and Polsky (1994) and Farber (1994).

42. See Stevens (1995*b*) who finds that while the probability of leaving poverty is 0.5 from one year to the next, the probability of re-entry after one year is 0.3, and that of those that fall into poverty in some year, over 50 per cent of the black individuals and 30 per cent of white individuals will spend at least five of the next ten years below the poverty threshold.

43. For example, pension contributions and health insurance benefits are tax deductible. Health and life insurance companies may be able to offer firms lower rates than individuals because employer-provided coverage reduces the adverse selection problem.

44. The literature on UI benefits, however, indicates that workers in highly cyclical or seasonal industries are well aware of the benefits provided by the programme and that their wages reflect the expectation of benefits. The perceived value of workers' compensation has not been examined in the literature.

45. This result has been disputed by Akerlof *et al.* (1996) who show that the data are plagued by measurement errors which result in spurious nominal wage cuts. That said, they do cite evidence that firms under stress do obtain significant nominal wage reductions.

46. See, for example, Abowd and Freeman (1991) and Borjas and Freeman (1992).

47. A simple back-of-the-envelope calculation based on a constant returns to scale Cobb-Douglas production function (with labour's share of income at 60 per cent of GDP) indicates that a $2\frac{3}{4}$ per cent rise in labour supply generates a $1\frac{3}{4}$ per cent rise in output (holding capital constant) which is split equi-proportionately between labour and capital so that the wage bill rises by $1\frac{3}{4}$ per cent; thus, real wages per worker fall by 1 per cent. As documented by Jaeger (1995), immigrants saw their wages decline relative to native workers with the same education level (in part due to changing relative amounts of work experience), and an increasing share of immigrants were low-skilled workers. Thus, the effective labour supply grew by even less than $2\frac{3}{4}$ per cent, and the 1 per cent estimate should serve as an upper bound.

48. Indeed, studies based on microeconomic data, such as Altonji and Card (1991), often find no effect of the level of immigrants in metropolitan areas and local wages. One reason for this is probably that capital will tend to expand in areas with growing labour supply. This can happen among regions in a country and among countries. The increased foreign capital inflows in the 1980s may in part reflect the additional labour supply. In addition, US labour is mobile and will also shift to equate wages across geographic areas.

49. The precise experiment is that in the counterfactual case the immigrant work force evolves in the same way as the native work force, that is the level of dropouts declines by 39 per cent and the level of college graduates rises by 43 per cent over the decade. The change in relative wages is based on an elasticity of substitution of 1.5 between college-educated workers (including 30 per cent of those with some college) and others and an elasticity of 9 between dropouts and high-school graduates (including 70 per cent of those with some college). Jaeger (1995) has calculated higher estimates, reflecting his use of data for the 50 largest metropolitan areas which experienced a stronger growth of low-skilled immigrants. Borjas, Freeman and Katz (1992) generally report smaller estimates, reflecting much higher elasticities of substitution between skill groups.

50. The literature concerning the effect of trade has recently been reviewed by Freeman (1995). He concludes that ''trade matters, but it is neither all that matters nor the primary cause of observed changes''. The literature on foreign investment and foreign outsourcing is perhaps more inconclusive still. Slaughter (1995) shows that outsourcing by multinationals contributed very little to the rise in relative demand towards skilled labour. Feenstra and Hanson (1996), however, find that outsourcing can account for 30 to 50 per cent of the increase in the relative demand for skilled labour. The main difference between the two papers is the definition of outsourcing. Slaughter includes transactions with foreign subsidiaries but, unlike Feenstra and Hanson, ignores transactions involving independent foreign suppliers. Both papers tend to overstate the effect of outsourcing by including the growing trade deficit as a source of job losses as opposed to job shifts from tradeables towards non-tradeables.

51. The trade deficit in goods and services is the result of the savings and investment imbalance. For example, in the Mundell-Fleming model an increase in government purchases (a decrease in domestic saving) is fully offset by an appreciation of the exchange rate and deterioration of the trade account (to import foreign saving). In this example, there is a shift in production from tradeable goods towards government purchases – the composition but not the level of employment is altered.

52. In the 1994 *OECD Employment Outlook*, the United States and United Kingdom were ranked as the countries with the lightest regulatory framework.

53. For example, the US Labor Department's employee benefits survey shows that 41 per cent of employees of medium and large establishments were covered by formal severance pay plans in 1991 and 15 per cent of the employees at small establishments were covered in 1992. One would expect that ''good employer behaviour'' is rewarded in the market place by greater employee loyalty and lower compensation costs; employees seem to trade lower pay for greater security. For example, recently concluded negotiations by the UAW focused on job security.

54. From the mid-1960s to the early 1990s average and marginal income tax rates were little changed for those at one-half median income, median income and twice median income,

while average and marginal Social Security tax rates rose. In 1965 the combined average and marginal tax rates were 12 and 17 per cent, respectively, for a four-person family at median income. Tax rates peaked in 1981 at 25 and 37 per cent, and in 1990 they were 25 and 30 per cent.

55. Leonesio (1990) reviewed the earnings test literature and found that eliminating the test would have only a minor impact on labour supply. Its impact on reported earnings may be more significant because some workers will shift compensation towards wages from other income (fringe benefits, company profits, etc.) when the implicit wage tax is dropped.

56. Lumsdaine (1995) provides a complete review of the literature on labour supply and the retirement decision.

57. In 1995, the tax base ranged from $7 000 in a dozen states to $25 500 in Hawaii; the average level, weighted by employment was about $9 000. The basic statutory tax rate is 5.4 per cent, but rates for individual employers vary from 0 to 10 per cent because of experience rating, the degree of which varies by state. The average rate on taxable payroll was 2.4 per cent, and the average rate on total payroll was 0.9 per cent.

58. The full range is from $130 to $5 200, but 32 states fall into the quoted range.

59. Those with only two quarters of employment are generally entitled to about 13 weeks of benefits. The extended benefits may be triggered if the state's total unemployment rate is over 6.5 per cent and is at least 110 per cent of the rate it was two years earlier or if its insured unemployment rate meets similar criteria. In addition, near the end of each recession since 1970, temporary extended benefit programmes have been enacted that in general were renewed until the national unemployment rate fell to around 7 per cent.

60. For example, 40 per cent of claimants exhausted their regular benefits in 1992, and a substantial portion of those receiving extended benefits exhausted these as well.

61. Statement of purpose in the original Social Security Act of 1935.

62. Specifically, they construct two measures of household welfare using consumption data and show that the welfare level of households receiving unemployment benefits is only 4 to 8 per cent lower than that of non-recipient households once adjusted for family size and other household characteristics, and the difference is particularly small for households with lower levels of education.

63. The *ad hoc* extension of time limits towards the ends of recessions probably is an important aid to benefit adequacy.

64. These figures are cited in the review article by Atkinson and Micklewright (1991). The same effect of benefit levels is found by Poterba and Summers (1995*b*).

65. For example, since unemployment benefits require prior work history, the potential for qualifying for benefits makes the transition to employment more attractive, particularly for jobs with uncertain tenures. Benefits may also improve job search if time spent and market expenditures are complements in job search. And the requirement to look for work may also boost labour market activity. The financing of benefits, to the extent its incidence falls on labour, may on the other hand reduce labour supply.

66. Anderson and Meyer (1995) find that the industry-specific portion of the payroll tax is shifted onto the worker, while the firm-specific portion is absorbed by the firm. Thus, more

complete experience rating would shift employment away from firms that engage in layoffs frequently to other firms within a market. Work by Meyer and Rosenbaum (1996) indicates that a large share of unemployment benefit claimants experience repeated temporary layoffs by the same employer. This is consistent with the hypothesis that incomplete experience rating leads some firms and industries to receive substantial cross-subsidies, particularly those with strong seasonal variations. The unemployment insurance system hence suffers from the moral hazard problem inherent in most insurance schemes.

67. This credit is fully refundable and for many workers is much larger than income taxes owed. For example, under the 1996 rate schedule, a single individual with two or more children and earning $20 000 would face an average income tax rate of 5 per cent and a marginal rate of 15 per cent. However, under the EITC, the average rate falls to –3 per cent and the marginal rate rises to 35 per cent.

68. Scholz (1996) estimates that the EITC would raise single parents' participation rates by about 7 percentage points and that labour force participation of married primary and secondary workers would barely move. In sum, this effect would boost aggregate hours worked by 145 million hours and raise the labour force participation rate by about 2 percentage points for the low income target group. Those already working would reduce hours worked by an estimated 55 million hours. The estimated increase of 90 million hours of work is about 0.3 per cent of potential hours of work (defined as the product of the target population and 1 800 hours per person) or .04 per cent of total hours worked by all employees.

69. In 1992, a family head with two children and no income could have received $4 875 per year from AFDC and $2 871 worth of Food Stamps. A single individual could have received $1 332 per year in Food Stamps.

70. The combined AFDC and Food Stamp benefit is about 70 per cent of the poverty level, and the typical AFDC head works about 10 hours per week. Assuming a benefit reduction rate of 100 per cent, the effect of these programmes is a 4.6 reduction in hours worked (*i.e.* they would have been about 15 hours without the programmes). Reducing the benefit reduction rate to 25 per cent would only boost hours by an estimated 0.7 per week (Moffitt, 1992).

71. At one end of the spectrum is Parsons (1984), who noted that there was a close correlation between the 4 percentage point increase in DI recipiency rate and the 5 percentage point decline in the participation rate of males aged 45-54 over the 1960s and 1970s. Others have found much smaller effects. Bound (1989), cited in OECD (1995*i*), found that a substantial number of men reported themselves disabled and out of the work force before the inception of DI, a disability rate that would have accounted for three-quarters of those on the DI rolls in 1980.

72. An economically disadvantaged individual is defined as one who is a member of a family that receives cash welfare payments or is a member of a family with income below the poverty line.

73. About 10 per cent of primary and secondary students attend private schools, and a small number are taught at home.

74. The funding disparity across states has narrowed considerably, reflecting the desegregation of the South and the narrowing of *per capita* incomes across regions. State governments,

sometimes at the insistence of state courts, have also reduced funding disparities within states. Thus states, in some cases, provide implicit input standards through their efforts to create more equitable financing. In principle, federal grants could also reduce disparities, but the current funding formulas do not achieve much in this regard.

75. See Lynch and Black (1995) for a study on the incidence and determinants of training in the United States.

76. Indeed, the most common reason offered by firms for not offering formal job skills training is that on-the-job training satisfies needs. Formal training is conducted for three main reasons: to provide skills specific to the establishment, to retain valuable workers and to upgrade employee skills in response to changes in technology.

77. The percentage of 25-29 year-old white high-school graduates with four or more years of college rose from 23 per cent in 1976 to 30 per cent in 1991, while the share of black high-school graduates rose from 13 per cent to about 15-16 per cent. Some have found a linkage with the cost of schooling, with the rise in real tuition and fee levels inhibiting black college participation relatively more severely because they are more likely to come from low-income households (Kane, 1994). Interestingly, the difference between the percentages of whites and blacks that have completed at least one year of college narrowed over the same period (45 per cent in 1971 to 55 per cent in 1991 for whites and from 25 per cent to 43 per cent for blacks).

78. The share of non-resident aliens among college students rose from 2 per cent in 1976 to 3 per cent in 1990.

79. Youth unemployment rates are much higher in the United States, but it is much more common for American youths to combine work and part-time schooling, while German university students are required to be enrolled full-time to receive free tuition. Accordingly, 60 per cent of unemployed American 16-19 year-olds and 15 per cent of 20-24 year-olds were enrolled in school, while only 8 per cent of unemployed German 20-24 year-olds were in school.

80. Wage dispersion is inversely related to size of firm, and many industries with large firms tend to lack effective competition. Larger firms may tend to offer standardised pay scales as productivity levels are more difficult to monitor (Davis and Haltiwanger, 1995). Unions may be more effective in industries where there are rents to share, but there seems to be no close correlation between unionisation and industry-specific wage-premia.

81. At the macroeconomic level the basic evidence is found in the faster relative growth of skilled workers. But this could simply reflect shifts in production among industries towards those with greater skill requirements for reasons other than technological change. However, most of the increase in the relative use of skilled workers reflects changes within industries (Berman *et al.*, 1994 and 1995; OECD, 1996*b*). Moreover, firm-level and establishment-level data also point to a positive correlation between use of advanced technologies and of highly skilled or highly educated workers. Siegel (1995), Doms *et al.* (1995) and Krueger (1993) present evidence for the United States.

82. This programme was reviewed in the 1994 *Survey*.

83. The legal framework of investor protection has recently been examined in a comparative context by La Porta *et al.* (1996).

84. In 1991, the United States had 15.1 million non-farm proprietorships and 1.5 million partnerships, as against only 3.8 million corporations, but the latter represented 90 per cent of total business receipts. The focus of this chapter will, therefore, be nearly entirely on corporations. It is only in services other than transportation, public utilities, trade and finance, insurance and real estate that the corporate share of business receipts is less than three-quarters (Annex Table A1). The corporate share of market GDP in the United States – at nearly 60 per cent – would appear to be higher than in most other OECD countries. More than half of the US corporate share is attributable to publicly listed firms, compared with only about a third in Japan and Germany (McKinsey Global Institute, 1996).

85. It has also produced sizeable benefits as well. Small investors could afford to become owners through the division of equity claims into small units. This not only enlarged the pool of prospective providers of capital and created deep and liquid financial markets but also allowed small investors to hold diversified portfolios, lowering risk premia. In addition, henceforth managers would be chosen for their ability and training rather than on the basis of family background. La Porta *et al.* (1996) have recently argued that dispersed ownership is likely only where investor protection is adequate.

86. This is perhaps not entirely accurate: in his *Wealth of Nations*, Adam Smith was already aware of the problem: ''The directors of (joint stock) companies, however, being the managers rather of other people's money than of their own, it cannot be expected that they should watch over it with the same anxious vigilance with which the partners in a private copartnery frequently watch over their own'' (Smith, 1937, p. 700).

87. Today, amongst the largest non-financial corporations the largest five stockholders own about 25 per cent of all shares, slightly more than in the United Kingdom (21 per cent), but well below similar figures for Japan (33 per cent), Germany (42 per cent) and especially Italy (87 per cent) (OECD, 1995*g*).

88. Corporate law in the United States is a state responsibility. Given that the vast majority of large US corporations are incorporated in Delaware, that state's law is especially important.

89. Prior to that, relationship banking, as exists today in most other OECD countries, was much stronger than it has been in recent decades. This appears to have had a number of governance advantages, exemplified by the fact that the mere presence of a representative of J.P. Morgan on a firm's board of directors boosted its stock price by an estimated 30 per cent (Delong, 1991).

90. State laws have also generally restricted interstate banking; only in 1997 will all such restraints be lifted for the first time in 50 years under the terms of the 1994 Riegle-Neal Interstate Banking and Branching Efficiency Act.

91. Even their trust departments are prevented from putting any more than 10 per cent of any trust's assets into any single firm's securities and must maintain what is called a ''Chinese wall'' between their trust and lending activities. The evidence is that they engage in excessive investment in conservative stocks and avoid futures and options due to ''prudent-person laws'' (Del Guercio, 1996); in any case, their holdings of corporate equities have been steadily declining in relative terms. In the governance domain, while generalisations are difficult due to varying trust terms, bank trusts are usually characterised by pro-management behaviour.

92. Similarly, in contrast with other OECD countries, large shareholders rarely hold any of the corporation's market debt (Prowse, 1994).

93. A recent addition in the public employees pension sector is a fund for federal employees set up under the terms of the 1986 Federal Employment Retirement System Act. It is expected eventually to become the largest institutional investor in the world, but it is not permitted to engage in active trading strategies, nor to exercise directly its proxy voting rights. Similar questions are being debated in the Social Security context (see Chapter II).

94. US institutional investors had $11.5 trillion in assets (159 per cent of GDP and 20 per cent of total domestically-held financial assets) at end-1995, up from $6.8 trillion only five years earlier (OECD, 1996*c*). This was over half of all institutional investor assets in the major seven countries (excluding Italy).

95. One very recent measure shows the ratio of CEO to average pay having risen from 42 in 1980 to 141 in 1995. In the late 1980s such multiples for the United States were already triple those found in the United Kingdom and over six times Japanese outcomes. Even if much of this remuneration is performance-based, it is almost always a one-way bet, with no sign that overall compensation varies over time more than that of non-executives. It was only in 1992 that the SEC began to require detailed reporting to shareholders of top executive pay and its relation to corporate performance to shareholders. The government tried to strengthen shareholders' position in 1993 by making the tax deduction for executive salaries in excess of $1 million per year available only if compensation is tied to specific corporate performance goals and if the package and performance criteria are approved by shareholders.

96. Hart and Moore (1995) have recently argued that managers should be compensated for maximising the total net market value of the firm, not just the value of its equity claims. Similarly, the optimal degree of pay-performance sensitivity is negatively related to the variability of firm value and leverage: only if debt is convertible will it be desirable for all providers of capital to the firm to see management compensation closely in line with share-price performance (John and John, 1993; Garen, 1994). For further discussion of this "stakeholder" view of the firm see below.

97. According to Jensen and Murphy (1990), the probability of CEO turnover for firms earning exactly the market rate of return in the previous two years is one in nine; it rises to about one in six (an increase of only about 6 percentage points) if it underperforms by 50 per cent. This represents an average loss to the CEO of $0.28 per $1 000 of shareholder loss; but the range is from $2.25 per $1 000 for small firms to $0.05 for large ones.

98. In particular, while the Modigliani-Miller theorem states that the choice between debt and equity financing has no bearing on the market value of the firm, it is now widely appreciated that this holds only if markets are perfect (in particular information must be complete), the tax treatment of the two is the same, there are no costs of bankruptcy and the two types of finance have no idiosyncratic effects on governance. Given that US taxation has always favoured debt, it is a relevant question why equity is ever supplied by outsiders. Higher risk-adjusted returns (the so-called "equity premium") and weak residual control rights, as well as the regulatory constraints on the banking system, are probably a large part of the answer.

99. Note that the effects on managerial discretion may vary according to the number of creditors and the type of debt: if it is widely dispersed (in the form of bills and bonds as opposed to bank loans), the costs of re-negotiation in times of distress will be higher, enhancing the disciplinary effects, unless the distress is beyond managerial control (Bolton and Scharfstein, 1996). But some observers (*e.g.* Bernanke *et al.*, 1990; Gertler and Hubbard, 1993) have claimed that the costs of re-negotiation fell in the 1980s, blurring the distinction among the various types of debt and between debt and equity.

100. There appear to be no agency costs of debt in Japan, despite evidence of its presence in the United States; higher agency costs may, therefore, explain 10-40 per cent of the average difference in leverage between the two economies (Prowse, 1990).

101. According to corporate law, however, directors have only what are referred to as a duty of care and a duty of loyalty (the avoidance of direct conflicts of interest), neither of which has much to do with either share value maximisation or fiduciary responsibilities (Sahlman, 1990*a*). Some states have gone to unusual lengths to limit directors' responsibilities: for example, in New Mexico directors are not liable even for reckless acts (Monks and Minow, 1995).

102. But proxy contests are relatively rare (there are only about 10 per year), and their effectiveness in boosting operating returns has also been questioned (Ikenberry and Lakonishok, 1993). Nevertheless, there is some evidence that when CEOs are fired, especially in cases of corporate underperformance, board turnover rises noticeably.

103. This pushes US practices further away from those in Japan where fully 59 per cent of boards have no outsiders at all and where banks and corporate blockholders have a more important monitoring role (Kaplan, 1994; Kaplan and Minton, 1994). According to the Investor Responsibility Research Center managers represent about 20 per cent of US board membership, comparable to the level in Canada and France, but well below the insider share of around 50 per cent in the United Kingdom.

104. Approximately 80 per cent of large firms in the 1980s had combined chairmen-CEOs, compared with 30 per cent in the United Kingdom, 11 per cent in Japan and zero in Germany, where it is forbidden by law (Jacobs, 1991). By 1995, however, combined CEO-chairmen were to be found in only 62 per cent of large US corporations, although the figure is still 80 per cent for the top 1 000 (NACD, 1995). Various observers, however, believe that such a separation generates a potential for rivalry and is useful only in a crisis or as part of a succession process.

105. To some extent banks benefit from the expansion of the banking relationship with the borrower, but US firms which get large enough will borrow directly in the commercial paper or bond market. Stiglitz (1985), therefore, recommends that banks be allowed to own equities, but he recognises the moral hazard problem which could ensue in the presence of public deposit insurance.

106. Kester (1992) contrasts the Anglo-American system of contractual and legalistic governance with those based on industrial groups in which agency problems are addressed *via* concentrated equity ownership, with control in the hands of key stakeholders with multiple commingled claims against other firms in the group. Note that US anti-trust laws also

restrain the formation of industrial groups: Dupont was forced to reduce its 25 per cent holding in General Motors in the 1950s, for example.

107. That large shareholders derive derive substantial private benefits from control is indicated by the premia paid for large controlling blocks of shares (Barclay and Holderness, 1989).

108. Of course, these barriers are most inhibiting for small shareholders. But a study by the Employee Benefits Research Institute reports that fully one-third of institutional investors did not have specific guidelines on proxy voting, three-quarters gave no policy guidance to their money managers and 31 per cent did not even know whether their proxies had been voted (Jacobs, 1991).

109. They may also have felt that greater activism was needed to offset the reduced discipline resulting from what was perceived to be the demise of the market for corporate control. As the head of TIAA-CREF, John Biggs, is quoted as saying in Hawley and Williams (1994): ''The significance of shareholder activism is not the three or four laggards you catch – it's that you get the herd to run. We need to scare all the animals''.

110. Union pension funds now hold some $250 billion in assets and, led by the Teamsters funds, have very recently been amongst the most active in terms of advocating corporate governance reforms.

111. Such a course of action goes even further than that favoured by former SEC Commissioner Joseph Grundfest (1993) who urged shareholders to just vote ''no'' on the proxy statement when dissatisfied with managerial performance.

112. In Gilson's (1990) sample of 111 publicly traded firms filing for bankruptcy or privately restructuring their debt, banks ended up with an average of 36 per cent of the firm's common stock. Their subsequent monitoring role more closely resembles that of banks in the Japanese and German systems (Prowse, 1994).

113. However, tax changes made in 1990 made debt forgiveness taxable to the firm and made it more difficult to structure non-taxable exchange offers, providing greater incentives to use the formal bankruptcy process (Wruck, 1990).

114. The determinants of the timing of these waves are discussed in Annex I.

115. Baumol (1991), paraphrasing Dr. Johnson's comment about hanging, says that the threat of hostile takeover ''focuses the mind wonderfully''.

116. This is not a trivial assumption: bidders lose small amounts of wealth on average, as bids may in part be driven by managers' empire-building or other objectives (Bradley *et al.*, 1988).

117. In August 1996 a law was passed retroactively providing tax deductibility to investment banking fees associated with leveraged buyouts.

118. Perhaps the most restrictive legislation was passed in Pennsylvania in April 1990. It contains a ''disgorgement'' provision whereby any owner of more than 20 per cent of a firm's shares must forfeit any profit earned on their sale if that sale occurs within 18 months after a failed tender offer or proxy fight. The result of this law was that after passage listed firms incorporated in the state lost over 9 per cent of their value, about $4 billion (Szewczyk and Tsetsekos, 1992). All told, in 12 states such legislation was passed to accommodate the needs of a single firm. Most other state laws and corporate anti-takeover measures have

probably led to only small reductions in shareholder wealth for firms incorporated or headquartered there – perhaps of the order of 1 per cent (Karpoff and Malatesta, 1989). Thus, with a takeover premium averaging around 40 per cent, they succeed in reducing the probability of takeover by only about 2½ percentage points.

119. This view bears some close resemblance to the systems in some other OECD Member countries where worker influence on corporate decisions is formalised, where creditors' role is traditionally greater and where inter-corporate holdings mean that the firm is more of a co-ordination device for aligning the various interests of the multiple stakeholders. The view is gaining strength among the US public at large as well: according to a Harris poll taken in February 1996 and published in the 11 March 1996 issue of Business Week only 5 per cent of 1 004 adults questioned agreed with the statement: ''US corporations should have only one purpose – to make the most profit for their shareholders – and their pursuit of that goal will be best for America in the long term''. The remaining 95 per cent chose the statement ''US corporations should have more than one purpose. They also owe something to their workers and the communities in which they operate, and they should sometimes sacrifice some profit for the sake of making things better for their workers and communities''.

120. Even in manufacturing and mining alone, the value of property, plant and equipment fell from 62.3 per cent of the aggregate market value of all large firms in 1982 to 37.9 per cent in 1991 (Blair, 1995).

121. The long-term value of loyalty – from customers and investors, as well as employees – has recently been emphasised by Reichheld (1996).

122. The idea that workers should hold stock to protect their firm-specific capital has recently been advocated in order to ensure greater worker support for socially efficient corporate policies – even with respect to layoffs (Lazear and Freeman, 1996). However, as noted in the text above with reference to executives, this proposal would pose a potential problem of overconcentration of workers' assets in the employer.

123. Friedman (1962, p. 133) probably stated this view as succinctly as anyone: ''Few trends could so thoroughly undermine the foundations of our free society as the acceptance by corporate officials of a social responsibility other than to make as much money for their stockholders as possible.''

124. NACD (1995) reports that 37 per cent of all firms which have recently been sued were alleged, following declines in their stock prices, to have violated disclosure rules. the costs of shareholder litigation could be reduced by: fixing a time period to avoid the rush to be first to sue; restricting attorney's fees; and extending the statute of limitations on securities fraud (CPC, 1995). Note that in late 1995 the Congress overrode a Presidential veto and enacted legislation to make it more difficult to win class-action securities fraud suits. It provides a ''safe harbour'' for executives making forward-looking statements about their company's prospects, providing that they are not intending to deceive investors.

125. However, for small business at least, the Act already envisages closed-end funds (business development companies) which offer significant managerial assistance to the portfolio company.

126. In some countries differential voting rights provide a means for separating the two purposes of equity – financing and control. In 1988 the SEC attempted to limit such differences, but this was overturned by the federal courts in 1990. However, all the major stock exchanges adopted rules to this effect in early 1995. Neverthless, a possible sign of the future was the recent floating of a new class of nonvoting stock in Berkshire Hathaway Corporation which will have greater liquidity at the cost of a lack of control. See below for further discussion.

127. In a similar vein Monks and Minow (1995) advocate moving the responsibility for incorporation from the state to the federal level to avoid a race to the bottom in terms of catering to management in the current system. But most corporate lawyers point out that states which count on substantial revenues from incorporation, such as Delaware, make a significant effort to give superior service to business clients.

128. Since stock commissions amounted to $13 billion in 1993, such a tax on equity transactions would not yield much in the way of revenue, however.

129. Various theoretical models have been built to describe how such short termism could be maintained in equilibrium (Stein, 1989; Shleifer and Vishny, 1990).

130. Another source of data, the Federation of European Stock Exchanges, reports that average holding periods for equities traded in Madrid and especially in Paris were also less than one year in 1995.

131. However, such event studies (based on stock price reactions to corporate announcements) may mislead to the extent that the relevant news may often be combined with other news regarding prospects for the investment. For example, firms announcing research efforts are usually convinced of their payoff, and they avoid announcing the abandoning of research projects. In any case, Miles (1993) found that the UK equities market discounts future cash flows excessively.

132. The 1991 figure represents 81.1 firms per million population. By way of comparison, there were only 61.9 in the United Kingdom, 57.8 in Italy and 40.0 in France in the early 1990s.

133. Such firms, in contrast to traditional ''Tayloristic'' companies allocate multiple tasks to their employees and, therefore, have flatter organisational structures, more decentralised decision-making, smaller scale, greater production flexibility and broader product lines. They also make greater use of computers.

134. According to CPC (1995), US employees currently own about $120 billion of equity in their employers, about 3 per cent of the total. But employee ownership programmes have been introduced in only about 4 per cent of all eligible firms, about 10 000 in all. These tend to be the largest publicly traded firms. The most common forms are stock-option programmes, especially 401(k) plans, with stock purchases of some $3 billion per year, and Employee Stock Ownership Plans (ESOPs). There were nearly 10 000 ESOPs covering over 11 million employees in the early 1990s; they benefit from federal tax incentives to the tune of about $1.1 billion per year. Such subsidies may be justified by the evidence they provide about the private performance gains which occur at employee-owned firms, due, in broad terms, to the transformation of the corporate culture they may bring about and by the favourable effects they may have on the overall distribution of income. For further discussion see Blair (1995, chapter 8) and Kruse and Blasi (1995).

Bibliography

Abowd, John M. and Richard B. Freeman (eds.) (1991), *Immigration, Trade, and the Labor Market*, University of Chicago Press, Chicago.

Abowd, J.M. and M.L. Bognanno (1993), ''International Differences in Executive and Managerial Compensation'', mimeo.

Aggarwal, Rajesh and Andrew A. Samwick (1996), ''Executive Compensation, Strategic Competition and Relative Performance Evaluation: Theory and Evidence'', National Bureau of Economic Reserach Working Paper No. 5648, July.

Aizcorbe, A.M. and P.C. Jackman (1993), ''The Commodity Substitution Effect in CPI Data, 1982-91'', *Monthly Labor Review*, 116, 12, December.

Akerlof, George A. (1970), ''The Market for 'Lemons': Qualitative Uncertainty and the Market Mechanism'', *Quarterly Journal of Economics*, 84, 3, August.

Akerlof, George A., William T. Dickens and George L. Perry (1996), ''The Macroeconomics of Low Inflation'', *Brookings Papers on Economic Activity*, 1.

Altonji, Joseph G. and David Card (1991), ''The Effects of Immigration on the Labor Market Outcomes of Less-Skilled Natives'', in J.M. Abowd and R.B. Freeman (eds.), *Immigration, Trade, and the Labor Market*, University of Chicago Press, Chicago.

Amihud, Yakov and Baruch Lev (1981), ''Risk Reduction as a Managerial Motive for Conglomerate Mergers'', *Bell Journal of Economics*, 12, 2, Autumn.

Anderson, Patricia M. and Bruce Meyer (1995), ''The Incidence of a Firm-Varying Payroll Tax: The Case of Unemployment Insurance'', National Bureau of Economic Research Working Paper No. 5201, August.

Armknecht, P.A., B.R. Moulton and K.J. Stewart (1994), ''Improvements to the Food at Home, Shelter and Prescription Drug Indexes in the US Consumer Price Index'', paper presented at the International Conference on Price Indices, 31 October – 2 November, Statistics Canada, Ottawa.

Asquith, Paul and Thierry A. Wizman (1990), ''Event Risk, Covenants and Bondholder Returns in Leveraged Buyouts'', *Journal of Financial Economics*, 27, 1, September.

Atkinson, Anthony B. (1996), ''Income Distribution in Europe and the United States'', *Oxford Review of Economic Policy*, 12, 1, Spring.

Atkinson, Anthony B. and John Micklewright (1991), ''Unemployment Compensation and Labour Market Transitions: A Critical Review'', *Journal of Economic Literature*, 29, 4, December.

Auerbach, Alan J. and David Reishus (1988), ''The Effects of Taxation on the Merger Decision'' in Alan J. Auerbach (ed.), *Corporate Takeovers: Causes and Consequences*, University of Chicago Press, Chicago and London.

Barclay, Michael J. and Clifford G. Holderness (1989), ''Private Benefits From Control of Public Corporations'', *Journal of Financial Economics*, 25, 2, December.

Barro, Robert J. (1995), ''Inflation and Economic Growth'', *Bank of England Quarterly Bulletin*, 35, 2, May.

Baumol, William J. (1991), ''Enterprising Pursuit of Rents and the Case of Takeovers'', *Applied Financial Economics*, 1.

Beatty, Anne (1995), ''The Cash Flow and Informational Effects of Employee Stock Ownership Plans'', *Journal of Financial Economics*, 38, 2, June.

Bebchuk, Lucian Arye (1994), ''Efficient and Inefficient Sales of Corporate Control'', *Quarterly Journal of Economics*, 109, 4, November.

Berle, Adolph A. and Gardiner C. Means (1932), *The Modern Corporation and Private Property*, Macmillan, New York.

Berman, Eli, John Bound and Zvi Griliches (1994), ''Changes in the Demand for Skilled Labor Within US Manufacturing: Evidence from the Annual Survey of Manufacturers'', *Quarterly Journal of Economics*, 109, 2, June.

Berman, Eli, John Bound and Steven Machin (1995), ''Implications of Skill Biased Technical Change: International Evidence'', paper presented at the Expert Workshop on ''Technology, Productivity, and Employment: Macroeconomic and Sectoral Evidence'', Paris, 19-20 June.

Bernanke, Ben S., John Y. Campbell and Toni M. Whited (1990), ''U.S. Corporate Leverage: Developments in 1987 and 1988'', *Brookings Papers in Economic Activity*, 1.

Bhagat, Sanjai, Andrei Shleifer and Robert W. Vishny (1990), ''Hostile Takeovers in the 1980s: The Return to Corporate Specialization'', *Brookings Papers on Economic Activity: Microeconomics*.

Bhagat, Sanjai and Richard H. Jefferis (1991), ''Voting Power in the Proxy Process: The Case of Antitakeover Charter Amendments'', *Journal of Financial Economics*, 30, 1, November.

Bhide, Amar (1993), ''The Hidden Costs of Stock Market Liquidity'', *Journal of Financial Economics*, 34, 1, August.

Bishop, John H. (1996), ''Is the Market for College Graduates Headed for a Bust? Demand and Supply Responses to Rising College Wage Premiums'', *New England Economic Review, May/June*.

Black, Bernard S. (1992), ''Next Steps in Proxy Reform'', *Journal of Corporation Law*, 18, 1, Fall.

Blackburn, McKinley L., David E. Bloom and Richard Freeman (1990), ''The Declining Economic Position of Less Skilled American Men'', in Gary Burtless (ed.), *A Future of Lousy Jobs?*, Brookings Institution, Washington.

Blair, Margaret M. (1995), *Ownership and Control: Rethinking Corporate Governance for the Twenty-First Century*, Brookings Institution, Washington.

Blair, Margaret M. and Martha A. Schary (1993), ''Industry Level Pressures to Restructure'' in Margaret M. Blair (ed.), *The Deal Decade*, Brookings Institution, Washington.

Blair, Margaret M. and Girish Uppal (1993), *The Deal Decade Handbook*, Brookings Institution, Washington.

Blanchard, Olivier Jean, Florencio Lopez-de Silanes and Andrei Shleifer (1994), ''What Do Firms Do With Cash Windfalls?'', *Journal of Financial Economics*, 36, 3, December.

Bolton, Patrick and David S. Scharfstein (1996), ''Optimal Debt Structure and the Number of Creditors'', *Journal of Political Economy*, 104, 1, February.

Borjas, George J. and Richard B. Freeman (eds.) (1992), *Immigration and the Work Force: Economic Consequences for the United States and Source Areas*, University of Chicago Press, Chicago.

Borjas, George J., Richard B. Freeman and Lawrence F. Katz (1992), ''On the Labor Market Effects of Immigration and Trade'', in G. Borjas and R.B. Freeman (eds.), *Immigration and the Work Force: Economic Consequences for the United States and Source Areas*, University of Chicago Press, Chicago.

Borjas, George J. and Lynette Hilton (1996), ''Immigration and the Welfare State: Immigrant Participation in Means-Tested Entitlement Programs'', *Quarterly Journal of Economics*, 111, 2, May.

Bound, John and George Johnson (1992), ''Changes in the Structure of Wages in the 1980s: An Evaluation of Alternative Explanations'', *American Economic Review*, 82, 3, June.

Bradley, M., A. Desai and E.H. Kim (1988), ''Synergistic Gains from Corporate Acquisitions and Their Division Between the Stockholders of Target and Acquiring Frims'', *Journal of Financial Economics*, 21, 1, May.

Brickley, James A. and Christopher M. James (1987), ''The Takeover Market, Corporate Board Composition, and Ownership Structure: The Case of Banking'', *Journal of Law and Economics*, 30 (1), April.

Brickley, James A., Jeffrey L. Coles and Rory L. Terry (1994), ''Outside Directors and the Adoption of Poison Pills'', *Journal of Financial Economics*, 35, 3, June.

Brophy, David J. (1995), ''Financing Innovation and Entrepreneurship in the Twenty First Century'', University of Michigan, Center for the Study of Private Equity, mimeo.

Burtless, Gary (1995), ''Widening US Income Inequality and the Growth of World Trade'', paper presented at the Tokyo Club in Dresden, Germany, September.

Byrd, John W. and Kent A. Hickman (1992), ''Do Outside Directors Monitor Bids? Evidence From Tender Offer Bids'', *Journal of Financial Economics*, 32, 2, October.

Cable, John (1985), ''Capital Market Information and Industrial Performance: The Role of West German Banks'', *Economic Journal*, 95, March.

Campbell, Thomas J., Daniel P. Kessler and George B. Shepherd (1995), ''The Causes and Effects of Liability Reform: Some Empirical Evidence'', National Bureau of Economic Research Working Paper No. 4989, January.

Card, David and Dean Hyslop (1996), ''Does Inflation 'Grease the Wheels of the Labor Market'?'', National Bureau of Economic Research Working Paper No. 5538, April.

Carlson, John B. and Benjamin D. Keen (1995), ''M2 Growth in 1995: A Return to Normalcy?'', *Economic Commentary*, Federal Reserve of Cleveland, December.

Carter, John R. and David Schap (1990), ''Line-Item Veto: Where is thy Sting?'', *Journal of Economic Perspectives*, 4, 2, Spring.

Chan, Sultan, John D. Martin and John W. Kensinger (1990), ''Corporate Research and Development Expenditures and Share Valuation'', *Journal of Financial Economics*, 26, 2, August.

Chevalier, Judith A. (1995), ''Capital Structure and Product-Market Competition: Empirical Evidence From the Supermarket Industry'', *American Economic Review*, 85, 3, June.

Coase, Ronald (1937), ''The Nature of the Firm'', *Economica*, 4.

Coffee, John C., Jr. (1991), ''Liquidity versus Control: The Institutional Investor as Corporate Monitor'', *Columbia Law Review*, 91, 6, October.

Cole, Rebel A. and John D. Wolken (1995), ''Financial Services Used by Small Businesses: Evidence from the 1993 National Survey of Small Business Finances'', *Federal Reserve Bulletin*, 81, July.

Comment, Robert and Gregg A. Jarrell (1995), ''Corporate Focus and Stock Returns'', *Journal of Financial Economics*, 37, 1, January.

Comment, Robert and G. William Schwert (1995), ''Poison or Placebo? Evidence on the Deterrance and Wealth Effects of Modern Antitakeover Measures'', *Journal of Financial Economics*, 39, 1, September.

Competitiveness Policy Council (1993), *The Will to Act*, Report of the Subcouncil on Corporate Governance and Financial Markets, Washington, March.

Competitiveness Policy Council (1995), *Lifting All Boats: Increasing the Payoff From Private Investment in the US Economy*, Report of the Capital Allocation Subcouncil, Washington, September.

Congressional Budget Office (1996), *The Economic and Budget Outlook: Fiscal Years 1997-2000*, May.

Council of Economic Advisers (1985), *Economic Report of the President*, Chapter 6, US Government Printing Office, Washington, February.

Council of Economic Advisers (1996), ''Job Creation and Employment Opportunities: The United States Labor Market, 1993-1996'', mimeo, April.

Currie, Janet and Duncan Thomas (1995), ''Does Head Start Make a Difference?'', *American Economic Review*, 85, 3, June.

Davis, Steven J., John Haltiwanger and Scott Schuh (1994), ''Small Business Job Creation: Dissecting the Myth and Reassessing the Facts'', *Business Economics*, 29, 3, July.

Davis, Steven J. and John Haltiwanger (1995), ''Employer Size and the Wage Structure in US Manufacturing'', National Bureau of Economic Research Working Paper No. 5393, December.

Del Guercio, Diane (1996), ''The Distorting Effect of the Prudent-Man Laws on Institutional Equity Investments'', *Journal of Financial Economics*, 40, 1, January.

Delong, J. Bradford (1991), ''Did Morgan's Men Add Value? An Economist's Perspective on Financial Capitalism'', in Peter Temin (ed.), *Inside the Business Enterprise: Historical Perspectives on the Use of Information*, University of Chicago Press, Chicago.

Demsetz, Harold and Kenneth Lehn (1985), ''The Structure of Corporate Ownership: Causes and Consequences'', *Journal of Political Economy*, 93, 6, December.

Denis, David J. and Diane K. Denis (1995*a*), ''Causes of Financial Distress Following Leveraged Recapitalisations'', *Journal of Financial Economics*, 37, 2, February.

Denis, David J. and Diane K. Denis (1995*b*), ''Performance Changes Following Top Management Dismissals'', *Journal of Finance*, 50, 4, September.

Diamond, Douglas W. (1984), ''Financial Intermediation and Delegated Monitoring'', *Review of Economic Studies*, 51(3), 166, July.

Dickerson, Andrew P., Heather D. Gibson and Euclid Tsakalotos (1995), ''Short-Termism and Underinvestment: The Influence of Financial Systems'', *The Manchester School*, 63, 4, December.

Diebold, Francis X., David Neumark and Daniel Polsky (1994), ''Job Stability in the United States'', National Bureau of Economic Research Working Paper No. 4859, September.

Diewert, W. Erwin (1996), ''Comment on CPI Biases'', *Business Economics*, 31, 2, April.

Doms, M., T. Dunne and K. Troske (1995), ''Workers, Wages, and Technology'', paper presented at the conference on ''The Effects of Technology and Innovation on Firm Performance and Employment'', Washington, 1-2 May.

Edey, Malcolm (1994), ''Costs and Benefits of Moving From Low Inflation to Price Stability'', *OECD Economic Studies* No. 23, Winter.

Edlin, Aaron S. and Joseph E. Stiglitz (1995), ''Discouraging Rivals: Managerial Rent Seeking and Economic Inefficiencies'', *American Economic Review*, 85, 5, December.

Edlin, Aaron S. and Stefan Reichelstein (1996), ''Holdups, Standard Breach Remedies and Optimal Investment'', *American Economic Review*, 86, 3, June.

Estrella, Arturo and Frederic S. Mishkin (1995), ''Predicting U.S. Recessions: Financial Variables as Leading Indicators'', National Bureau of Economic Research Working Paper No. 5379, November.

Fama, Eugene F. (1980), ''Agency Problems and the Theory of the Firm'', *Journal of Political Economy*, 88, 2, April.

Farber, Henry S. (1994), ''Are Lifetime Jobs Disappearing? Job Duration in the United States 1973-1993'', unpublished manuscript, Princeton University.

Farber, Henry S. (1996), ''The Changing Face of Job Loss in the United States, 1981-1993'', National Bureau of Economic Research Working Paper No. 5596, May.

Feenstra, Robert C. and Gordon H. Hanson (1996), ''Globalization, Outsourcing, and Wage Inequality'', National Bureau of Economic Research Working Paper No. 5424, January.

Feldstein, Martin and Daniel Feenberg (1995), ''The Effect of Increased Tax Rates on Taxable Income and Economic Efficiency: A Preliminary Analysis of the 1993 Tax Rate Increases'', National Bureau of Economic Research Working Paper No. 5370, November.

Feldstein, Martin (1996), ''The Costs and Benefits of Going From Low Inflation to Price Stability'', National Bureau of Economic Research Working Paper No. 5469, February.

Fleming, Michael J. (1995), ''New Evidence on the Effectiveness of the Proxy Mechanism'', Federal Reserve Bank of New York Research Paper No. 9503, March.

Fleming, Michael J. and John J. Moon (1995), ''Preserving Firm Value Through Exit: The Case of Voluntary Liquidations'', Federal Reserve Bank of New York Staff Report Number 8, December.

Frank, Robert and Philip J. Cook (1995), *The Winner Take All Society*, The Free Press, New York.

Frankel, Jeffrey A. (1991), ''Cost of Capital in Japan: Update'', *Business Economics*, 26, 2, April.

Franks, Julian R. and Walter N. Torous (1992), ''Lessons From a Comparison of US and UK Insolvency Codes'', *Oxford Review of Economic Policy*, 8, 3, Autumn.

Franks, Julian R. and Walter N. Torous (1994), ''A Comparison of Financial Recontracting in Distressed Exchanges and Chapter 11 Reorganizations'', *Journal of Financial Economics*, 35, 3, June.

Frazis, Harley J., Diane E. Hertz and Michael W. Horigan (1995), ''Employer Provided Training: Results From A New Survey'', *Monthly Labor Review*, 118, 5, May.

Freeman, Richard B. (1995), ''Are Your Wages Set in Beijing?'', *Journal of Economic Literature*, 9, 3, Summer.

Friedman, Benjamin M. (1995), ''Economic Implications of Changing Share Ownership'', National Bureau of Economics Research Working Paper No. 5141, June.

Friedman, Milton (1962), *Capitalism and Freedom*, University of Chicago Press, Chicago.

Froot, Kenneth A., Andre F. Perold and Jeremy C. Stein (1992), ''Shareholder Trading Practices and Corporate Investment Horizons'', *Journal of Applied Corporate Finance*, 5, 2, Summer.

Fukao, Mitsuhiro (1995), *Financial Integration, Corporate Governance, and the Performance of Multinational Companies*, Brookings Institution, Washington.

Fukuyama, Francis (1995), *Trust: The Social Virtues and the Creation of Prosperity*, Free Press, New York.

Gabriel, Stuart A., Joe P. Mattey and William L. Wascher (1995), ''The Demise of California Reconsidered: Interstate Migration over the Economic Cycle'', *Economic Review*, Federal Reserve Bank of San Francisco, No. 2.

Gardner, Jennifer (1995), ''Worker Displacement: A Decade of Change'', *Monthly Labor Review*, 118, 4, April.

Garen, John E. (1994), ''Executive Compensation and Principal – Agent Theory'', *Journal of Political Economy*, 102, 6, December.

Gertler, Mark and R. Glenn Hubbard (1993), ''Corporate Finance Policy, Taxation and Macroeconomic Risk'', *Rand Journal of Economics*, 24, 2, Summer.

Gilson, Ronald J. and Reinier Kraakman (1991), ''Reinventing the Outside Director: An Agenda for Institutional Investors'', *Stanford Law Review*, 43.

Gilson, Ronald J. and Reinier Kraakman (1993), ''Investment Companies as Guardian Shareholders: The Place of the MSIC in the Corporate Governance Debate'', *Stanford Law Review*, 45, 4, April.

Gilson, Stuart C. (1990), ''Bankruptcy, Boards, Banks and Blockholders: Evidence on Changes in Corporate Ownership and Control When Firms Default'', *Journal of Financial Economics*, 27, 2, October.

Gittleman, Maury and Mary Joyce (1995), ''Earnings Mobility in the United States, 1967-91'', *Monthly Labor Review*, 118, 9, September.

Gokhale, Jagadeesh, Erica L. Groshen and David Neumark (1995), ''Do Hostile Takeovers Reduce Extramarginal Wage Payments?'', *Review of Economics and Statistics*, 77, 3, August.

Golbe, Devra L. and Lawrence J. White (1988), ''A Time-Series Analysis of Mergers and Acquisitions'' in Alan J. Auerbach (ed.), *Corporate Takeovers: Causes and Consequences*, University of Chicago Press, Chicago and London.

Gordon, Lilli A. and John Pound (1990), ''ESOPs and Corporate Control'', *Journal of Financial Economics*, 27, 2, October.

Gordon, Lilli A. and John Pound (1993), ''Active Investing in the US Equity Market: Past Performance and Future Prospects'', a Report prepared for the California Public Employees' Retirement System, 11 January.

Greenwald, Bruce C. and Joseph E. Stiglitz (1990), ''Asymmetric Information and the New Theory of the Firm: Financial Constraints and Risk Behavior'', American Economic Association, *Papers and Proceedings*, 80, 2, May.

Grossman, Sanford J. and Oliver D. Hart (1980), ''Takeover Bids, the Free-Rider Problem, and the Theory of the Corporation'', *Bell Journal of Economics*, 11, 1, Spring.

Grundfest, Joseph A. (1990), ''Subordination of American Capital'', *Journal of Financial Economics*, 27, 1, September.

Grundfest, Joseph A. (1993), ''Just Vote No: A Minimalist Strategy for Dealing With Barbarians Inside the Gates'', *Stanford Law Review*, 45, 4, April.

Haldane, Andrew (1995), ''Inflation Targets'', *Bank of England Quarterly Bulletin*, 35, 3, August.

Hall, Bronwyn H. (1990), ''The Impact of Corporate Restructuring on Industrial Research and Development'', *Brookings Papers on Economic Activity: Microeconomics*.

Hall, Bronwyn H. and Robert H. Hall (1993), ''The Value and Performance of US Corporations'', *Brookings Papers on Economic Activity*, 1.

Hamermesh, Daniel S. and Daniel T. Slesnick (1995), ''Unemployment Insurance and Household Welfare: Microeconomic Evidence 1980-93'', National Bureau of Economic Research Working Paper No. 5315, October.

Harhoff, Dietmar and Thomas J. Kane (1996), ''Is the German Apprenticeship System a Panacea for the US Labour Market?'', Centre for Economic Policy Research Discussion Paper No. 1311, January.

Hart, Oliver D. (1983), ''The Market Mechanism as an Incentive Scheme'', *Bell Journal of Economics*, 14, 2, Autumn.

Hart, Oliver D. (1995), ''Corporate Governance: Some Theory and Implications'', *Economic Journal*, 105, 430, May.

Hart, Oliver and John Moore (1995), ''Debt and Seniority: An Analysis of the Role of Hard Claims in Constraining Management'', *American Economic Review*, 85, 3, June.

Haubrich, Joseph G. (1994), ''Risk Aversion, Performance Pay, and the Principal – Agent Problem'', *Journal of Political Economy*, 102, 2, April.

Hawley, James P., Andrew T. Williams and John U. Miller (1994), ''Getting the Herd to Run: Shareholder Activism at the California Public Employees' Retirement System (CalPERS)'', *Business and the Contemporary World*, 6, 4.

Hawley, James P. and Andrew T. Williams (1996), ''Corporate Governance in the United States: The Rise of Fiduciary Capitalism – A Review of the Literature'', background consultants' paper for the OECD, 31 January.

Healy, Paul M., Krishna G. Palepu and Richard S. Ruback (1992), ''Does Corporate Performance Improve After Mergers?'', *Journal of financial Economics*, 31, 2, April.

Helwege, Jean and Paul Kleiman (1996), ''Understanding Aggregate Default Rates of High Yield Bonds'', *Current Issues in Economics and Finance*, Federal Reserve Bank of New York, 2, 6, May.

Hermalin, Benjamin E. (1992), ''The Effects of Competition on Executive Behavior'', *Rand Journal of Economics*, 23, 3, Autumn.

Herman, Edward S. (1981), *Corporate Control, Corporate Power*, Cambridge University Press, Cambridge.

Holderness, Clifford G. and Dennis P. Sheehan (1988), ''The Role of Majority Shareholders in Publicly Held Corporations: An Exploratory Analysis'', *Journal of Financial Economics*, 20, 1/2, January/March.

Hubbard, R. Glenn (ed.) (1990), *Asymmetric Information, Corporate Finance and Investment*, University of Chicago Press, Chicago and London.

Hubbard, R. Glenn and Darius Palia (1995), ''Benefits of Control, Managerial Ownership and the Stock Returns of Acquiring Firms'', *Rand Journal of Economics*, 26, 4, Winter.

Ikenberry, David and Josef Lakonishok (1993), ''Corporate Governance through the Proxy Contest: Evidence and Implications'', *Journal of Business*, 66, 3.

Ippolito, Richard A. and William H. James (1992), ''LBOs, Reversions and Implicit Contracts'', *Journal of Finance*, 47, 1, March.

Jacobs, Michael T. (1991), *Short-Term America: The Causes and Cures of Our Business Myopia*, Harvard Business School Press, Boston.

Jaeger, David A. (1995), ''Skill Differences and the Effect of Immigrants on the Wages of Natives'', US Department of Labor, Working Paper No. 273, December.

James, Christopher (1984), ''An Analysis of the Effect of State Acquisition Laws on Managerial Efficiency: The Case of Bank Holding Company Acquisitions'', *Journal of Law and Economics*, 27, April.

James, Christopher M. and Peggy Wier (1987), ''Returns to Acquirers and Competition in the Acquisition Market: The Case of Banking'', *Journal of Political Economy*, 95, 2.

Jarrell, Gregg A. and Annette B. Poulsen (1987), ''Shark Repellants and Stock Prices: The Effects of Antitakeover Amendments Since 1980'', *Journal of Financial Economics*, 19, 1, September.

Jenkinson, Tim and Colin Mayer (1992), ''The Assessment: Corporate Governance and Corporate Control'', *Oxford Review of Economic Policy*, 8, 3, Autumn.

Jensen, Michael C. (1986), ''Agency Costs of Free Cash Flow, Corporate Finance, and Takeovers'', American Economic Association, *Papers and Proceedings*, 76, 2, May.

Jensen, Michael C. (1989), ''Eclipse of the Public Corporation'', *Harvard Business Review*, 89, 5, September-October.

Jensen, Michael C. (1993), ''The Modern Industrial Revolution, Exit and the Failure of Internal Control Systems'', *Journal of Finance*, 48, 3, July.

Jensen, Michael C. and William Meckling (1976), ''Theory of the Firm, Managerial Behavior, Agency Costs and Ownership Structure'', *Journal of Financial Economics*, 3, 2, October.

Jensen, Michael C. and Kevin J. Murphy (1990), ''Performance Pay and Top-Management Incentives'', *Journal of Political Economy*, 98, 2, April.

John, Teresa A. and Kose John (1993), ''Top-Management Compensation and Capital Structure'', *Journal of Finance*, 48, 3, July.

Johnson, H. Thomas and Robert S. Kaplan (1991), *Relevance Lost: The Rise and Fall of Management Accounting*, Harvard Business School Press, Boston.

Jones, Jonathan, Kenneth Lehn and J. Harold Mulherin (1991), ''Institutional Ownership of Equity: Effects on Stock Market Liquidity and Corporate Long-Term Investments'', in Arnold W. Sametz (ed.), *Institutional Investing: Challenges and Responsibilities for the 21st Century*, Business One Irwin, Homewood, Illinois.

Juhn, Chinhui (1992), ''Decline of Male Labor Market Participation: The Role of Declining Market Opportunities'', *Quarterly Journal of Economics*, 107, 2, February.

Kane, Thomas (1994), ''College Entry by Blacks Since 1970: The Roles of College Costs, Family Background, and the Returns to Education'', *Journal of Political Economy*, 102, 5, October.

Kaplan, Steven N. (1989a), ''The Effects of Management Buyouts on Operating Performance and Value'', *Journal of Financial Economics*, 24, 2, October.

Kaplan, Steven N. (1989b), ''Management Buyouts: Evidence on Taxes as a Source of Value'', *Journal of Finance*, 44, 3, July.

Kaplan, Steven N. and David Reishus (1990), ''Outside Directorships and Corporate Performance'', *Journal of Financial Economics*, 27, 2, October.

Kaplan, Steven N. and Michael S. Weisbach (1992), ''The Success of Acquisitions: Evidence from Divestitures'', *Journal of Finance*, 47, 1, March.

Kaplan, Steven N. and Jeremy C. Stein (1993), ''The Evolution of Buyout Pricing and Financial Structure in the 1980s'', *Quarterly Journal of Economics*, 108, 2, May.

Kaplan, Steven N. (1994), ''Top Executive Awards and Firm Performance: A Comparison of Japan and the United States'', *Journal of Political Economy*, 102, 3, June.

Kaplan, Steven N. and Bernadette A. Minton (1994), ''Appointments of Outsiders to Japanese Boards: Determinants and Implications for Managers'', *Journal of Financial Economics*, 36, 2, October.

Karoly, Lynn A. (1996), ''Anatomy of the US Income Distribution: Two Decades of Change'', *Oxford Review of Economic Policy*, 12, 1, Spring.

Karpoff, Jonathan M. and Paul H. Malatesta (1989), ''The Wealth Effects of Second-Generation State Takeover Legislation'', *Journal of Financial Economics*, 25, 2, December.

Karpoff, Jonathan M., Paul H. Malatesta and Ralph A. Walking (1995), ''Corporate Governance and Shareholder Initiatives: Empirical Evidence'', mimeo, August.

Kessler, Daniel and Mark McClellan (1996), ''Do Doctors Practice Defensive Medecine?'', *Quarterly Journal of Economics*, 111, 2, May.

Kester, W. Carl (1992), ''Industrial Groups as Systems of Corporate Governance'', *Oxford Review of Economic Policy*, 8, 3, Autumn.

Krueger, Alan B. (1993), ''How Computers Have Changed the Wage Structure: Evidence from Microdata, 1984-1989'', *Quarterly Journal of Economics*, 108, 1, February.

Kruse, Douglas and Joseph Blasi (1995), ''Employee Ownership, Employee Attitudes and Firm Performance'', National Bureau of Research Working Paper No. 5277, September.

Lalonde, Robert J. (1995), ''The Promise of Public Sector-Sponsored Training Programs'', *Journal of Economic Perspectives*, 9, 2, Spring.

Lamont, Owen (1996), ''Cash Flow and Investment: Evidence from Internal Capital Markets'', National Bureau of Economic Research Working Paper No. 5499, March.

Lang, Larry H.P., Rene M. Stulz and Ralph A. Walkling (1991), ''A Test of the Free Cash Flow Hypothesis: The Case of Bidder Returns'', *Journal of Financial Economics*, 29, 2, October.

Lang, Larry H.P. and Rene M. Stulz (1992), ''Contagion and Competitive Intra-Industry Effects of Bankruptcy Announcements'', *Journal of Financial Economics*, 32, 1, August.

Lang, Larry H.P. and Rene M. Stulz (1994), ''Tobin's q, Corporate Diversification and Firm Performance'', *Journal of Political Economy*, 102, 6, December.

Lang, Larry H.P., Annette Poulsen and Rene M. Stulz (1995), ''Asset Sales, Firm Performance and the Agency Costs of Managerial Discretion'', *Journal of Financial Economics*, 37, 1, January.

Lang, Larry H.P., Eli Ofek and Rene M. Stulz (1996), ''Leverage, Investment and Firm Growth'', *Journal of Financial Economics*, 40, 1, January.

La Porta, Rafael, Florencio Lopez-de-Silanes, Andrei Shleifer and Robert W. Vishny (1996), ''Law and Finance'', National Bureau of Economic Research Working Paper No. 5661, July.

Lazear, Edward P. and Richard B. Freeman (1996), ''Relational Investing: The Worker's Perspective'', National Bureau of Economic Research Working Paper No. 5436, January.

Lebow, David E., David J. Stockton and William L. Wascher (1995), ''Inflation, Nominal Wage Rigidity, and the Efficiency of Labor Markets'', Finance and Economics Discussion Series, No. 94-45, Federal Reserve Board, October.

Leech, Dennis (1987), ''Corporate Ownership and Control: A New Look at the Evidence of Berle and Means'', *Oxford Economic Papers*, 39, 3, September.

Leonesio, Michael V. (1990), ''The Effects of the Social Security Earnings Test on the Labor-Market Activity of Older Americans: A Review of the Evidence'', *Social Security Bulletin*, 53, 5.

Levine, David (1995), *Reinventing the Workplace*, Brookings Institution, Washington.

Levy, Frank and Richard J. Murnane (1992), ''US Earnings Levels and Earnings Inequality: A Review of Recent Trends and Proposed Explanations'', *Journal of Economic Literature*, 30, 3, September.

Lichtenberg, Frank R. and Donald Siegel (1990), ''The Effects of Leveraged Buyouts on Productivity and Related Aspects of Firm Behavior'', *Journal of Financial Economics*, 27, 1, September.

Lindbeck, Assar and Dennis J. Snower (1996), ''Reorganisation of Firms and Labour Market Inequality'', Centre for Economic Policy Research Discussion Paper No. 1375, March.

Longhofer, Stanley D. and Charles T. Carlstrom (1995), ''Absolute Priority Rule Violations in Bankruptcy'', *Economic Review*, Federal Reserve Bank of Cleveland, 34, 4, Quarter 4.

Lowenstein, Louis (1996), ''Financial Transparency and Corporate Governance: You Manage What You Measure'', *Columbia Law Review*, forthcoming.

Lumsdaine, Robin L. (1995), ''Factors Affecting Labor Supply Decisions and Retirement Income'', National Bureau of Economic Research Working Paper No. 5223, August.

Lumsdaine, Robin L., James H. Stock and David A. Wise (1995), ''Why are Retirement Rates so High at Age 65?'', National Bureau of Economic Research Working Paper No. 5190, July.

Lynch, Lisa M. and Sandra E. Black (1995), ''Beyond the Incidence of Training: Evidence from a National Employers Survey'', National Bureau of Economic Research Working Paper No. 5231, August.

Macavoy, Paul W. *et al.* (1983), ''ALI Proposals for Increased Control of the Corporation by the Board of Directors: An Economic Analysis'', xerox.

Mace, Myles (1971), *Directors, Myth and Reality*, Harvard Business School Press, Boston.

Mahoney, James M., Chamu Sundaramurthy and Joseph T. Mahoney (1995), ''The Differential Impact on Stockholder Wealth of Various Antitakeover Provisions'', Federal Reserve Bank of New York Research Paper No. 9512, June.

Manne, Henry G. (1965), ''Mergers and the Market for Corporate Control'', *Journal of Political Economy*, 73, April.

Martin, Kenneth J. and John J. McConnell (1991), ''Corporate Performance, Corporate Takeovers, and Management Turnover'', *Journal of Finance*, 46, 2, June.

Mason, Edward S. (ed.) (1959), *The Corporation in Modern Society*, Harvard University Press, Cambridge, Massachusetts.

May, Don O. (1995), ''Do Managerial Motives Influence Firm Risk Reduction Strategies?'', *Journal of Finance*, 50, 4, September.

Mayer, Colin (1996), ''Corporate Governance, Competition and Performance'', OECD Economics Department Working Paper 164.

McCauley, Robert N. and Steven A. Zimmer (1989), ''Explaining International Differences in the Cost of Capital'', *Federal Reserve Bank of New York Quarterly Review*, 14, 2, Summer.

McCauley, Robert N. and Steven A. Zimmer (1994), ''Exchange Rates and International Differences in the Cost of Capital'' in Y. Amihud and R. Levich (eds.), *Exchange Rates and Corporate Performance,* Irwin, Burr Ridge, Illinois.

McConnell, John J. and Chris Muscarella (1985), ''Corporate Capital Expenditure Decisions and the Market Value of the Firm'', *Journal of Financial Economics*, 14, 3, September.

McConnell, John J. and Henri Servaes (1990), ''Additional Evidence on Equity Ownership and Corporate Value'', *Journal of Financial Economics*, 27, 2, October.

McConnell, John J. and Henri Servaes (1995), ''Equity Ownership and the Two Faces of Debt'', *Journal of Financial Economics*, 39, 1, September.

McKinsey Global Institute (1996), *Capital Productivity,* Washington, D.C.

McWilliams, Victoria B. (1990), ''Managerial Share Ownership and the Stock Price Effects of Antitakeover Amendment Proposals'', *Journal of Finance*, 45, 5, December.

Mehran, Hamid (1995), ''Executive Compensation Structure, Ownership and Firm Performance'', *Journal of Financial Economics*, 38, 2, June.

Meyer, Bruce D. (1995), ''Lessons from the US Unemployment Insurance Experiments'', *Journal of Economic Literature*, 33, 1 March.

Meyer, Bruce D. and Dan T. Rosenbaum (1996), ''Repeat Use of Unemployment Insurance'', National Bureau of Economic Research Working Paper No. 5423, January.

Miles, David (1993), ''Testing for Short Termism in the UK Stock Market'', *Economic Journal*, 103, 421, November.

Milgrom, Paul and John Roberts (1992), *Economics, Organization and Management*, Prentice Hall, Englewood Cliffs, N.J.

Millstein, Ira M. (1995*a*), ''Corporate Governance in the United States'', xerox.

Millstein, Ira M. (1995*b*), ''The Professional Board'', *The Business Lawyer*, 46, November.

Mitchell, Mark L. and Kenneth Lehn (1990), ''Do Bad Bidders Become Good Targets?'', *Journal of Political Economy*, 98, 2, April.

Mitchell, Mark L. and J. Harold Mulherin (1996), ''The Impact of Industry Shocks on Takeover and Restructuring Activity'', *Journal of Financial Economics*, 41, 2, June.

Moffitt, Robert and Peter Gottschalk (1994), ''The Growth of Earnings Instability in the US Labor Market'', *Brookings Papers on Economic Activity*, 2.

Monks, Robert A.G. and Nell Minow (1995), *Corporate Governance*, Blackwell, Cambridge, Massachusetts and Oxford.

Morck, Randall, Andrei Shleifer and Robert W. Vishny (1988), ''Management Ownership and Market Valuation: An Empirical Analysis'', *Journal of Financial Economics*, 20, 1/2, January/March.

Morck, Randall, Andrei Shleifer and Robert W. Vishny (1989), ''Alternative Mechanisms for Corporate Control'', *American Economic Review*, 79, 4, September.

Morck, Randall, Andrei Shleifer and Robert W. Vishny (1990), ''Do Managerial Objectives Drive Bad Acquisitions?'', *Journal of Finance*, 45, 1, March.

Myers, Stewart C. (1989), ''Signaling and Accounting Information'', National Bureau of Economic Research Working Paper No. 3193, December.

National Association of Corporate Directors and Deloitte and Touche LLP (1995), ''The 1995 Corporate Governance Survey'', March.

Neiva, Elizabeth MacIver (1995), ''The Current State of American Corporate Governance'', draft, Institutional Investor Project, Columbia University, December.

Nesbitt, Stephen L. (1994), ''Long-Term Rewards From Shareholder Activism: A Study of the 'CalPERS' Effect'', *Journal of Applied Corporate Finance*, 6, Winter.

Novaes, Walter and Luigi Zingales (1995), ''Capital Structure Choice When Managers are in Control: Entrenchment versus Efficiency'', National Bureau of Economic Research Working Paper No. 5384, December.

OECD (1993), *Economic Survey of the United States 1993*, Paris, November.

OECD (1994*a*), *Economic Survey of the United States 1994*, Paris, November.

OECD (1994*b*), *OECD Employment Outlook*, Paris, July.

OECD (1995*a*), ''Framework Conditions for Industry Project: Corporate Governance Environments in OECD Countries'', unpublished, February.

OECD (1995*b*), ''Structural Changes in Financial Markets and Implications for Corporate Governance'', unpublished, June.

OECD (1995*c*), *Economic Survey of the United States 1995*, Paris, November.

OECD (1995*d*), *OECD Employment Outlook*, Paris, July.

OECD (1995*e*), *Economic Survey of Germany 1995*, Paris, August.

OECD (1995*f*), ''Social Transfers: Spending Patterns, Institutional Arrangements and Policy Reforms'', unpublished, September.

OECD (1995*g*), *Economic Survey of Italy*, Paris, January.

OECD (1995*h*), *Education at a Glance*, Paris.

OECD (1995*i*), *The Labour Market and Older Workers*, Paris.

OECD (1996*a*), *OECD Employment Outlook*, Paris, July.

OECD (1996*b*), ''Technology, Productivity and Job Creation'', unpublished, February.

OECD (1996*c*), ''Institutional Investors and Financial Markets in OECD Countries'', unpublished, June.

OECD (1996*d*), ''Venture Capital in OECD Countries'', *Financial Market Trends*, 63, February.

OECD (1996*e*) ''The Distribution of Earnings in Selected OECD Countries'', unpublished, July.

OECD and Statistics Canada (1995), *Literacy, Economy and Society: Results of the First International Adult Literacy Survey,* Paris.

Oliner, Stephen D. and Daniel E. Sichel (1994), ''Computers and Output Growth Revisited: How Big is the Puzzle?'', *Brookings Papers on Economic Activity*, 2.

O'Neill, June (1990), ''The Role of Human Capital in Earnings Differences Between Black and White Men'', *Journal of Economic Perspectives*, 4, 4, Fall.

Opler, Tim C. and Jonathan Sokobin (1995), ''Does Coordinated Institutional Activism Work? An Analysis of the Activities of the Council of Institutional Investors'', mimeo, August.

Orphanides, Athanasios and David W. Wilcox (1996), ''The Opportunistic Approach to Disinflation'', Board of Governors of the Federal Reserve System, May.

Parsons, Donald O. (1984), ''Disability Insurance and Male Labor Force Participation: A Response to Haveman and Wolfe'', *Journal of Political Economy*, 92, 3, June.

Petersen, Mitchell A. (1992), ''Pension Reversions and Worker-Stockholder Wealth Transfers'', *Quarter Journal of Economics*, 107, 3, August.

Phillips, Gordon M. (1995), ''Increased Debt and Industry Product Markets: An Empirical Analysis'', *Journal of Financial Economics*, 37, 2, February.

Pontiff, Jeffrey, Andrei Shleifer and Michael S. Weisbach (1990), ''Reversions of Excess Pension Assets After Takeovers'', *Rand Journal of Economics*, 21, 4, Winter.

Porter, Michael E. (1992), *Capital Choices: Changing the Way America Invests in Industry*, Council on Competitiveness and Harvard Business School.

Poterba, James M. and Lawrence H. Summers (1995*a*), ''A CEO Survey of US Companies' Time Horizons and Hurdle Rates'', *Sloan Management Review*, Fall.

Poterba, James M. and Lawrence H. Summers (1995*b*) ''Unemployment Benefits and Labour Market Transitions: A Multinominal Logit Model with Errors in Classification'', *Review of Economics and Statistics*, 72, 2, May.

Pound, John (1991), ''Proxy Voting and the SEC: Investor Protection Versus Market Efficiency'', *Journal of Financial Economics*, 29, 2, October.

Prowse, Stephen D. (1990), ''Institutional Investment Patterns and Corporate Financial Behavior in the United States and Japan'', *Journal of Financial Economics*, 27, 1, September.

Prowse, Stephen (1994), ''Corporate Governance in an International Perspective: A Survey of Corporate Control Mechanisms Among Large Firms in the United States, the United Kingdom, Japan and Germany'', Bank for International Settlements Economic Papers No. 41, July, Basel.

Ravenscraft, David J. and F.M. Scherer (1987), *Mergers, Sell-offs, and Economic Efficiency*, Brookings Institution, Washington.

Reichheld, Frederick F. (1996), *The Loyalty Effect*, Harvard Business School Press, Boston.

Reinsdorf, M. (1993), ''The Effect of Outlet Price Differentials in the US Consumer Price Index'' in M.F. Foss, M.E. Manser and A.H. Young (eds.), *Price Measurement and Their Uses*, National Bureau of Economic Research Studies in Income and Wealth, 57.

Reinsdorf, M. and B.R. Moulton (1996), ''The Construction of Basic Components of Cost of Living Indexes'', to appear in T. Bresnahan and R.J. Gordon (eds.), *New Goods*, National Bureau of Economic Research.

Roe, Mark J. (1990), ''Political and Legal Constraints on Ownership and Control of Public Companies'', *Journal of Financial Economics*, 27, 1, September.

Roe, Mark J. (1993), ''Mutual Funds in the Boardroom'', *Journal of Applied Corporate Finance*.

Roe, Mark J. (1994), *Strong Managers, Weak Owners: The Political Roots of American Corporate Finance*, Princeton University Press, Princeton.

Romano, Roberta (1993), ''Public Pension Fund Activism in Corporate Governance Reconsidered'', *Columbic Law Review*, 93, 4, May.

Rosenstein, Stuart and Jeffrey G. Wyatt (1990), ''Outside Directors, Board Independence and Shareholder Wealth'', *Journal of Financial Economics*, 26, 2, August.

Rosett, Joshua G. (1990), ''Do Union Wealth Concessions Explain Takeover Premiums? The Evidence on Contract Wages'', *Journal of Financial Economics*, 27, 1, September.

Ross, Stephen (1973), ''The Economic Theory of Agency: The Principal's Problem'', *American Economic Review*, 63, 1, March.

Ruhm, Christopher J. (1994), ''Do Pensions Increase Labor Supply of Older Men?'', National Bureau of Economic Research Working Paper No. 4925, November.

Rydqvist, Kristian (1992), ''Dual-Class Shares: A Review'', *Oxford Review of Economic Policy*, 8, 3, Autumn.

Sahlman, William A. (1990*a*), ''Why Sane People Shouldn't Serve on Public Boards'', *Harvard Business Review*, 90, 3, May-June.

Sahlman, William A. (1990*b*), ''The Structure and Governance of Venture Capital Organizations'', *Journal of Financial Economics*, 27, 2, October.

Samuel, Cherian (1996), ''Stock Market and Investment: The Governance Role of the Market'', World Bank Policy Research Working Paper 1578, March.

Scharfstein, David (1988), ''The Disciplinary Role of Takeovers'', *Review of Economic Studies*, 55(2), 182, April.

Schmidt, Klaus M. (1996), ''Managerial Incentives and Product Market Competition'', Centre for Economic Policy Research Discussion Paper No. 1382, April.

Scholz, John Karl (1996), ''In-Work Benefits in the United States: The Earned Income Tax Credit'', *Economic Journal*, 106, 1, January.

Schranz, Mary C. (1993), ''Takeovers Improve Firm Performance: Evidence From the Banking Industry'', *Journal of Political Economy*, 101, 2, April.

Servaes, Henri (1991), ''Tobin's Q and the Gains From Takeovers'', *Journal of Finance*, 46, 1, March.

Sharpe, Steven A. (1994), ''Financial Market Imperfections, Firm Leverage and the Cyclicality of Employment'', *American Economic Review*, 84, 4, September.

Shiller, Robert J. (1992), ''Who is Minding the Store?'' in Twentieth Century Fund (1992).

Shleifer, Andrei and Robert W. Vishny (1986), ''Large Shareholders and Corporate Control'', *Journal of Political Economy*, 94, 3, Part 1, June.

Shleifer, Andrei and Lawrence H. Summers (1988), ''Breach of Trust in Hostile Takeovers'' in Alan J. Auerbach (ed.), *Corporate Takeovers: Causes and Consequences*, University of Chicago Press, Chicago and London.

Shleifer, Andrei and Robert W. Vishny (1990), ''Equilibrium Short Horizons of Investors and Firms'', American Economic Association, *Papers and Proceedings*, 80, 2, May.

Shleifer, Andrei and Robert W. Vishny (1996), ''A Survey of Corporate Governance'', National Bureau of Economic Research Working Paper No. 5554, April, *Journal of Finance*, forthcoming.

Short, Helen (1994), ''Ownership, Control, Financial Structure and the Performance of Firms'', *Journal of Economic Surveys*, 8, 3, September.

Siegel, Donald (1995), ''The Impact of Computers on Manufacturing Productivity Growth: A Multiple Indicators, Multiple-Causes Approach'', *Review of Economics and Statistics* (forthcoming).

Slaughter, Matthew J. (1995), ''Multinational Corporations, Outsourcing, and American Wage Divergence'', National Bureau of Economic Research Working Paper No. 5253, September.

Smith, Abbie J. (1990), ''Corporate Ownership Structure and Performance: The Case of Management Buyouts'', *Journal of Financial Economics*, 27, 1, September.

Smith, Adam (1937), *The Wealth of Nations*, Modern Library, New York.

Smith, Michael P. (1996), ''Shareholder Activism by Institutional Investors: Evidence from CalPERS'', *Journal of Finance*, 51, 1, March.

Stein, Jeremy C. (1989), ''Efficient Capital Markets, Inefficient Firms: A Model of Myopic Corporate Behavior'', *Quarterly Journal of Economics*, 104, 4, November.

Stevens, Ann Huff (1995*a*), ''Long-term Effects of Job Displacement: Evidence from the Panel Study of Income Dynamics'', National Bureau of Economic Research Working Paper No. 5343, November.

Stevens, Ann Huff (1995*b*), ''Climbing Out of Poverty, Falling Back In: Measuring the Persistence of Poverty over Multiple Spells'', National Bureau of Economic Research Working Paper No. 5390, December.

Stiglitz, Joseph E. (1985), ''Credit Markets and the Control of Capital'', *Journal of Money, Credit and Banking*, 17, 2, May.

Strickland, Deon, Kenneth W. Wiles and Marc Zenner (1996), ''A Requiem for USA: Is Small Shareholder Monitoring Effective?'', *Journal of Financial Economics*, 40, 2, February.

Stulz, Rene M. (1990), ''Managerial Discretion and Optimal Financial Policies'', *Journal of Financial Economics*, 26, 1, July.

Sundaramurthy, Chamu, James M. Mahoney and Joseph T. Mahoney (1995), ''Board Structure, Antitakeover Provisions and Stockholder Wealth'', Federal Reserve Bank of New York Research Paper No. 9516, July.

Szewczyk, Samuel H. and George T. Tsetsekos (1992), ''State Intervention in the Market for Corporate Control: The Case of Pennsylvania Senate Bill 1310'', *Journal of Financial Economics*, 31, 1, February.

Tevlin, Stacey (1996), ''CEO Incentive Contracts, Monitoring Costs and Corporate Performance'', *New England Economic Review*, Federal Reserve Bank of Boston, January/February.

Thompson, Steve and Mike Wright (1995), ''Corporate Governance: The Role of Restructuring Transactions'', *Economic Journal*, 105, 430, May.

Thornton, Daniel L. (1996), ''The Costs and Benefits of Price Stability: An Assessment of Howitt's Rule'', *Federal Reserve Bank of St. Louis Review*, 78, 2, March/April.

Thurow, Lester (1988), ''Let's Put Capitalists Back into Capitalism'', *Sloan Management Review*, 30, Fall.

Tobin, James (1984), ''On the Efficiency of the Financial System'', *Lloyds Bank Review*, July.

Twentieth Century Fund (1992), *Report of the Task Force on Market Speculation and Corporate Governance*, Twentieth Century Fund Press, New York.

US Department of Commerce (1994), *Statistical Abstract of the United States*, US Government Printing Office, Washington.

US Department of Labor (1994), *Report on the American Workforce*, US Government Printing Office, Washington.

US Department of Labor (1995), *What's Working (and what's not): A Summary of Research on the Economic Impacts of Employment and Training Programs*, Office of the Chief Economist, January.

Visser, Jelli (1996), ''Unionisation Trends Revisited'', unpublished manuscript, University of Amsterdam.

Wahal, Sunil (1995), ''Pension Fund Activism and Firm Performance'', mimeo, University of North Carolina, Chapel Hill.

Wallman, Steven M.H. (1991), ''The Proper Interpretation of Corporate Constituency Statutes and Formulation of Director Duties'', *Stetson Law Review*, 21, 1, Fall.

Warner, Jerold B., Ronald L. Watts and Karen H. Wruck (1988), ''Stock Prices and Top Management Changes'', *Journal of Financial Economics*, 20, 1/2, January/March.

Weisbach, Michael S. (1988), ''Outside Directors and CEO Turnover'', *Journal of Financial Economics*, 20, 1/2, January/March.

Weiss, Lawrence (1990), ''Bankruptcy Resolution: Direct Costs and Violation of Priority of Claims'', *Journal of Financial Economics*, 27, 2, October.

White, Michelle J. (1989), ''The Corporate Bankruptcy Decision'', *Journal of Economic Perspectives*, 3, 2, Spring.

Williamson, Oliver E. (1988), ''Corporate Finance and Corporate Governance'', *Journal of Finance*, 43, 3, July.

Winston, Clifford (1993), ''Economic Deregulation: Days of Reckoning for Microeconomists'', *Journal of Economic Literature*, 31, 3, September.

Wright, Peter (1996), Research reported in *Business Week*, International Edition, 6 May, p. 8.

Wruck, Karen Hopper (1990), ''Financial Distress, Reorganization and Organizational Efficiency'', *Journal of Financial Economics*, 27, 2, October.

Yermack, David (1995), ''Do Corporations Award CEO Options Effectively?'', *Journal of Financial Economics*, 39, 2 and 3, October-November.

Yermack, David (1996), ''Higher Market Valuation of Companies With a Small Board of Directors'', *Journal of Financial Economics*, 40, 2, February.

Annex I

Supporting material for Chapter IV

How managers use their discretion

The orthodox view[1] of corporations is that they are nexuses of contracts: transactions-cost-minimising institutions which exist in order solely to maximise shareholder wealth. In this approach the core governance problem is the divorce of ownership from control and the resulting informational asymmetries,[2] and the key question is, therefore, how to overcome or at least to minimise these agency costs by making managers more responsive to shareholder interests. At a basic level managers can expropriate shareholder capital once it is committed to the firm (Shleifer and Vishny, 1996). In this context outright theft is relatively rare, but less egregious violations may not draw legal intervention due to the so-called ''business judgement rule'' which allows management a substantial degree of leeway. Thus, opportunism could, in theory, be avoided by shareholders writing complete explicit contracts with management or, failing that, utilising optimal incentive mechanisms, but neither is feasible, so contracting remains implicit, and residual control rights are necessarily allocated to managers. The likelihood of rent-seeking behaviour reduces the willingness of investors to provide the firm with capital and, despite constraints on managerial ability to exploit its discretionary powers, leads to a less efficient outcome than if the firm had been entirely managerially financed. Furthermore, overt bargaining between the two groups cannot take place because of management's fiduciary duty (''the duty of loyalty'' in legal parlance). Overall, some observers have claimed that it is more of a puzzle to explain managerial discipline than discretion (Edlin and Stiglitz, 1995).

There are a number of ways in which managers can maximise their own utility and behave opportunistically. Since their pay is generally related to the size of the firm, they are often said to pursue sales or growth (rather than profit) maximisation motives and thereby to build empires. There is an old and fairly lengthy literature to this effect. Much of the fear of empire-building was the result of the conglomeration boom of the 1960s: managers were said at the time to be diversifying in order to achieve synergies, but the subsequent evidence was that such advantages were overblown and that the economies of scale and scope just did not exist; the result was a substantial number of divestitures in the 1980s.[3] In an international perspective, it could be claimed that a size-maximising firm will respond to changing costs by attempting to maintain or increase market share: thus, for example, upward pressures on export prices from currency appreciation will be resisted even if the result is to reduce profitability. This characterisation might well still apply to many Japanese and some European firms who are not under strong financial market pressures to increase shareholder value.

A second area in which it is alleged that managers use their discretion is in their investment strategies. Since their earned incomes devolve entirely from the employer-firm, they cannot diversify their income risks as easily as shareholders can; thus, they may choose investment projects with a risk/return combination involving excessively low risk, through conglomerate mergers, for example (Amihud and Lev, 1981), particularly if they have large ownership stakes (Wright, 1996); on the other hand, executive stock options may encourage risk-taking due to the asymmetric returns involved. Such efforts to diversify are generally not in shareholders' interests (Morck *et al.*, 1990; Lang and Stulz, 1994), especially as they have increasingly achieved the benefits of diversification through mutual fund holdings. An additional investment distortion might be that too little capital is built in relationship-specific forms such as firm-specific human capital (Edlin and Reichelstein, 1996). It has also been argued that managers avoid returning capital to shareholders and waste free cash flow in unproductive uses (Jensen, 1986); the example of the oil industry in the 1980s continuing to invest in exploration after the world price plummeted is often cited.[4] A more general manifestation has been pointed out: firms facing low marginal returns on investment, as measured by low values of Tobin's Q, achieve stock-price returns after announcing a bid to acquire another firm which are inversely related to their free cash flow positions (Lang, Stulz and Walkling, 1991). Another piece of evidence comes from the record of what happens when firms receive unexpected cash windfalls as legal settlements: they often proceed to borrow even more in order to make an acquisition which turns out poorly and is subsequently divested (Blanchard *et al.*, 1994). They also boost executive compensation, buy out blockholders and, when they refrain from making acquisitions, horde cash and are themselves acquired. Finally, Lang, Poulsen and Stulz (1995) argue that, if managers are acting only in shareholders' interests, asset sales should respond to the dictates of operating efficiency. But they find instead that they are undertaken especially when pre-sale performance is poor and that the stock price effect is positive only if the proceeds are paid out: markets implicitly discount the proceeds of the sale if they are retained and, therefore, used to pursue managerial objectives.

A third way in which management may act counter to the best interests of shareholders is by paying themselves excessively (given their dominance of the board of directors) and consuming perquisites. The hypothesis is to some extent unprovable, as trends in managerial productivity are not observable. Executive pay has become a highly controversial subject in recent years, with compensation occasionally going beyond $100 million per year. The median[5] compensation package of chief executive officers (CEOs) of the largest non-financial corporations rose by 68 per cent in real terms in the decade to 1993, a period over which most other employees saw stagnant real wages.[6] Already by 1989 US executives were allegedly earning (in purchasing power parity terms) twice what their European counterparts were being paid and three times Japanese levels, although it is possible that their fringe benefits are lower and that they face greater income risks due to stronger reputational effects and shorter employment contract duration. Also, there seems to be a larger gap between the pay of CEOs and other senior management than in other countries, possibly to provide stronger incentives (sometimes called "tournament effects"). In any case, in the late 1980s the multiple of CEO over average worker pay was 109 in the United States, compared to only 35 in the United Kingdom and 17 in Japan (Jacobs, 1991).

The supposed justification of such apparently generous rewards is that they are performance-based, but the sensitivity of executive compensation to share price performance has been questioned: executive compensation has varied no more over time than that of non-executives – indeed, the variation has been lower for just salary and bonus pay – and is relatively unrelated to share price outcomes,[7] given executives' meagre stockholdings in their firms – a median value of only 0.25 per cent and much less for the largest firms (Jensen and Murphy, 1990; Jensen, 1993). Recently there has been a shift toward stock-options-based executive pay, but in the past firms have ratcheted down strike prices on CEO options (so-called "underwater options") when overall equity market performance was weak; and concerns have also been raised when options are issued at below market prices. The result of the heightened public concern was that in 1992 the SEC enacted reforms requiring the reporting and disclosure of top executive pay to shareholders, and in 1993 the government decided that the tax deduction for executive salaries in excess of $1 million per year would no longer be granted to firms unless the compensation is tied to specific corporate performance goals and the package and performance criteria are approved by shareholders.[8] Finally, there is some, albeit not much, evidence showing managerial discretion in the area of perquisites: executive salaries and occupancy expenses are higher for banks in states which do not permit acquisitions (James, 1984).

A last means by which managers display opportunistic behaviour is to attempt to entrench themselves[9] by weakening the mechanisms which exist in order to discipline or replace them, the takeover mechanism in particular (see below). Strategies to enhance entrenchment include: increasing leverage to reduce the risk of takeovers (Novaes and Zingales, 1995); investing in projects that are in some sense specific to themselves or that they can manage better than their rivals (Novaes and Zingales, 1995) or the choice of an organisational structure which makes the team indispensable. Edlin and Stiglitz (1995) have argued that management may actually invest in order to create informational asymmetries, for example by overindulging in acquisitions which promise potential but uncertain synergies for which they have earlier or better signals as to their realisation than do their rivals. In addition, their bargaining position is strengthened the noisier are the returns on the firm's investment projects.

Evidence of the effects of various managerial control mechanisms

Higher managerial ownership has been shown to boost share value, all else equal (Mehran, 1995), especially for firms with poor investment opportunities (McConnell and Servaes, 1995), although eventually higher managerial ownership may indicate entrenchment and the opportunity to pursue private benefits, and the relationship may invert (McConnell and Servaes, 1990).[10] It may also influence management's appetite for investment risk. Finally, high insider ownership has been shown to promote efficient voluntary liquidations (Fleming and Moon, 1995).

Some evidence on the use of *executive compensation* and incentives to curb managerial discretion is also available. Greater use of stock options is made when book profits contain lots of noise (making managerial performance more difficult to monitor). However, CEO options are not awarded according to a variety of proxies for agency cost reductions nor to financial contracting theories; rather they are often used more heavily when the firm is confronted by internal liquidity problems (Yermack, 1995).

Restructuring transactions, including leveraged buyouts (LBOs), management buyouts (MBOs) and leveraged recapitalisations all involve a reconcentration of equity in the hands of insiders, increased incentives and capabilities to monitor corporate performance and, most importantly perhaps, a substantial *substitution of debt for equity*. All are likely to lead to increased management efforts to minimise costs, a reversal of unprofitable diversification and a reduction in the response time for adaptation to market conditions (Thompson and Wright, 1995). LBOs have led to improved productivity performance, especially at the white-collar level (Lichtenberg and Siegel, 1990), although perhaps not for manufacturing firms (Bernanke *et al.*, 1990). LBOs undertaken in the period ending in 1986 boosted financial results due to more effective management of working capital: receivables were collected more quickly and inventory holding periods were cut back (Smith, 1990). But research and development efforts fell sharply for those firms with the largest increases in leverage (Hall, 1990). There is also some evidence that as the LBO boom proceeded the logic behind the transactions became less certain, with its forward momentum maintained to some extent by the value of equity cashed out by management and by the magnitude of the fees and commissions that were being generated – up to 6 per cent of the median firm's capital (Kaplan and Stein, 1993) and more than $1 billion in the RJR Nabisco case alone. While in most cases management's share of equity rose sharply after the buyout (on average from about 5 to around 22 per cent), thereby enhancing incentives, the dollar value of their equity holdings fell by an average of more than half. Thus, Baumol (1991) calls LBOs a ''vehicle for spectacularly lucrative rent seeking'', even if many are efficiency-enhancing. Ultimately, a surprisingly high per centage of firms which underwent leveraged recapitalisations were the victims of financial distress, although possibly not because the deals were poorly structured (Denis and Denis, 1995*a*).

Monitoring by the board of directors is a governance process which has not worked well in practice. One important reason for this is that nearly 5 per cent of all directors held fewer than 5 shares in the firm in the 1980s (Jacobs, 1991) and many more owned not many more than that. Even by 1995 only one-third of all firms required their directors to own any of the firm's common stock (NACD, 1995). However, the mechanism has worked to the extent that top executives of firms in financial distress or even reducing their dividends have been shown to be significantly less likely to receive additional outside directorships and to have a higher probability of resigning or losing existing outside directorships than others (Kaplan and Reishus, 1990; Gilson, 1990).

However, there is evidence that boards were not totally unresponsive to poor performance. Non-takeover-related complete management turnover has been shown to be more likely for the largest firms when they underperform their industry average (as proxied by Tobin's Q) (Morck *et al.*, 1989; Warner, Watts and Wruck, 1988). Following top management changes profit increases modestly if the change is due to a normal retirement and more substantially after a forced resignation, but such dismissals are probably attributable to external forces rather than normal board monitoring (Denis and Denis, 1995*b*).

There are some signs that the board is becoming a more effective monitoring mechanism. Blair (1995) cites data from Korn/Ferry International that the average director spent about 94 hours per year on board matters in 1991; more recently, that has risen to 123 hours. But that rapid rise only reversed the downtrend in the 1980s: the same source said directors spent 125 hours per year on board duties in 1983 (Jacobs, 1991). Individual directors are also serving on fewer boards: even if such restrictions are not self-imposed, 18 per cent of directors surveyed by Korn/Ferry International in 1995 said that their boards had limited the number of other boards the CEO could serve on – usually to two (Millstein, 1995*b*).

Perhaps most importantly boards are shrinking and increasingly comprised of outsiders. Yermack (1996) has shown that having smaller boards of directors is associated with better corporate performance using a number of different measures. The evidence that having a larger share of directors comprised of outsiders has led to governance and performance improvements is even stronger. First, it may limit managerial recourse to sales-maximisation objectives, thereby boosting rates of return (Macavoy *et al.*, 1983), and consequently stock prices (Rosenstein and Wyatt, 1990). Second, it may reduce management consumption of perquisites (Brickley and James, 1987). Third, it may boost the board's willingness to replace the CEO following a period of poor performance (Weisbach, 1988). Fourth, it may ensure better outcomes when the firm engages in takeovers (Byrd and Hickman, 1992). Finally, it may lead to a greater share of equity-based executive compensation (Mehran, 1995). Directors at 19 per cent of the top 1 000 corporations currently have some equity-based compensation, up from less than 2 per cent in 1983 (CPC, 1995). This higher share ownership by directors is associated with higher share prices (Morck *et al.*, 1988), despite the aforementioned effects on risk-taking. Boards now routinely have separate compensation committees to determine managerial pay, and since 1992 the SEC has required that its composition be public and that it explain the factors it uses to determine pay. The SEC also decided in 1992 that, even with this greater disclosure, executive pay is an appropriate matter for shareholder proposals, since only one firm in ten requires shareholder approval of top officer compensation plans (NACD, 1995), but thus far shareholder proposals on executive compensation have been rare.

Concentrated share ownership is a further means to incite additional monitoring by minimising the free-rider problem. But its importance has declined since Berle and Means (1932) found controlling blocks (holdings of least 20 per cent) in 110 of the 200 (that is 55 per cent) largest corporations in 1929. By 1975 the figure had fallen to about 17 per cent (Herman, 1981), primarily where control is exercised by a single family (Holderness and Sheehan, 1988). In 1984 some 13 per cent of all publicly-traded firms had a majority owner, although for those listed on the New York or American Exchanges the figure was only around 5 per cent (Bebchuk, 1994). Of course, effective control may require much less than a 20 per cent holding (Leech, 1987).

But the effect of concentrated ownership on performance is unclear. Tobin's Q seems to rise with the size of the largest block of shares in the firm until it reaches about 25 per cent (Gilson and Kraakman, 1993). Price-earnings ratios are significantly higher for firms whose largest shareholders have at least 15 per cent of their equity, but the effect holds only for firms in industries with research and development spending below 1 per cent of sales: these large holders may be able to reduce information-related costs in capital markets (Zeckhauser and Pound in Hubbard, 1990). But there appears to be no impact of concentrated ownership on book profits: lower shirking costs may be offset by higher capital acquisition costs (Demsetz and Lehn, 1985). Other unpublished evidence shows that share prices rise in the first two months after the purchase of a large stake, but significant declines ensue in the next two years if the blockholder does not later acquire the firm (Blair, 1995).

The main text makes clear that it is only large shareholders, that is institutional investors, who can possibly have sufficient incentives to do much in the way of monitoring management. However, greater institional monitoring may face a number of potential problems. First, US financial institutions have not even fully exploited their statutory rights to own equities, and even where such constraints are less binding, as in the United Kingdom and Germany, for example, most financial institutions do not have much higher shares of equity in individual firms. As capital markets have deepened and become more globally integrated, competition may have reduced the advantages of bank-based monitoring; even in the 1920s, J.P. Morgan was already retreating from its monitoring role (Coffee, 1991). Second, many institutions, mutual funds in particular, have a strong need for liquidity and thus short-term horizons which, even were regulations to be eased, would probably prevent them from accepting the responsibilities of control (Coffee, 1991). There is a basic conflict between liquidity and own monitoring: liquidity discourages monitoring by reducing the (transactions) costs of exit, while monitoring inhibits liquidity by creating informational asymmetries and the potential for a "lemons" problem (Bhide, 1993);[11] for this reason the United States, with its low transactions costs, has high liquidity and little monitoring. Third, as mentioned above, banks and insurance companies suffer from potential conflicts of interest – rocking the boat might cause providers of financial services to lose business – as do employer-provided pension funds, while trustees of Taft-Hartley and public-employee pension funds are suspected of, respectively, having political agendas or of being subject to political pressure, at least as regards "economically targeted investments" (Romano, 1993). Fourth, institutions' (possibly excessive) desire for diversification may prevent active institutional monitoring. Fifth, it is less than self-evident that monitoring skills are the same as investment management skills, and unbundling the activities might be required for the monitoring activity to be adequately compensated (Coffee, 1991).[12] And finally, of course, having large institutions monitoring corporations might even worsen agency problems by adding another layer of oversight, further distancing management from the ultimate owners (Blair, 1995). Large shareholders acting as monitors can also behave opportunistically, at the expense of minority shareholders or managers; also their preferences for risk-taking may be quite different. Ultimately, it is by no means clear who would monitor the monitor.

Shareholder resolutions are another means of disciplining management, but they are too infrequent to have much effect. In the six years ending in September 1990, only 0.35 per cent of all boards faced a proxy challenge, and only 28 per cent of these were fully successful (Grundfest, 1993). It is, therefore, not entirely surprising that a recent study showed that while such governance-related resolutions in the period 1986-90 tended to target poorly performing firms, there is little evidence that they led to higher stock prices (Karpoff *et al.*, 1995).

Shareholder and especially *institutional activism* has been the system's latest spontaneous response to the need for more monitoring and to SEC rule changes. The main text describes how a number of institutions began to target the governance practices of underperforming corporations in order to boost overall corporate performance. It should be pointed out, however, that there is only mixed evidence as to whether many such governance arrangements make much difference to share prices. Blair, in a background paper for CPC (1995), concludes that only supermajority amendments, poison pills and cumulative voting rights provisions have statistically significant albeit small effects. On the other hand, Gordon and Pound, in unpublished work cited by Hawley and Williams (1996), find that less restrictive governance structures lead to systematically better performance using some measures (return on assets, operating margins and cash flow-to-price ratios) but not others (price-earnings ratios and one- and five-year stock returns). In any case, the results of these institutional targeting efforts have begun to be analysed. The market-adjusted share prices of the 42 firms which CalPERS targeted from 1987 to 1992 improved dramatically in the years following targeting (Nesbitt, 1994). Similar results have been claimed for the CII "focus list" (Opler and Sokobin, 1995) and for the firms targeted by the United Shareholders Association, disbanded in 1993 (Strickland *et al.*, 1996). Yet in a more careful analysis of activism by CalPERS, Smith (1996) confirms a positive stock-price effect, but only for the sub-sample of targets where the resolution was successful (72 per cent of the post-1988 sample); for the others, shareholder wealth declined, possibly due to the capitalisation of costs incurred to resist the resolution and greater probability of entrenchment.[13] In the same vein, other research finds that only institutional activism using methods other than shareholder proposals had any positive abnormal returns in the years 1987-93 (Wahal, 1995).

The main text argues that it is the *market for corporate control* which is the most important disciplinary device in the US governance process. Activity in this market varies substantially over time. There are a variety of hypotheses that have been advanced as to why historical fluctuations in merger rates have occurred, given that it is unlikely that managerial incentives to behave opportunistically vary much over time. They seem to have a clear pro-cyclical component, in part due to the need for a ready supply of credit to fund them. Higher values of Tobin's Q have also been shown to boost merger rates (Golbe and White, 1988). Innovations in the 1980s such as high-yield "junk bond" financing also boosted the ability to launch tender offers: no longer could sheer size provide effective deterrence against takeovers (Jensen, 1993). It has been argued that the 1980s takeover boom was the result of the squeeze on net returns resulting from the high real interest rates associated with the battle against inflation and the still reduced investment yields due to the supply shocks of the 1970s (Blair and Schary, 1993). The timing of takeover waves is also to some extent related to industry-specific shocks, such as deregulation, and the subsequent need for restructuring (Mitchell and Mulherin, 1996). In any case, when the junk bond boom came to an end at the close of the decade and when credit supply dried up (the hypothesised "credit crunch"), the boom came to a fairly abrupt end.

While takeovers often have a clear rent-seeking motive, it is likely that they enhance overall efficiency: *i)* target, bidder and thus total returns are higher when bidders have high and targets have low values of Tobin's Q (Servaes, 1991); *ii)* firms were more likely to be the object of a hostile takeover in the 1980s when their performance lagged that of their industry peers in terms of returns on equity, sales growth and Tobin's Q and when they were in poorly performing industries (Morck *et al.*, 1989; Jacobs, 1991); *iii)* managers' probability of departure is higher after a successful takeover than for the average firm or after a failed attempt (Martin and McConnell, 1991); and *iv)* the 50 largest mergers from 1979 to mid-1984 resulted in improved post-acquisition operating performance using a number of different measures (Healy *et al.*, 1992).[14]

Takeovers may boost efficiency in a number of different ways. First, they may correct the hoarding of cash flow and resulting unwise investment. This is widely seen to have been important in the oil sector in the 1980s, when exploration activities continued at a high level despite low prices, but its importance elsewhere has been disputed. However, besides being small and having below-average sales growth and low Q values, takeover target firms have higher cash positions and lower leverage (Comment and Schwert, 1995). Second, they may correct an overmanning problem. Bhagat *et al.* (1990) find that post-takeover layoffs occurred mainly among white-collar and headquarters staff and explain an average of 10 to 20 per cent of bid premia in the 62 large hostile takeovers which occurred in the years 1984-86, but sometimes all of it. Their general conclusion is that layoffs are more a by-product of the hostile takeover process than the driving force behind it. Kaplan (1989*a*) also examines layoffs in the context of management buyouts. A third inefficiency is excessive executive compensation and related expenses. James (1984) found lower bank salary and occupancy expenses in states permitting bank holding company acquisitions than in those prohibiting them. Schranz (1993) also observed that banks in states with active takeover markets are more profitable; and that where this market was prohibited, there was a greater recourse to other mechanisms (such as managerial stock ownership) to align managerial interests with those of shareholders, but that they failed to compensate in full.

But takeovers may also be driven by factors other than correcting failures and exploiting synergies. Since there is evidence that rivals' stock prices rise when horizontal mergers are announced, it is possible that some additional rents are being realised in these cases, although that may just indicate a higher probability of takeovers of other firms in the industry. Also rivals' stock prices seem to rise when mergers are challenged by the anti-trust authorities. Such merger challenges were much less frequent in the 1980s. In the banking sector there is no evidence that bidder gains are the result of increased market power or collusion (James and Wier, 1987), although they are a function of the degree of competition in the market for acquisitions as defined by the number of potential rival bidders and the number of alternative targets available.

Another incentive to engage in a takeover is to exploit tax-saving strategies. The incentive is to merge a profitable firm with one having tax losses. This may have been important in about 5 per cent of all mergers in the 1980s (Auerbach and Reishus, 1988), but for management buyouts tax benefits could have accounted for an average of anywhere from 21 to 143 per cent of the premium paid to pre-buyout shareholders (Kaplan, 1989*b*). The 1986 tax reform also closed a number of other tax loopholes which had made mergers attractive. Of course, if the target firm had a sub-optimal amount of leverage, then the acquirer could change its capital structure and reap the resulting tax savings.

Some observers have also argued that takeovers are driven by the opportunity to expropriate extramarginal wage premia. That these quasi-rents exist can be attributed to rent-sharing, optimising long-term incentives and forced saving. The possibility that takeovers may bring about the abrogation of long-term implicit contracts with deleterious effects on the parties' willingness to engage in such contracting was first advanced by Shleifer and Summers (1988). Recently, Gokhale *et al.* (1995) found that extramarginal wage payments were reduced by 3-4 per cent (consistent with a 10 per cent increase in profit) following hostile takeovers involving a sample of takeovers in the Mid-West in 1980-91; there was no evidence of breaches of implicit contracts where control changes were non-hostile. However, Rosett (1990) found quite the opposite: union wage concessions following non-hostile acquisitions in the years 1973-87 accounted for about 5 per cent of bid premia, whereas where the transaction resulted in a change of CEO, union members' wealth actually rose by some 10 per cent.

Similarly, terminating overfunded defined-benefit pension plans (called "reversion") and expropriating the gains can be a strong incentive to acquire a firm. Among all workers covered by defined-benefit plans, those covered by overfunded plans represented 30 per cent of workers in 1980 and 76 per cent in 1985. A peak of nearly 700 000 workers and pension assets of $6.7 billion were subjected to reversions in 1985, before a 10 per cent excise tax on reverted assets was imposed in 1986. Thereafter, the number of plans, workers and assets subject to reversion fell sharply.

Finally, takeovers may be driven by short-sighted cutbacks in the target firm's investment activities. The evidence here is that mergers lead to a small but persistent reduction in the ratio of research and development spending to sales which is not likely due to the elimination of duplication (Hall, 1990). Increased leverage for whatever reason has a much larger negative effect on such activities.

Table A1. **Organisational form by industry, 1990**

	Corporations				Partnerships				Non-farm proprietorships			
	Number thousand	Share [1] %	Business receipts $ billion	Share [1] %	Number thousand	Share [1] %	Business receipts $ billion	Share [1] %	Number thousand	Share [1] %	Business receipts $ billion	Share [1] %
Agricultural services, forestry, fishing	127	21	83	75	125	20	10	9	363	59	17	16
Mining	40	19	97	78	41	19	20	16	132	62	7	6
Construction	407	18	523	80	59	3	31	5	1 782	79	99	15
Manufacturing	302	43	3 433	98	28	4	65	2	380	54	22	1
Transportation, public utilities	161	20	874	93	25	3	33	4	615	77	31	3
Wholesale and retail trade	1 022	27	3 217	90	176	5	98	3	2 650	69	250	7
Finance, insurance and real estate	610	22	1 955	92	822	30	122	6	1 331	48	49	2
Other services	1 029	12	726	64	267	3	162	14	7 335	85	252	22
Total [2]	3 717	19	10 914	90	1 554	8	541	4	14 783	74	731	6

1. Totals may not add because of rounding.
2. Includes businesses not allocable to individual industries.

Source: US Department of Commerce, *Statistical Abstract of the United States, 1994*, Table No. 834.

Notes

1. This view is most often associated with Coase (1937), Mason (1959), Manne (1965), Ross (1973), Jensen and Meckling (1976), Fama (1980) and Williamson (1988). It is apposite perhaps only for the case of the United States; elsewhere firms may serve more as co-ordination devices for aligning the interests of its ''stakeholders'' by means of inter-corporate shareholdings, employee ownership and representation, for example.
2. However, Fama (1980) and Blair (1995) remind their readers that separation of ownership from control (or, alternatively, management from risk-bearing) has produced obvious sizeable benefits as well: capital markets are deeper and risk premia lower; and managers are chosen for their ability and training, rather than their family backgrounds. For a recent survey of the effects of separating ownership from control on corporate performance see Short (1994).
3. Some 44 per cent of all unrelated acquisitions completed from 1971-82 were divested by the end of the 1980s (Kaplan and Weisbach, 1992).
4. Indeed, oil firms cut back on their non-oil investments after the oil price decline (Lamont, 1996).
5. Given some especially large increases the mean rise was even larger.
6. In fact, this difference is much more long-lived: according to Tevlin (1996), the contrast is even more massive taking the twenty-year period from 1970 to 1990. This trend is still ongoing: according to Business Week (International Edition, 22 April 1996), the ratio of CEO to average pay has risen from 42 in 1980 to 141 in 1995, with real CEO pay increasing by 27 per cent in 1995 alone. However, it should be pointed out that, given that the share of total CEO compensation provided in long-term forms (mostly stock options) doubled from 34 to 68 per cent from 1983 to 1992 according to one source (Blair, 1995), the remainder may actually have declined (by some 18 per cent) in real terms. Another source (Yermack, 1995) claims that options represented one-third of total compensation in 1990-91, up from one-fifth in 1984.
7. In the period 1974-86 average CEO wealth rose only $3.25 for every $1 000 increase in shareholder wealth: $2.50 from direct stock ownership, about $0.75 from salary revisions, outstanding stock options and the impact of performance-related dismissals and just over a penny from salary and bonuses. Note that this last figure was $0.175 (in constant 1986 prices) in 1934-38; at that point in history real executive pay (including bonus but not the value of options) was greater than in the 1980s, as were the proportion of shares in the largest firms held by CEOs. For more details see Jensen and Murphy (1990) and for a claim that these figures are down-biased, possibly seriously so, see Tevlin (1996). A comparison with Japanese CEOs

reveals that the latter hold even less equity in their firms and that the sensitivity of their rewards to firm performance is quite similar, although these rewards are more sensitive to negative profits but less to overall stock returns (Kaplan, 1994).

8. One influential institutional investor, however, has claimed that the relevant Treasury interpretation has not been drafted sufficiently clearly so that there is usually not enough information to cast an informed vote.
9. Of course, entrenchment is not by itself proof of inefficiency: higher agency costs might be more than offset by lower transactions costs (Kester, 1992).
10. There is a similar non-monotonic relationship between managerial ownership shares and the tendency to overpay when acquiring other firms, as measured by the premium offered in takeovers: initially, increased managerial ownership lowers bid premia as interests are aligned, but at higher levels of ownership this is more than offset by the twin attractions of diversification and maintenance of control (Hubbard and Palia, 1995).
11. The concept of ''lemons'' problems originates with Akerlof (1970). It refers to the effects on product and factor markets of difficulties in discerning quality. Here it means that a monitoring agent trying to sell out its equity position will have difficulties because potential buyers are aware that the monitor has more information about the firm than they do.
12. Related to this is the fact that money managers' compensation is not very sensitive to performance: incentive compensation based on capital appreciation is restricted under the terms of the Investment Advisers Act of 1940.
13. He also finds targeting is followed by improvement in operating performance, reductions in undistributed cash flow and increases in asset sales, but none of these effects is statistically significant relative to control samples. Nevertheless, he does confirm the benefits to CalPERS of its targeting strategy: its holdings increased by $19 million for a cumulative outlay on its behalf of only around $3 million. CalPERS representatives have claimed the return has been around $150 million.
14. However, a number of earlier studies found no such improvements; see Ravenscraft and Scherer (1987), for example. It is possible that takeovers result from industry-specific shocks and that post-takeover failure is the product of an inability to overcome those shocks, rather than from the takeovers themselves (Mitchell and Mulherin, 1996).

Annex II

Calendar of main economic events

1995

October

Federal government begins FY 96 without enactment of any of the thirteen annual appropriations bills; a Continuing Resolution is passed to fund the government until mid-November. In the last week of October the House and Senate pass Reconciliation Bills to implement the tax cuts and mandatory spending changes outlined in the Budget Resolution in order to balance the budget in seven years.

Job training reform programme passes the Senate after having passed the House in September.

November

The President vetoes bills to lift the debt limit and temporarily fund the government on 13 November. The Treasury continues issuing new debt by manipulating intragovernmental funds which affect the debt limit calculations but which do not affect public borrowing. On 15 November Federal government shuts down, with only essential civilian employees reporting for work in those agencies whose annual appropriations bills have not passed, idling an estimated 800 000 workers (only three of thirteen bills had been enacted by 14 November). The government reopens 19 November when another Continuing Resolution is passed to fund the government until 15 December. Agreement is made to balance budget over seven years.

At its November meeting the Federal Reserve leaves monetary policy unchanged, with the federal funds rate at 5¾ per cent.

December

The FY 96 Budget Reconciliation bill is vetoed 6 December and the President announces his own plan to balance the budget in seven years which makes greater spending cuts than the ten-year plan announced in June, but it proposes less deficit reduction than the Congressional plan, reflecting more optimistic assumptions.

On 15 December portions of the government are again shut down as six of the annual appropriations bills have yet to be enacted and the Continuing Resolution expires. An estimated 280 000 federal employees are furloughed and another 476 000 work without pay. Another Continuing Resolution is signed 5 January bringing employees back to work and authorising back pay.

The Federal Reserve eases monetary policy by cutting the federal funds target rate to 5½ per cent, citing favourable developments in inflation since July and moderation in inflation expectations.

1996

January

Welfare reform bill is vetoed 9 January. Earlier versions had passed the House in March 1995 and the Senate in September.

Negotiations are suspended on reaching an agreement for a programme to balance the budget. According to press reports the final negotiating positions were (cumulative deficit reduction over seven years in billions of dollars, excluding interest savings):

	Congress		Administration	
	Initial	January	Initial	January
Medicare	226	168	97	102
Medicaid	133	85	38	52
Discretionary	409	349	138	295
Welfare	64	60	38	43
Other mandatory	49	69	–6	60
Total spending cuts	881	731	305	552
Tax cuts (–)	–245	–203	–105	–87
Total deficit reduction	636	528	200	465

On 31 January, the Federal Reserve lowered the discount rate from 5¼ to 5 per cent and the target for the federal funds rate to 5¼ per cent. The announcement stated that the change was "consistent with contained inflation and sustainable growth".

Bureau of Economic Analysis releases revised national accounts data (see Box 1, Chapter I).

February

President releases an outline of FY 97 budget. It incorporates much of the Administration's recent proposals, balancing the the budget by 2001 using its own assumptions and 2002 using Congressional Budget Office assumptions.

In its biannual report to Congress the Federal Reserve sets the same ranges for monetary aggregates and debt as for the previous year. Economic projections by the Federal Reserve governors and Reserve Bank presidents are for real GDP to grow by 2 to $2^1/_4$ per cent over the four quarters of 1996, consumer prices to rise by $2^3/_4$ to 3 per cent and the civilian unemployment rate to remain in the $5^1/_2$ to $5^3/_4$ per cent range.

Landmark telecommunications bill is enacted.

March

Farm bill is passed and is signed into law in early April.

Signing of the so-called Helms-Burton Act, which targets foreign companies that invest in Cuba.

The Federal Reserve leaves interest rates unchanged.

The debt limit is raised to $5.5 trillion which is expected to allow the Treasury unrestricted operation until October 1997.

April

A health insurance reform bill passes Senate, after a similar bill passed the House in March.

Line-item veto is enacted, but authority to use it is delayed until January 1997.

Final Continuing Resolution is signed 26 April to fund for the rest of the fiscal year the agencies covered by the five appropriations bills that have yet to be enacted.

May

No changes in monetary policy stance are made by the Federal Reserve.

House passes bill to raise the minimum wage from $4.25 to $5.25 over two years.

Continuing drought conditions in the mid-west and south-west lead to lower grain harvest forecasts and higher prices.

June

FY 97 Budget Resolution is passed by both houses which proposes to balance the budget by 2002 and sets discretionary spending near FY 96 levels.

July

At its July meeting, the Federal Reserve leaves its short-term interest rates unchanged. In its report to Congress, the Federal Reserve reaffirmed the 1996 ranges for money and debt growth and provisionally adopted the same ranges for 1997. The economic projections by the Federal Reserve governors and Reserve Bank presidents are for real GDP to grow by $2^1/_2$ to 3 per cent over the four quarters of 1996 and $1^1/_2$ to 2 per cent in 1997. The Consumer Price Index is projected to rise by 3 to $3^1/_4$ per cent over the four quarters of 1996, slipping to $2^3/_4$ to 3 per cent in 1997.

The right to sue under title III of the Helms-Burton Act is suspended for six months.

August

The minimum wage is increased from $4.25 to $4.75 beginning 1 October 1996 and to $5.15 in September 1997. The new law also includes a temporary training wage, small reductions to income taxes paid by businesses and persons, and a temporary renewal of the Generalised System of Preferences tariffs for the least developed nations.

The Safe Drinking Water Act is reauthorised, refocusing federal regulatory efforts on the substances that pose the most serious health threats.

Welfare reform is enacted. The bill replaces the Aid to Families with Dependent Children programme by the Temporary Assistance for Needy Families block grant to states. Food Stamps and Supplemental Security Income programmes are scaled back and restrictions are placed on aid to both legal and illegal immigrants.

Health care reform legislation is passed. It increases the tax deductibility of insurance premiums for the self-employed, guarantees portability between jobs, offers tax breaks for premiums on long-term care and begins a pilot programme of medical care savings accounts.

Iran and Libya Sanctions Act is signed. The act gives the President a choice of six sanctions against firms that invest in the energy industries of either country or those that sell petroleum related products or chemical, biological or nuclear weapons to Libya.

The Federal Reserve leaves interest rates unchanged.

September

Despite press reports indicating that eight of the twelve Bank presidents asked for an increase in the discount rate, the Federal Reserve does not change either the target federal funds rate or discount rate.

As the fiscal year ends, only seven of the thirteen annual appropriations bills have been enacted. The remaining bills are folded into an omnibus bill, granting all departments and agencies full year funding. The bill also includes provisions to restrict illegal immigration, shore up funding for the insurer of savings and loans institutions and auction another portion of the electromagnetic spectrum.

A securities regulation reform bill is passed.

It is announced that the share of the population living below the poverty line fell from 14.5 per cent in 1994 to 13.8 per cent in 1995.

An Information Technology Agreement is reached with the European Union. The EU will drop tariffs on semiconductors and be admitted to the World Semiconductor Council.

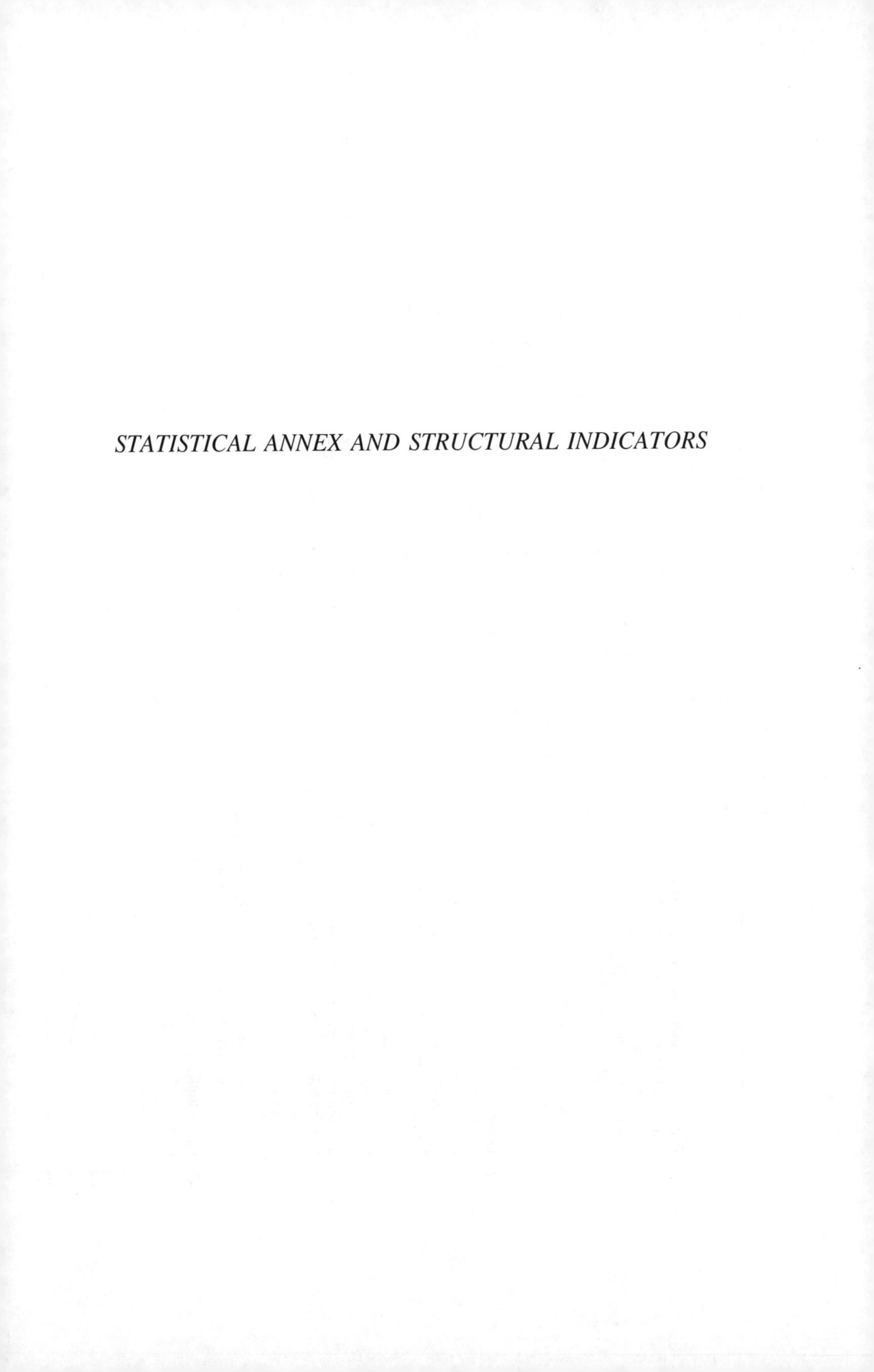

STATISTICAL ANNEX AND STRUCTURAL INDICATORS

Table A. **Selected background statistics**

	Average 1986-95	1986	1987	1988	1989	1990	1991	1992	1993	1994	1995
A. Percentage change from previous year at constant 1992 prices											
Private consumption	2.5	4.0	3.1	3.9	2.3	1.7	–0.6	2.8	2.8	3.1	2.3
Public consumption	1.4	4.6	2.2	2.0	2.7	2.3	1.0	–0.1	0.0	0.2	–0.3
Gross fixed capital formation	2.1	2.1	0.4	1.5	2.0	–1.4	–6.6	5.2	5.1	7.9	5.3
Private residential	2.4	–3.5	–1.1	4.4	4.0	–0.6	–6.4	1.9	6.4	9.8	9.5
Private non-residential	1.8	12.0	0.2	–2.0	–3.7	–9.3	–12.3	16.6	7.6	10.8	–2.3
Public	2.2	7.6	5.2	–2.0	3.4	6.3	–1.1	3.4	–1.2	–1.3	1.9
GDP	2.4	3.0	2.9	3.8	3.4	1.3	–1.0	2.7	2.3	3.5	2.0
GDP price deflator	3.2	2.7	3.1	3.7	4.2	4.3	4.0	2.7	2.6	2.3	2.5
Industrial production	2.6	0.9	5.0	4.4	1.5	0.0	–1.8	3.5	3.5	5.8	3.3
Employment	1.6	2.3	2.6	2.3	2.0	1.3	–0.9	0.7	1.5	2.3	1.6
Compensation of employees (current prices)	5.7	6.1	7.2	7.8	6.0	6.4	3.1	5.4	4.5	5.3	5.3
Productivity (GDP/employment)[1]	0.6	1.3	0.1	0.7	1.0	–0.1	–0.2	3.1	0.3	0.5	–0.4
Unit labour costs (compensation/GDP)	3.2	3.0	4.2	3.9	2.5	5.0	4.1	2.6	2.2	1.7	3.2
B. Percentage ratios											
Gross fixed capital formation as per cent of GDP at constant prices	16.8	18.0	17.5	17.1	16.9	16.5	15.5	15.9	16.3	17.0	17.6
Stockbuilding as per cent of GDP at constant prices	0.3	0.2	0.5	0.2	0.5	0.2	0.0	0.1	0.3	0.9	0.5
Foreign balance as per cent of GDP at constant prices	–1.5	–3.0	–2.8	–2.0	–1.4	–1.0	–0.4	–0.5	–1.1	–1.6	–1.6
Compensation of employees as per cent of GDP at current prices	58.3	58.2	58.8	58.9	57.9	58.4	58.4	58.4	58.1	57.8	58.2
Direct taxes as per cent of household income	14.6	14.3	15.2	14.7	15.1	14.7	14.0	13.9	14.3	14.8	15.2
Household saving as per cent of disposable income	5.2	6.4	5.2	5.3	5.0	5.2	5.8	5.7	4.7	4.2	4.9
Unemployment as per cent of total labour force	6.2	7.0	6.2	5.5	5.3	5.6	6.8	7.5	6.9	6.1	5.6
C. Other indicator											
Current balance (billion dollars)	–110.9	–150.9	–166.3	–127.1	–103.8	–92.7	–7.4	–61.5	–99.9	–151.2	–148.2

1. Ratio of business sector GDP to business sector employment.

Source: US Department of Commerce, *Survey of Current Business*, and OECD.

Table B. **National product and expenditure**

Seasonally adjusted, percentage changes from previous period, annual rates, 1992 prices

	Average 1985-95	1985	1986	1987	1988	1989	1990	1991	1992	1993	1994	1995
Private consumption	2.7	4.7	4.0	3.1	3.9	2.3	1.7	–0.6	2.8	2.8	3.1	2.3
Public consumption	1.7	4.8	4.6	2.2	2.0	2.7	2.3	1.0	–0.1	0.0	0.2	–0.3
Gross fixed investment	2.5	6.0	2.1	0.4	1.5	2.0	–1.4	–6.6	5.2	5.1	7.9	5.3
Private residential	1.7	1.3	12.0	0.2	–2.0	–3.7	–9.3	–12.3	16.6	7.6	10.8	–2.3
Private non-residential	2.8	6.2	–3.5	–1.1	4.4	4.0	–0.6	–6.4	1.9	6.4	9.8	9.5
Public	3.1	12.2	7.6	5.2	–2.0	3.4	6.3	–1.1	3.4	–1.2	–1.3	1.9
Final domestic demand	2.5	4.9	3.7	2.4	3.2	2.3	1.3	–1.3	2.7	2.7	3.4	2.4
Stockbuilding[1]	–0.1	–0.9	–0.4	0.3	–0.3	0.4	–0.4	–0.2	0.2	0.2	0.6	–0.4
Total domestic demand	2.4	4.0	3.4	2.7	2.9	2.7	0.9	–1.6	2.8	2.9	4.0	2.0
Exports of goods and services	8.2	2.7	7.4	11.0	15.9	11.7	8.5	6.3	6.6	2.9	8.2	8.9
Imports of goods and services	6.2	6.5	8.4	6.1	4.0	3.9	3.9	–0.7	7.5	9.2	12.0	8.0
Foreign balance[1]	0.0	–0.4	–0.3	0.1	0.7	0.5	0.3	0.6	–0.1	–0.7	–0.5	0.0
GDP	2.5	3.7	3.0	2.9	3.8	3.4	1.3	–1.0	2.7	2.3	3.5	2.0

	1995 levels (Current $ billions)	1993	1994				1995				1996	
		Q4	Q1	Q2	Q3	Q4	Q1	Q2	Q3	Q4	Q1	Q2
Private consumption	4 924.9	2.8	2.8	3.5	2.8	3.1	1.0	3.1	2.4	1.1	3.5	3.4
Public consumption	1 136.4	0.3	–2.1	–0.9	5.4	–0.9	–1.8	–0.1	–0.5	–3.1	–0.6	7.8
Gross fixed investment	1 250.2	17.1	3.9	7.1	10.2	6.1	7.6	–0.2	4.7	1.2	10.9	7.1
Private residential	289.8	24.4	12.8	12.7	–1.9	0.0	–6.4	–13.4	9.2	6.4	7.4	16.3
Private non-residential	738.5	17.6	7.2	7.2	13.8	12.1	15.3	3.5	4.9	2.4	11.6	3.8
Public	221.9	7.8	–15.1	–0.2	15.8	–4.0	2.0	5.5	–0.9	–9.0	13.1	7.2
Final domestic demand	7 311.5	4.6	2.2	3.4	4.4	3.0	1.6	2.0	2.4	0.4	4.1	4.7
Stockbuilding[1]	37.0	0.0	0.4	0.5	–0.2	–0.1	0.0	–0.4	0.0	–0.3	–0.3	0.1
Total domestic demand	7 348.5	4.5	3.6	5.5	3.7	2.4	1.5	0.6	2.5	–0.7	3.1	5.3
Exports of goods and services	807.4	23.4	–1.6	15.9	9.7	16.5	2.5	5.9	10.8	10.7	1.8	5.7
Imports of goods and services	902.1	17.5	8.2	18.3	10.7	10.3	11.2	4.5	0.0	1.6	10.6	10.0
Foreign balance[1]	–94.7	0.1	–0.3	–0.1	–0.1	0.1	–0.3	0.0	0.3	0.2	–0.3	–0.2
GDP	7 253.8	4.8	2.5	5.0	3.5	3.0	0.4	0.7	3.8	0.3	2.0	4.7

1. Changes as a percentage of previous period GDP.

Source: US Department of Commerce, *Survey of Current Business*.

Table C. **Labour market**

Seasonally adjusted

	1987	1988	1989	1990	1991	1992	1993	1994	1995	1995			1996	
										Q2	Q3	Q4	Q1	Q2
1. Number of persons, millions														
Population of working age[1, 2]	182.8	184.6	186.4	188.0	189.8	192.0	194.8	196.8	198.6	198.3	198.8	199.4	199.8	200.3
Civilian labour force[1]	119.9	121.7	123.9	125.9	126.4	128.1	129.2	131.0	132.4	132.5	132.4	132.4	133.2	133.6
Unemployment[1]	7.4	6.7	6.5	7.1	8.6	9.6	8.9	8.0	7.4	7.5	7.5	7.3	7.5	7.3
Employment[1]	112.4	115.0	117.3	118.8	117.7	118.5	120.3	123.1	125.0	125.0	124.9	125.1	125.7	126.4
Employment[3]	102.0	105.2	107.9	109.4	108.3	108.6	110.7	114.2	117.2	117.0	117.4	117.9	118.5	119.3
Federal government	2.9	3.0	3.0	3.1	3.0	3.0	2.9	2.9	2.8	2.8	2.8	2.8	2.8	2.8
State and local	14.1	14.4	14.8	15.2	15.4	15.7	15.9	16.3	16.5	16.5	16.5	16.5	16.6	16.7
Manufacturing	19.0	19.3	19.4	19.1	18.4	18.1	18.1	18.3	18.5	18.5	18.4	18.4	18.3	18.3
Construction	5.0	5.1	5.2	5.1	4.7	4.5	4.7	5.0	5.2	5.1	5.2	5.2	5.3	5.4
Other	61.0	63.4	65.6	66.9	66.8	67.4	69.1	71.7	74.3	74.0	74.5	75.0	75.5	76.2
2. Percentage change from previous period (s.a.a.r.)														
Population of working age[1, 2]	1.2	1.0	1.0	0.9	0.9	1.2	1.5	1.0	0.9	0.8	1.0	1.1	0.9	1.0
Civilian labour force	1.7	1.5	1.8	1.6	0.4	1.4	0.8	1.4	1.0	0.9	–0.4	0.2	2.3	1.4
Employment[1]	2.6	2.3	2.0	1.3	–0.9	0.7	1.5	2.3	1.6	0.5	–0.4	0.6	1.9	2.3
Employment[3]	2.6	3.2	2.6	1.4	–1.1	0.3	2.0	3.1	2.7	1.6	1.7	1.7	1.8	2.8
Federal government	1.5	1.0	0.6	3.3	–3.9	0.0	–1.8	–1.5	–1.7	–0.8	–1.5	–3.4	–2.1	–1.6
State and local government	2.0	2.5	2.6	2.9	1.4	1.5	1.6	2.0	1.5	0.9	1.4	0.7	0.9	2.0
Manufacturing	0.3	1.7	0.4	–1.6	–3.5	–1.6	–0.2	1.4	0.8	–0.7	–1.9	–1.5	–1.3	–0.3
Construction	3.1	2.8	1.5	–0.9	–9.2	–3.5	3.8	6.8	3.6	–0.3	2.8	3.6	7.6	5.6
Other	3.6	4.0	3.4	2.1	–0.2	0.8	2.7	3.7	3.5	2.6	2.7	2.7	2.5	3.7
3. Unemployment rates														
Total	6.2	5.5	5.3	5.6	6.8	7.5	6.9	6.1	5.6	5.6	5.6	5.5	5.6	5.4
Married men	3.9	3.2	3.1	3.4	4.4	5.1	4.4	3.7	3.3	3.4	3.4	3.2	3.1	3.0
Females	6.2	5.6	5.4	5.5	6.4	7.0	6.6	6.0	5.6	5.7	5.7	5.5	5.6	5.4
Youths	16.9	15.3	15.0	15.6	18.7	20.1	19.1	17.6	17.3	17.1	17.7	17.6	17.4	16.3
4. Activity rate[4]	61.5	62.3	62.9	63.2	62.0	61.7	61.7	62.5	62.9	63.1	62.8	62.8	62.9	63.1

1. Household survey. Data from the household survey for 1994 are not directly comparable to data for 1993 and earlier years because of the implementation in January 1994 of a major redesign of the survey and the introduction of 1990 Census-based population controls, adjusted for the estimated undercount.
2. Non-institutional population aged 16 and over.
3. Non-agricultural payroll.
4. Employment as percentage of population aged from 16 to 64.

Source: US Department of Labor, *Monthly Labor Review.*

Table D. **Costs and prices**

Percentage changes from previous period, s.a.a.r.

	1987	1988	1989	1990	1991	1992	1993	1994	1995	1995			1996	
										Q2	Q3	Q4	Q1	Q2
Rates of pay														
Major wage settlements[1]	3.1	2.6	3.2	3.5	3.5	3.0	2.9	2.7	2.4	3.2	3.2	2.0	..	..
Hourly earnings index[2]	2.5	3.3	4.0	3.7	3.1	2.4	2.4	2.7	2.9	2.9	3.3	3.5	2.3	3.7
Wages and salaries per person	4.6	4.7	3.4	4.7	3.4	5.6	1.5	1.8	3.4	3.7	6.2	5.2	2.5	5.5
Compensation per person	4.5	5.5	3.9	5.1	4.1	4.7	3.0	2.9	3.7	3.5	5.9	4.5	2.2	4.9
Productivity, non-farm business														
Hourly	–0.2	0.6	0.5	0.5	0.6	3.2	0.2	0.5	0.6	2.0	2.0	–1.2	2.0	0.0
Per employee	0.4	0.9	0.7	–0.6	–0.4	2.7	0.8	0.7	–0.1	–0.6	3.0	–1.0	0.5	1.6
Unit labour cost, non-farm business	4.1	3.7	2.1	5.0	4.3	1.9	2.1	1.6	2.9	2.7	1.9	5.3	1.5	3.7
Prices														
GDP deflator	3.1	3.7	4.2	4.3	4.0	2.7	2.6	2.3	2.5	2.4	2.1	2.0	2.2	1.8
Private consumption deflator	3.8	4.2	4.9	5.1	4.2	3.3	2.6	2.4	2.4	2.7	1.5	1.6	2.2	2.9
Consumer price index	3.7	4.1	4.8	5.4	4.2	3.0	3.0	2.6	2.8	3.6	1.8	1.9	3.7	4.0
Food	4.2	4.1	5.8	5.8	2.9	1.2	2.2	2.4	2.8	3.4	2.2	2.7	1.8	4.3
Wholesale prices	2.6	4.0	5.0	3.6	0.2	0.6	1.5	1.3	3.6	5.0	0.9	0.9	2.7	5.1
Crude products	6.7	2.5	7.4	5.7	–7.0	–0.8	2.0	–0.7	1.0	4.5	–5.9	8.7	25.8	17.4
Intermediate products	2.4	5.5	4.6	2.2	0.0	0.2	1.4	2.0	5.4	6.5	2.3	–2.4	–0.8	3.3
Finished products	2.1	2.5	5.1	4.9	2.1	1.2	1.2	0.6	1.9	3.5	0.3	2.4	2.5	4.5

1. Total effective wage adjustment in all industries under collective agreements in non-farm industry covering at least 1 000 workers, not seasonally adjusted.
2. Production or non-supervisory workers on private non-agricultural payrolls.

Source: US Department of Labor, Bureau of Labor Statistics, *Monthly Labor Review*; US Department of Commerce, *Survey of Current Business*.

Table E. **Monetary indicators**

	1987	1988	1989	1990	1991	1992	1993	1994	1995	1995			1996	
										Q2	Q3	Q4	Q1	Q2
Monetary aggregates (percentage changes from previous period s.a.a.r)														
M1	11.6	4.2	1.0	3.6	6.0	12.4	11.6	6.2	–0.3	–0.4	–1.4	–5.0	–2.6	–0.7
M2	6.5	5.4	4.2	5.5	3.7	2.0	1.2	1.4	2.0	3.5	6.8	4.2	5.9	4.0
M3	6.9	6.4	4.5	2.7	1.7	0.6	0.2	1.7	4.3	6.2	8.0	4.6	7.3	5.4
Velocity of circulation														
GDP/M1	6.3	6.5	7.0	7.1	6.9	6.5	6.1	6.1	6.4	6.3	6.4	6.5	6.6	6.7
GDP/M2	1.7	1.7	1.8	1.8	1.8	1.8	1.9	2.0	2.0	2.0	2.0	2.0	2.0	2.0
GDP/M3	1.3	1.3	1.4	1.4	1.4	1.5	1.6	1.6	1.6	1.6	1.6	1.6	1.6	1.6
Federal Reserve Bank reserves ($ billion)														
Non-borrowed	38.6	37.8	38.7	39.9	42.7	50.0	57.2	59.8	57.4	57.5	57.2	56.3	55.4	54.3
Borrowed	0.8	2.4	1.1	0.9	0.4	0.2	0.2	0.3	0.2	0.2	0.3	0.2	0.0	0.2
Total	39.4	40.1	39.8	40.9	43.1	50.2	57.4	60.0	57.6	57.7	57.5	56.5	55.4	54.5
Required	38.4	39.1	38.9	39.9	41.9	49.2	56.3	59.0	56.6	56.9	56.5	55.4	54.2	53.5
Excess	1.0	1.0	1.0	1.0	1.2	1.0	1.1	1.1	1.0	0.9	1.0	1.1	1.2	1.0
Free (excess – borrowed)	0.3	–1.3	–0.2	0.0	0.8	0.9	0.9	0.8	0.8	0.7	0.7	0.9	1.1	0.8
Interest rates (%)														
Federal funds rate	6.7	7.6	9.2	8.1	5.7	3.5	3.0	4.2	5.8	6.0	5.8	5.7	5.4	5.2
Discount rate[1]	5.7	6.2	7.0	7.0	5.4	3.3	3.0	3.6	5.2	5.3	5.3	5.3	5.1	5.0
Prime rate[2]	8.2	9.3	10.9	10.0	8.5	6.3	6.0	7.1	8.8	9.0	8.8	8.7	8.3	8.3
3-month Treasury bills	5.8	6.7	8.1	7.5	5.4	3.4	3.0	4.2	5.5	5.6	5.4	5.3	4.9	5.0
AAA rate[3]	9.4	9.7	9.3	9.3	8.8	8.1	7.2	8.0	7.6	7.7	7.4	7.0	7.1	7.6
10-year Treasury notes	8.4	8.8	8.5	8.6	7.9	7.0	5.9	7.1	6.6	6.6	6.3	5.9	5.9	6.7

1. Rate for Federal Reserve Bank of New York.
2. Prime rate on short-term business loans.
3. Corporate Bonds, AAA rating group, quoted by Moody's Investors Services.

Source: Board of the Governors of the Federal Reserve System, *Federal Reserve Bulletin.*

Table F. **Balance of payments, OECD basis**

Millions of dollars

	1986	1987	1988	1989	1990	1991	1992	1993	1994	1995
Exports, fob[1]	223 344	250 208	320 230	362 120	389 307	416 913	440 352	456 823	502 485	574 879
Imports, fob[1]	368 425	409 765	447 189	477 365	498 337	490 981	536 458	589 441	668 584	749 348
Trade balance	–145 081	–159 557	–126 959	–115 245	–109 030	–74 068	–96 106	–132 618	–166 099	–174 469
Services, net[2]	18 413	16 326	24 900	37 511	49 763	59 776	66 705	66 776	50 615	51 650
Balance on goods and services	–126 671	–143 232	–102 060	–77 734	–59 269	–14 293	–29 402	–65 842	–115 484	–122 818
Private transfers, net	–10 126	–10 600	–12 010	–12 698	–13 043	–13 865	–13 330	–13 988	–15 700	–15 954
Official transfers, net	–14 063	–12 507	–13 024	–13 409	–20 352	20 703	–18 817	–20 095	–20 061	–14 141
Current balance	–150 860	–166 339	–127 083	–103 840	–92 662	–7 425	–61 551	–99 926	–151 245	–152 913
US assets abroad other than official reserves	–105 131	–80 591	–95 447	–143 451	–68 205	–57 275	–65 411	–146 519	–131 197	–270 354
US private assets, net[3]	–103 109	–81 597	–98 414	–144 710	–70 512	–60 175	–63 759	–146 213	–130 875	–270 028
Reported by US banks	–59 975	–42 119	–53 927	–58 160	12 379	–610	20 895	29 947	915	–59 004
US government assets[4]	–2 022	1 006	2 967	1 259	2 307	2 900	–1 652	–306	–322	–326
Foreign assets in the United States										
Liabilities to foreign official monetary agencies[5]	35 648	45 387	39 758	8 503	33 910	17 199	40 858	71 681	39 409	110 483
Other liabilities to foreign monetary agencies[6]	190 463	197 596	200 507	209 987	88 282	80 935	105 646	159 017	251 956	315 842
Reported by US banks	76 737	86 537	63 744	51 780	–3 824	3 994	15 461	20 859	114 396	19 906
Allocation of SDR's	–	–	–	–	–	–	–	–	–	–
Errors and omissions	31 501	–4 029	–13 096	54 094	44 480	–28 936	–26 398	35 985	–14 269	6 684
Change in reserves (+ = increase)										
a) Gold	–	–	–	–	–	–	–	–	–	–
b) Currency assets	942	–7 589	5 065	25 229	2 697	–6 307	–4 276	798	–5 293	6 468
c) Reserve position in IMF	–1 501	–2 070	–1 024	–471	–731	366	2 691	43	–494	2 466
d) Special drawing rights	246	510	–127	535	193	176	–2 316	537	441	808

1. Excluding military goods.
2. Services include reinvested earnings of incorporated affiliates.
3. Including: Direct investment financed by reinvested earnings of incorporated affiliates; foreign securities; US claims on unaffiliated foreigners reported by US non-banking concerns; and U.S. claims reported by US banks, not included elsewhere.
4. Including: US credits and other long-term assets; repayments on US credits and other long-term assets, US foreign currency holdings and US short-term assets, net.
5. Including: US Government securities and other US Government liabilities, US liabilities reported by US banks not included elsewhere and other foreign official assets.
6. Including direct investment; US Treasury securities; other US securities; US liabilities to unaffiliated foreigners reported by US non-banking concerns; US liabilities reported by US banks not included elsewhere.

Source: US Department of Commerce, *Survey of Current Business.*

Table G. **Public sector**

Per cent of GDP

	1960	1970	1980	1990	1993	1994	1995
A. General government accounts							
Receipts							
Total direct taxes	13.6	13.8	14.3	13.3	13.0	13.4	14.0
Social security contributions	4.2	6.0	8.1	9.0	9.1	9.1	9.1
Indirect taxes	8.6	9.1	7.6	7.7	8.2	8.3	8.2
Total current receipts	26.4	28.9	30.0	30.1	30.3	30.7	31.3
Disbursements							
Government consumption	16.2	18.5	17.1	17.0	16.5	15.9	15.7
Property income payable	1.3	1.2	1.1	2.1	2.0	2.0	2.3
Susbsidies	0.1	0.5	0.5	0.4	0.5	0.4	0.3
Transfers	5.6	8.1	11.4	11.8	13.8	13.7	14.0
Total current disbursements	23.1	28.3	30.2	31.4	32.8	32.0	32.2
Saving	3.3	0.6	–0.2	–1.3	–2.4	–1.3	–0.9
Gross investment	5.4	4.2	3.5	3.5	3.2	3.1	3.1
Consumption of fixed capital	2.8	2.5	2.3	2.0	2.0	2.0	2.0
Total expenditure	25.7	30.0	31.4	32.8	33.9	33.0	33.3
Net lending	0.7	–1.1	–1.4	–2.7	–3.6	–2.3	–2.0
B. Central government accounts							
Current receipts	18.4	18.8	20.2	19.7	19.5	19.9	20.4
Total non-interest expenditure	16.5	18.8	20.4	19.5	20.5	19.6	19.3
Primary deficit	2.0	0.1	–0.3	0.2	–1.0	0.2	1.1
Interest expenditure	1.3	1.4	1.9	3.1	2.9	2.9	3.2
Net Lending	0.7	–1.3	–2.2	–3.0	–3.9	–2.7	–2.1
Net lending excluding Social Security	0.6	–1.7	–2.0	–3.9	–4.7	–3.5	–2.9
C. State and local government accounts							
Current receipts	9.2	12.5	13.0	12.7	13.7	13.7	13.7
Total non-interest expenditure	9.2	12.5	13.0	13.5	14.3	14.2	14.5
Primary deficit	0.0	0.0	0.0	–0.8	–0.6	–0.6	–0.7
Interest expenditure	0.0	–0.2	–0.8	–1.1	–1.0	–0.9	–0.8
Net Lending	0.0	0.2	0.7	0.2	0.3	0.3	0.1
D. Government debt (% GDP)							
General government gross debt	56.9	41.5	37.0	55.6	63.5	63.7	64.3
Net debt	45.1	29.5	21.8	39.7	48.8	49.6	50.7

Source: Bureau of Economic Analysis; OECD.

Table H. **Financial markets**

	1970	1975	1980	1990	1991	1992	1993	1994
A. Financial and corporate flows								
Share of private financial institutions' financial assets in national net assets (%)[1]	49.0	43.9	41.0	67.2	73.3	78.7	83.9	83.2
Market value of equities including corporate farm equities (billions of dollars)[1]	631	635	1 256	3 011	4 126	4 609	5 127	5 003
Debt-to-equity ratio in non-financial corporate business excluding farms (%)[1]	56.5	87.6	70.5	82.0	59.5	54.2	46.9	53.5
Ratio of market value to net worth[1]	77.8	39.0	41.3	73.2	106.8	126.3	136.1	126.8
B. Foreign sector (billions of dollars)								
Net foreign assets outstanding[1, 3]	68.7	81.4	278.6	–266.9	–346.0	–472.5	–632.6	–886.3
Changes in net foreign investment[2]	3.0	24.0	25.7	–51.8	–46.4	–85.0	–82.8	–188.9
of which net financial investment of:								
Private sector	17.1	93.3	81.2	202.3	270.7	306.9	204.5	51.3
Public sector	–22.2	–80.0	–63.3	–217.6	–306.3	–389.1	–339.4	–285.9
Foreign purchases of US corporate equities[2]	0.7	3.1	4.2	–16.0	10.4	–5.8	20.5	0.3
US purchases of foreign equities[2]	1.1	–0.9	2.4	7.4	30.7	30.7	60.6	43.0
C. Net worth (billions of dollars)[1]								
Total, all sectors	3.070	5.558	10.666	18.323	18.459	18.500	19.052	20.014
Private, consolidated	3.488	6.203	11.689	20.941	21.321	21.592	22.336	23.287
Household	3.349	5.109	9.666	19.059	20.900	21.879	23.054	23.714
Total owner-occupied real estate	0.867	1.572	3.289	6.016	6.484	6.709	7.010	7.390
Home mortgages as a per cent of owner-occupied real estate	31.5	27.9	27.5	40.8	40.3	41.5	42.4	42.7
D. Debt to net worth ratios, private sector (%)[4]								
Household	13.5	14.3	14.4	19.0	18.1	18.3	18.6	19.6
Non-farm non-corporate business	38.3	46.5	42.5	64.5	65.5	64.8	63.8	61.8
Farm business	18.3	16.8	17.6	16.9	17.0	16.8	16.5	16.4
Non-financial corporate business excluding farms	44.0	34.2	29.1	60.1	63.6	68.5	67.9	67.9
Private financial institutions	65.2	73.9	77.3	114.7	108.5	109.6	109.1	124.0

1. Data are year-end outstandings.
2. Data are annual flows.
3. Net foreign assets exclude US holdings of foreign equities and foreign holdings of US equities.
4. Debt is credit market debt.

Source: Board of Governors of the Federal Reserve System, *Balance Sheets for the US Economy*, 1945-94.

Table I. **Labour market indicators**

	Peak	Trough	1991	1992	1993	1994	1995
A. Evolution							
Standardised unemployment rate	1982: 9.6	1969: 3.4	6.8	7.4	6.9	6.0	5.5
Unemployment rate							
Total	1982: 9.5	1969: 3.4	6.8	7.5	6.9	6.0	5.5
Male	1983: 9.7	1969: 2.7	7.1	7.8	7.1	6.1	5.5
Female	1982: 9.4	1969: 4.7	6.5	7.1	6.6	6.0	5.6
Youth[1]	1982: 17.0	1969: 7.4	13.4	14.2	13.4	12.5	12.1
Share of long-term unemployment[2]	1983: 13.4	1969: 1.9	6.3	11.2	11.7	12.2	9.7
Productivity index, 1992 = 100[3]			102.8	104.9	105.7	106.8	107.3

	1970	1980	1991	1992	1993	1994	1995
B. Structural or institutional characteristics							
Participation rate[4]							
Global	60.4	63.8	66.6	66.7	66.3	66.6	66.7
Male	79.7	76.0	75.2	75.3	74.9	75.0	75.0
Female	43.3	51.4	57.5	58.0	58.2	58.8	59.0
Employment/population between 16 and 64 years	57.4	59.2	62.0	61.7	61.7	62.5	62.9
Employment by sector							
Agriculture – per cent of total	4.5	3.6	2.9	2.9	2.7	2.9	2.9
– per cent change	–3.6	0.6	1.0	–0.2	–3.4	8.6	0.3
Industry – per cent of total	34.3	30.5	25.3	24.6	24.0	24.0	24.0
– per cent change	–1.8	–1.9	–4.4	–2.0	–0.8	2.2	1.5
Services – per cent of total	61.1	65.9	71.8	72.5	73.2	73.1	73.1
– per cent change	3.0	1.7	0.3	1.6	2.5	2.2	1.5
of which: Government – per cent of total	0.2	0.2	0.2	0.2	0.2	0.2	0.2
– per cent change	3.0	1.8	0.6	1.3	1.1	1.5	1.0
Voluntary part-time work[5]	13.9	14.2	13.7	13.4	13.4		
Social insurance as a per cent of compensation	10.8	16.7	18.2	18.1	18.9	19.1	18.8
Government unemployment insurance benefits[6]	12.3	12.6	10.6	13.1	12.0	9.1	8.7
Minimum wage: as a percentage of average wage[7]	49.6	46.6	40.1	40.2	39.2	38.2	37.1

1. People between 16 and 24 years as a percentage of the labour force of the same age group.
2. People looking for a job since one year or more as a percentage of total unemployment.
3. Production as a percentage of employment.
4. Labour force as a percentage of the corresponding population aged between 16 and 64 years.
5. As a percentage of salary workers.
6. Value of the unemployment benefits per unemployed divided by the compensation per employee.
7. Private non-agricultural sector.

Source: US Department of Labor, Bureau of Labor Statistics, Data Resources Incorporated, and OECD.

BASIC STATISTICS

BASIC STATISTICS:

INTERNATIONAL COMPARISONS

	Units	Reference period[1]	Australia	Austria
Population				
Total	Thousands	1994	17 840	8 031
Inhabitants per sq. km	Number	1994	2	96
Net average annual increase over previous 10 years	%	1994	1.4	0.6
Employment				
Total civilian employment (TCE)[2]	Thousands	1994	7 680 (93)	3 737
of which: Agriculture	% of TCE	1994	5.3 (93)	7.2
Industry	% of TCE	1994	23.7 (93)	33.2
Services	% of TCE	1994	71 (93)	59.6
Gross domestic product (GDP)				
At current prices and current exchange rates	Bill. US$	1994	331.6	198.1
Per capita	US$	1994	18 588	24 670
At current prices using current PPP's[3]	Bill. US$	1994	327.9	162.3
Per capita	US$	1994	18 382	20 210
Average annual volume growth over previous 5 years	%	1994	2.2	2.5
Gross fixed capital formation (GFCF)	% of GDP	1994	21.4	24.8
of which: Machinery and equipment	% of GDP	1993	9.8	8.7
Residential construction	% of GDP	1993	5.2	6.3
Average annual volume growth over previous 5 years	%	1994	0.8	3.7
Gross saving ratio[4]	% of GDP	1994	16.8	25.3
General government				
Current expenditure on goods and services	% of GDP	1994	17.5	
Current disbursements[5]	% of GDP	1993	36.9	48.4
Current receipts	% of GDP	1993	33.5	48.6
Net official development assistance	% of GNP	1993	0.34	0.31
Indicators of living standards				
Private consumption per capita using current PPP's[3]	US$	1993	10 803	10 546
Passenger cars, per 1 000 inhabitants	Number	1990	430	382
Telephones, per 1 000 inhabitants	Number	1991	464	432
Television sets, per 1 000 inhabitants	Number	1991	480	478
Doctors, per 1 000 inhabitants	Number	1993	2.2 (91)	2.3
Infant mortality per 1 000 live births	Number		6.1	6.5
Wages and prices (average annual increase over previous 5 years)				
Wages (earnings or rates according to availability)	%	1994	3	5.5
Consumer prices	%	1994	3	3.4
Foreign trade				
Exports of goods, fob*	Mill. US$	1994	47 363	44 881
As % of GDP	%	1994	14.3	22.7
Average annual increase over previous 5 years	%	1994	5	6.7
Imports of goods, cif*	Mill. US$	1994	49 731	55 071
As % of GDP	%	1994	15	27.8
Average annual increase over previous 5 years	%	1994	4	7.2
Total official reserves[6]	Mill. SDRs	1994	7 730	11 523
As ratio of average monthly imports of goods	Ratio	1994	1.9	2.5

* At current prices and exchange rates.

1. Unless otherwise stated.
2. According to the definitions used in OECD *Labour Force Statistics*.
3. PPPs = Purchasing Power Parities.
4. Gross saving = Gross national disposable income minus private and government consumption.
5. Current disbursements = Current expenditure on goods and services plus current transfers and payments of property income.
6. Gold included in reserves is valued at 35 SDRs per ounce. End of year.

EMPLOYMENT OPPORTUNITIES

Economics Department, OECD

The Economics Department of the OECD offers challenging and rewarding opportunities to economists interested in applied policy analysis in an international environment. The Department's concerns extend across the entire field of economic policy analysis, both macroeconomic and microeconomic. Its main task is to provide, for discussion by committees of senior officials from Member countries, documents and papers dealing with current policy concerns. Within this programme of work, three major responsibilities are:

- to prepare regular surveys of the economies of individual Member countries;
- to issue full twice-yearly reviews of the economic situation and prospects of the OECD countries in the context of world economic trends;
- to analyse specific policy issues in a medium-term context for the OECD as a whole, and to a lesser extent for the non-OECD countries.

The documents prepared for these purposes, together with much of the Department's other economic work, appear in published form in the *OECD Economic Outlook, OECD Economic Surveys, OECD Economic Studies* and the Department's *Working Papers* series.

The Department maintains a world econometric model, INTERLINK, which plays an important role in the preparation of the policy analyses and twice-yearly projections. The availability of extensive cross-country data bases and good computer resources facilitates comparative empirical analysis, much of which is incorporated into the model.

The Department is made up of about 80 professional economists from a variety of backgrounds and Member countries. Most projects are carried out by small teams and last from four to eighteen months. Within the Department, ideas and points of view are widely discussed; there is a lively professional interchange, and all professional staff have the opportunity to contribute actively to the programme of work.

Skills the Economics Department is looking for:

a) Solid competence in using the tools of both microeconomic and macroeconomic theory to answer policy questions. Experience indicates that this normally requires the equivalent of a Ph.D. in economics or substantial relevant professional experience to compensate for a lower degree.

b) Solid knowledge of economic statistics and quantitative methods; this includes how to identify data, estimate structural relationships, apply basic techniques of time series analysis, and test hypotheses. It is essential to be able to interpret results sensibly in an economic policy context.

c) A keen interest in and extensive knowledge of policy issues, economic developments and their political/social contexts.

d) Interest and experience in analysing questions posed by policy-makers and presenting the results to them effectively and judiciously. Thus, work experience in government agencies or policy research institutions is an advantage.

e) The ability to write clearly, effectively, and to the point. The OECD is a bilingual organisation with French and English as the official languages. Candidates must have excellent knowledge of one of these languages, and some knowledge of the other. Knowledge of other languages might also be an advantage for certain posts.

f) For some posts, expertise in a particular area may be important, but a successful candidate is expected to be able to work on a broader range of topics relevant to the work of the Department. Thus, except in rare cases, the Department does not recruit narrow specialists.

g) The Department works on a tight time schedule with strict deadlines. Moreover, much of the work in the Department is carried out in small groups. Thus, the ability to work with other economists from a variety of cultural and professional backgrounds, to supervise junior staff, and to produce work on time is important.

General information

The salary for recruits depends on educational and professional background. Positions carry a basic salary from FF 305 700 or FF 377 208 for Administrators (economists) and from FF 438 348 for Principal Administrators (senior economists). This may be supplemented by expatriation and/or family allowances, depending on nationality, residence and family situation. Initial appointments are for a fixed term of two to three years.

Vacancies are open to candidates from OECD Member countries. The Organisation seeks to maintain an appropriate balance between female and male staff and among nationals from Member countries.

For further information on employment opportunities in the Economics Department, contact:

Administrative Unit
Economics Department
OECD
2, rue André-Pascal
75775 PARIS CEDEX 16
FRANCE

E-Mail: compte.esadmin@oecd.org

Applications citing ''ECSUR'', together with a detailed *curriculum vitae* in English or French, should be sent to the Head of Personnel at the above address.

MAIN SALES OUTLETS OF OECD PUBLICATIONS
PRINCIPAUX POINTS DE VENTE DES PUBLICATIONS DE L'OCDE

AUSTRALIA – AUSTRALIE
D.A. Information Services
648 Whitehorse Road, P.O.B 163
Mitcham, Victoria 3132 Tel. (03) 9210.7777
Fax: (03) 9210.7788

AUSTRIA – AUTRICHE
Gerold & Co.
Graben 31
Wien I Tel. (0222) 533.50.14
Fax: (0222) 512.47.31.29

BELGIUM – BELGIQUE
Jean De Lannoy
Avenue du Roi, Koningslaan 202
B-1060 Bruxelles
Tel. (02) 538.51.69/538.08.41
Fax: (02) 538.08.41

CANADA
Renouf Publishing Company Ltd.
1294 Algoma Road
Ottawa, ON K1B 3W8 Tel. (613) 741.4333
Fax: (613) 741.5439

Stores:
61 Sparks Street
Ottawa, ON K1P 5R1 Tel. (613) 238.8985

12 Adelaide Street West
Toronto, ON M5H 1L6 Tel. (416) 363.3171
Fax: (416)363.59.63

Les Éditions La Liberté Inc.
3020 Chemin Sainte-Foy
Sainte-Foy, PQ G1X 3V6 Tel. (418) 658.3763
Fax: (418) 658.3763

Federal Publications Inc.
165 University Avenue, Suite 701
Toronto, ON M5H 3B8 Tel. (416) 860.1611
Fax: (416) 860.1608

Les Publications Fédérales
1185 Université
Montréal, QC H3B 3A7 Tel. (514) 954.1633
Fax: (514) 954.1635

CHINA – CHINE
China National Publications Import
Export Corporation (CNPIEC)
16 Gongti E. Road, Chaoyang District
P.O. Box 88 or 50
Beijing 100704 PR Tel. (01) 506.6688
Fax: (01) 506.3101

CHINESE TAIPEI – TAIPEI CHINOIS
Good Faith Worldwide Int'l. Co. Ltd.
9th Floor, No. 118, Sec. 2
Chung Hsiao E. Road
Taipei Tel. (02) 391.7396/391.7397
Fax: (02) 394.9176

CZECH REPUBLIC – RÉPUBLIQUE TCHÈQUE
National Information Centre
NIS – prodejna
Konviktská 5
Praha 1 – 113 57 Tel. (02) 24.23.09.07
Fax: (02) 24.22.94.33
(*Contact* Ms Jana Pospisilova, nkposp@dec.niz.cz)

DENMARK – DANEMARK
Munksgaard Book and Subscription Service
35, Nørre Søgade, P.O. Box 2148
DK-1016 København K Tel. (33) 12.85.70
Fax: (33) 12.93.87

J. H. Schultz Information A/S,
Herstedvang 12,
DK – 2620 Albertslung Tel. 43 63 23 00
Fax: 43 63 19 69
Internet: s-info@inet.uni-c.dk

EGYPT – ÉGYPTE
The Middle East Observer
41 Sherif Street
Cairo Tel. 392.6919
Fax: 360-6804

FINLAND – FINLANDE
Akateeminen Kirjakauppa
Keskuskatu 1, P.O. Box 128
00100 Helsinki

Subscription Services/Agence d'abonnements :
P.O. Box 23
00371 Helsinki Tel. (358 0) 121 4416
Fax: (358 0) 121.4450

FRANCE
OECD/OCDE
Mail Orders/Commandes par correspondance :
2, rue André-Pascal
75775 Paris Cedex 16 Tel. (33-1) 45.24.82.00
Fax: (33-1) 49.10.42.76
Telex: 640048 OCDE
Internet: Compte.PUBSINQ@oecd.org

Orders via Minitel, France only/
Commandes par Minitel, France exclusivement :
36 15 OCDE

OECD Bookshop/Librairie de l'OCDE :
33, rue Octave-Feuillet
75016 Paris Tél. (33-1) 45.24.81.81
(33-1) 45.24.81.67

Dawson
B.P. 40
91121 Palaiseau Cedex Tel. 69.10.47.00
Fax: 64.54.83.26

Documentation Française
29, quai Voltaire
75007 Paris Tel. 40.15.70.00

Economica
49, rue Héricart
75015 Paris Tel. 45.75.05.67
Fax: 40.58.15.70

Gibert Jeune (Droit-Économie)
6, place Saint-Michel
75006 Paris Tel. 43.25.91.19

Librairie du Commerce International
10, avenue d'Iéna
75016 Paris Tel. 40.73.34.60

Librairie Dunod
Université Paris-Dauphine
Place du Maréchal-de-Lattre-de-Tassigny
75016 Paris Tel. 44.05.40.13

Librairie Lavoisier
11, rue Lavoisier
75008 Paris Tel. 42.65.39.95

Librairie des Sciences Politiques
30, rue Saint-Guillaume
75007 Paris Tel. 45.48.36.02

P.U.F.
49, boulevard Saint-Michel
75005 Paris Tel. 43.25.83.40

Librairie de l'Université
12*a*, rue Nazareth
13100 Aix-en-Provence Tel. (16) 42.26.18.08

Documentation Française
165, rue Garibaldi
69003 Lyon Tel. (16) 78.63.32.23

Librairie Decitre
29, place Bellecour
69002 Lyon Tel. (16) 72.40.54.54

Librairie Sauramps
Le Triangle
34967 Montpellier Cedex 2
Tel. (16) 67.58.85.15
Fax: (16) 67.58.27.36

A la Sorbonne Actual
23, rue de l'Hôtel-des-Postes
06000 Nice Tel. (16) 93.13.77.75
Fax: (16) 93.80.75.69

GERMANY – ALLEMAGNE
OECD Bonn Centre
August-Bebel-Allee 6
D-53175 Bonn Tel. (0228) 959.120
Fax: (0228) 959.12.17

GREECE – GRÈCE
Librairie Kauffmann
Stadiou 28
10564 Athens Tel. (01) 32.55.321
Fax: (01) 32.30.320

HONG-KONG
Swindon Book Co. Ltd.
Astoria Bldg. 3F
34 Ashley Road, Tsimshatsui
Kowloon, Hong Kong Tel. 2376.2062
Fax: 2376.0685

HUNGARY – HONGRIE
Euro Info Service
Margitsziget, Európa Ház
1138 Budapest Tel. (1) 111.62.16
Fax: (1) 111.60.61

ICELAND – ISLANDE
Mál Mog Menning
Laugavegi 18, Pósthólf 392
121 Reykjavik Tel. (1) 552.4240
Fax: (1) 562.3523

INDIA – INDE
Oxford Book and Stationery Co.
Scindia House
New Delhi 110001 Tel. (11) 331.5896/5308
Fax: (11) 371.8275

17 Park Street
Calcutta 700016 Tel. 240832

INDONESIA – INDONÉSIE
Pdii-Lipi
P.O. Box 4298
Jakarta 12042 Tel. (21) 573.34.67
Fax: (21) 573.34.67

IRELAND – IRLANDE
Government Supplies Agency
Publications Section
4/5 Harcourt Road
Dublin 2 Tel. 661.31.11
Fax: 475.27.60

ISRAEL – ISRAËL
Praedicta
5 Shatner Street
P.O. Box 34030
Jerusalem 91430 Tel. (2) 52.84.90/1/2
Fax: (2) 52.84.93

R.O.Y. International
P.O. Box 13056
Tel Aviv 61130 Tel. (3) 546 1423
Fax: (3) 546 1442

Palestinian Authority/Middle East:
INDEX Information Services
P.O.B. 19502
Jerusalem Tel. (2) 27.12.19
Fax: (2) 27.16.34

ITALY – ITALIE
Libreria Commissionaria Sansoni
Via Duca di Calabria 1/1
50125 Firenze Tel. (055) 64.54.15
Fax: (055) 64.12.57

Via Bartolini 29
20155 Milano Tel. (02) 36.50.83

Editrice e Libreria Herder
Piazza Montecitorio 120
00186 Roma Tel. 679.46.28
Fax: 678.47.51

Libreria Hoepli
Via Hoepli 5
20121 Milano Tel. (02) 86.54.46
Fax: (02) 805.28.86

Libreria Scientifica
Dott. Lucio de Biasio 'Aeiou'
Via Coronelli, 6
20146 Milano Tel. (02) 48.95.45.52
Fax: (02) 48.95.45.48

JAPAN – JAPON
OECD Tokyo Centre
Landic Akasaka Building
2-3-4 Akasaka, Minato-ku
Tokyo 107 Tel. (81.3) 3586.2016
Fax: (81.3) 3584.7929

KOREA – CORÉE
Kyobo Book Centre Co. Ltd.
P.O. Box 1658, Kwang Hwa Moon
Seoul Tel. 730.78.91
Fax: 735.00.30

MALAYSIA – MALAISIE
University of Malaya Bookshop
University of Malaya
P.O. Box 1127, Jalan Pantai Baru
59700 Kuala Lumpur
Malaysia Tel. 756.5000/756.5425
Fax: 756.3246

MEXICO – MEXIQUE
OECD Mexico Centre
Edificio INFOTEC
Av. San Fernando no. 37
Col. Toriello Guerra
Tlalpan C.P. 14050
Mexico D.F. Tel. (525) 665 47 99
Fax: (525) 606 13 07

NETHERLANDS – PAYS-BAS
SDU Uitgeverij Plantijnstraat
Externe Fondsen
Postbus 20014
2500 EA's-Gravenhage Tel. (070) 37.89.880
Voor bestellingen: Fax: (070) 34.75.778

Subscription Agency/Agence d'abonnements :
SWETS & ZEITLINGER BV
Heereweg 347B
P.O. Box 830
2160 SZ Lisse Tel. 252.435.111
Fax: 252.415.888

NEW ZEALAND – NOUVELLE-ZÉLANDE
GPLegislation Services
P.O. Box 12418
Thorndon, Wellington Tel. (04) 496.5655
Fax: (04) 496.5698

NORWAY – NORVÈGE
NIC INFO A/S
Ostensjoveien 18
P.O. Box 6512 Etterstad
0606 Oslo Tel. (22) 97.45.00
Fax: (22) 97.45.45

PAKISTAN
Mirza Book Agency
65 Shahrah Quaid-E-Azam
Lahore 54000 Tel. (42) 735.36.01
Fax: (42) 576.37.14

PHILIPPINE – PHILIPPINES
International Booksource Center Inc.
Rm 179/920 Cityland 10 Condo Tower 2
HV dela Costa Ext cor Valero St.
Makati Metro Manila Tel. (632) 817 9676
Fax: (632) 817 1741

POLAND – POLOGNE
Ars Polona
00-950 Warszawa
Krakowskie Prezdmiescie 7 Tel. (22) 264760
Fax: (22) 265334

PORTUGAL
Livraria Portugal
Rua do Carmo 70-74
Apart. 2681
1200 Lisboa Tel. (01) 347.49.82/5
Fax: (01) 347.02.64

SINGAPORE – SINGAPOUR
Ashgate Publishing
Asia Pacific Pte. Ltd
Golden Wheel Building, 04-03
41, Kallang Pudding Road
Singapore 349316 Tel. 741.5166
Fax: 742.9356

SPAIN – ESPAGNE
Mundi-Prensa Libros S.A.
Castelló 37, Apartado 1223
Madrid 28001 Tel. (91) 431.33.99
Fax: (91) 575.39.98

Mundi-Prensa Barcelona
Consell de Cent No. 391
08009 – Barcelona Tel. (93) 488.34.92
Fax: (93) 487.76.59

Llibreria de la Generalitat
Palau Moja
Rambla dels Estudis, 118
08002 – Barcelona
(Subscripcions) Tel. (93) 318.80.12
(Publicacions) Tel. (93) 302.67.23
Fax: (93) 412.18.54

SRI LANKA
Centre for Policy Research
c/o Colombo Agencies Ltd.
No. 300-304, Galle Road
Colombo 3 Tel. (1) 574240, 573551-2
Fax: (1) 575394, 510711

SWEDEN – SUÈDE
CE Fritzes AB
S–106 47 Stockholm Tel. (08) 690.90.90
Fax: (08) 20.50.21

For electronic publications only/
Publications électroniques seulement
STATISTICS SWEDEN
Informationsservice
S-115 81 Stockholm Tel. 8 783 5066
Fax: 8 783 4045

Subscription Agency/Agence d'abonnements :
Wennergren-Williams Info AB
P.O. Box 1305
171 25 Solna Tel. (08) 705.97.50
Fax: (08) 27.00.71

SWITZERLAND – SUISSE
Maditec S.A. (Books and Periodicals/Livres et périodiques)
Chemin des Palettes 4
Case postale 266
1020 Renens VD 1 Tel. (021) 635.08.65
Fax: (021) 635.07.80

Librairie Payot S.A.
4, place Pépinet
CP 3212
1002 Lausanne Tel. (021) 320.25.11
Fax: (021) 320.25.14

Librairie Unilivres
6, rue de Candolle
1205 Genève Tel. (022) 320.26.23
Fax: (022) 329.73.18

Subscription Agency/Agence d'abonnements :
Dynapresse Marketing S.A.
38, avenue Vibert
1227 Carouge Tel. (022) 308.08.70
Fax: (022) 308.07.99

See also – Voir aussi :
OECD Bonn Centre
August-Bebel-Allee 6
D-53175 Bonn (Germany)
Tel. (0228) 959.120
Fax: (0228) 959.12.17

THAILAND – THAÏLANDE
Suksit Siam Co. Ltd.
113, 115 Fuang Nakhon Rd.
Opp. Wat Rajbopith
Bangkok 10200 Tel. (662) 225.9531/2
Fax: (662) 222.5188

TRINIDAD & TOBAGO, CARIBBEAN TRINITÉ-ET-TOBAGO, CARAÏBES
SSL Systematics Studies Limited
9 Watts Street
Curepe, Trinadad & Tobago, W.I.
Tel. (1809) 645.3475
Fax: (1809) 662.5654

TUNISIA – TUNISIE
Grande Librairie Spécialisée
Fendri Ali
Avenue Haffouz Imm El-Intilaka
Bloc B 1 Sfax 3000 Tel. (216-4) 296 855
Fax: (216-4) 298.270

TURKEY – TURQUIE
Kültür Yayinlari Is-Türk Ltd. Sti.
Atatürk Bulvari No. 191/Kat 13
06684 Kavaklidere/Ankara
Tél. (312) 428.11.40 Ext. 2458
Fax : (312) 417.24.90
et 425.07.50-51-52-53

Dolmabahce Cad. No. 29
Besiktas/Istanbul Tel. (212) 260 7188

UNITED KINGDOM – ROYAUME-UNI
HMSO
Gen. enquiries Tel. (0171) 873 0011
Fax: (0171) 873 8463

Postal orders only:
P.O. Box 276, London SW8 5DT
Personal Callers HMSO Bookshop
49 High Holborn, London WC1V 6HB

Branches at: Belfast, Birmingham, Bristol, Edinburgh, Manchester

UNITED STATES – ÉTATS-UNIS
OECD Washington Center
2001 L Street N.W., Suite 650
Washington, D.C. 20036-4922
Tel. (202) 785.6323
Fax: (202) 785.0350
Internet: washcont@oecd.org

Subscriptions to OECD periodicals may also be placed through main subscription agencies.

Les abonnements aux publications périodiques de l'OCDE peuvent être souscrits auprès des principales agences d'abonnement.

Orders and inquiries from countries where Distributors have not yet been appointed should be sent to: OECD Publications, 2, rue André-Pascal, 75775 Paris Cedex 16, France.

Les commandes provenant de pays où l'OCDE n'a pas encore désigné de distributeur peuvent être adressées aux Éditions de l'OCDE, 2, rue André-Pascal, 75775 Paris Cedex 16, France.

8-1996

OECD PUBLICATIONS, 2, rue André-Pascal, 75775 PARIS CEDEX 16
PRINTED IN FRANCE
(10 96 02 1) ISBN 92-64-15340-3 – No. 49121 1996
ISSN 0376-6438